University of the State of New York

Celebration of the centennial Anniversary of the University of the State of New York

And the twenty-second University Convocation, held July 8-10, 1884. Second Edition

University of the State of New York

Celebration of the centennial Anniversary of the University of the State of New York
And the twenty-second University Convocation, held July 8-10, 1884. Second Edition

ISBN/EAN: 9783337188160

Printed in Europe, USA, Canada, Australia, Japan

Cover: Foto ©ninafisch / pixelio.de

More available books at **www.hansebooks.com**

STATE OF NEW YORK:

CELEBRATION

OF THE

CENTENNIAL ANNIVERSARY

OF THE

University of the State of New York,

AND THE

TWENTY-SECOND UNIVERSITY CONVOCATION,

HELD JULY 8-10, 1884.

SECOND EDITION.

PRINTED BY THE AUTHORITY OF THE LEGISLATURE.

ALBANY:
WEED, PARSONS & COMPANY, PRINTERS.
1885.

PREFATORY NOTE.

The University of the State of New York was established by an act of the Legislature, passed May 1, 1784. By this act, and subsequent amendatory acts, the supervision of the institutions of secondary and superior education in the State was intrusted to the Regents of the University. They were thus constituted a State board of education which, in priority of establishment, antedates all others in the United States. The century which has since elapsed has witnessed the inception, organization and development of the present noble system of education in the State. In this work the part of the Board of Regents has been so conspicuous and honorable that it has been deemed appropriate to celebrate, in some suitable manner, the centennial anniversary of its establishment. It was accordingly arranged that special commemorative services should be held in connection with the usual University Convocation of 1884. The following pages comprise the proceedings of this centennial celebration, together with the papers and discussions of the Twenty-second Convocation. The fame of the orators, the excellence of the special historical discourses, the unparalleled dignity and importance of the educational discussions combined to render the occasion a worthy and fitting memorial of a century of disinterested service.

D. M.

ALBANY, *November*, 1884.

CONTENTS.

	PAGE.
Proceedings of the Convocation and the Centennial Celebration.........	1
Address of welcome by Chancellor Pierson......................	1
Report of the Executive Committee............................	2
Presentation of the portrait of Chancellor Pruyn.................	7
Portrait of Governor George Clinton, the first Chancellor, remarks by Vice-Chancellor George W. Clinton.............................	9
Remarks of Governor Cleveland................................	12
Appointment of Executive Committee for 1885	15
Degrees conferred.	15
Closing address by Chancellor Pierson.........................	15
Register of the Twenty-second Convocation.....................	17
Centennial oration by Hon. George William Curtis.................	23
The American College, an address by Hon. Charles E. Fitch...........	41
Academic education in New York, one hundred years ago, by Noah T. Clarke, Ph.D	57
Remarks by Principal Alonzo Flack............................	79
Remarks by Principal Joseph E. King...........................	84
Remarks by Principal Elisha Curtiss............................	87
Remarks by Professor W. D. Wilson............................	89
Remarks by President A. W. Cowles...........................	89
Remarks by Principal T. K. Wright.............................	90
The Growth and Development of the Teaching of Science in the Schools and Colleges of New York, by Dr. J. Dorman Steele.............	93
Remarks by Dr. Noah T. Clarke................................	110
Remarks by Principal Joseph E. King..........................	112
Remarks by Principal Solomon Sias...........................	113
Remarks by Principal John E. Bradley.........................	114
Remarks by Regent Martin I. Townsend........................	116
Remarks by Professor Cady Staley............................	116
The Relations of the University to the Colleges of the State and to Higher Education, by Professor W. D. Wilson........................	117
Remarks by Principal Joseph E. King	129
Remarks by Professor C. W. Bennett..	132
Remarks by Principal Alonzo Flack..	133
Remarks by Chancellor Pierson................................	134

Contents.

	PAGE.
The Relations of the Public School System of the State of New York to Higher Education, by Hon. William B. Ruggles, Superintendent of Public Instruction....	137
Remarks by Principal Solomon Sias...	142
Remarks by President Ebenezer Dodge...	143
Remarks by Conductor Eugene Bouton...	145
Remarks by Principal J. W. Cole..	147
Remarks by Superintendent A. J. Robb...	148
Remarks by President Ebenezer Dodge...	148
Remarks by Principal A. Mattice...	149
Remarks by Professor Eugene Bouton	150
Remarks by Principal Elisha Curtiss...	151
Remarks by President A. W. Cowles...	152
Remarks by President M. B. Anderson...	153
Remarks by Professor W. D. Wilson...	154
Conference of the presidents of the colleges of the State of New York....	157
Remarks by President M. B. Anderson, chairman...	157
Remarks by President A. D. White...	165
Remarks by President Ebenezer Dodge...	175
Remarks by President Anthony...	179
Remarks by President A. S. Webb...	180
Remarks by President E. N. Potter...	182
Remarks by Warden R. B. Fairbairn...	185
Remarks by President White...	188
Remarks by Brother Justin...	189
The Limits of Normal School Training, by Professor James M. Milne....	193
Remarks by Inspector A. B. Watkins...	202
Remarks by Dr. Noah T. Clarke...	202
Remarks by Principal C. T. R. Smith	203
Remarks by Professor J. M. Milne...	203
Remarks by Principal E. A. Sheldon...	203
Remarks by Superintendent A. J. Robb...	205
Remarks by Principal E. A. Sheldon...	206
Remarks by Principal Elisha Curtiss...	207
Remarks by Principal James A. Cassety...	207
Remarks by Principal D. C. Farr...	209
Remarks by Principal N. W. Benedict	209
Remarks by Principal E. A. Sheldon...	210
Remarks by Professor J. M. Milne...	210
Some Suggestions on the Study of Modern German Poets, by Vice-President M. J. Kircher...	213
The Study of English, by Conductor Eugene Bouton...	225
Medical Education — Its Objects and Requirements, by Professor F. R. Sturgis, M. D...	241
Report of the Committee on Necrology, by Principal John E. Bradley, chairman...	261

CONTENTS.   vii

Notices of — *Continued :*

PAGE.

Notices of —
Rev. Dr. Simeon North.................................. 262
Professor Benjamin N. Martin 264
Professor Arnold Guyot................................. 272
Orlando Meads, LL. D.................................. 277
General S. D. Hungerford.............................. 278
Professor Jacob S. Mosher, M. D....................... 280
Elisha Harris, M. D 286
Rev. Michael P. Costin, S. J........................... 288
Professor Arthur Spielman............................. 289
Dr. John C. Gallup..................................... 290
John A. Gillett.. 291
Stephen G. Taylor...................................... 292
Alonzo M. Winchester.................................. 294

I.

CELEBRATION OF THE CENTENNIAL ANNIVERSARY AND THE PROCEEDINGS OF THE TWENTY-SECOND CONVOCATION, HELD JULY 8-10, 1884.

MINUTES OF THE PROCEEDINGS.

The Convocation was called to order by Chancellor Henry R. Pierson, in the Senate chamber of the Capitol. The invocation was pronounced by the Rev. A. W. Cowles, D. D., President of Elmira Female College.

Chancellor Pierson, in opening the proceedings of the Convocation, made the following address of welcome:

GENTLEMEN OF THE CONVOCATION: — I have very few prepared words that I shall say to greet you, but I greet you gladly and I give you hearty welcome. The Regents of the University look forward to this annual meeting with very great interest; and now twenty-two years have proved that its organization has been one of the strongest arms of our success. To the meeting of this year we have looked with peculiar interest, not only because as years go on the Convocation improves both in its methods and in its work, but because it marks an important era in the existence of the Board, the attainment of its centennial epoch. The education of the people is held to be the duty of the government toward the Commonwealth. To discharge that obligation, governments have instituted organizations, conferring upon them powers of administration and trusts to be executed. Early, very early in the history of this State, among its very first works, was the establishment of the University of the State, and the creation of the Regents to take charge of higher education in the State. A hundred years have passed with very slight changes in the fundamental law which established that Board. It has grown as other things have grown, and matured as other things have matured in the State, until to-day it stands represented not only by the institutions of education in the State, but by you men and women who are now here, and who come up here to give us advice and counsel in our work year by year. Hence you are our witnesses. You are the evidence of our growth and our progress. You tell us what we have done well, and caution us against turning aside into places where we ought not to go.

The executive committee having the Convocation in charge have prepared a programme which will commend itself to you as being full of interest. We ask you to give it that consideration in its government of your action and in its guidance of your discussions, which is due to the care taken by them. You know in this Convocation we have few restrictions. Every man carries his own lance; and he may parry or thrust as he wishes, taking the consequences; and it is that freedom of discussion — it is that general liberty which has done us so much good — so much good to the Board itself. I may say to those who are not members of the Board, we believe that the progress of education has been as great during the last as in any preceding year. It gives me particular pleasure to say that the State in its benefactions, and in consideration of the work, has been very liberal. We have asked for nothing which we have not obtained.

Gentlemen, as I said in the beginning, I shall not detain you. There are others here. This programme tells you that there are others here prepared to do this work. Again I thank you for your presence. I greet you with great pleasure. I look upon the three days to come as of great promise of good to the cause of education in the State. I am glad you come here — men of thought and men of culture — men who arrange, men who make and mark progress, who come here and make your impress upon the work of education as represented by this Board. The next thing in order is the report of the Executive Committee by Prof. J. H. Gilmore, Chairman.

Report of the Executive Committee.

Mr. CHANCELLOR AND MEMBERS OF THE CONVOCATION : — A pernicious custom prevails in Congress of permitting Senators and Representatives to print in the *Congressional Record*, speeches which they have never delivered. But they have never been permitted — so far as I am aware — to deliver speeches which they themselves had already printed and which were in the hands of their associates, who could follow them, line by line, and see how faithful they were to the printed copy.

It would be somewhat akin to such an absurdity, if I were to go, minutely, into the programme for this occasion; and orally recite, session by session, the appointments which you can read at your leisure. Permit me, however, as chairman of the executive committee, to call your attention to a few salient points.

Although this occasion is one of especial historical significance, it has not seemed to your committee wise, wholly to abandon that discussion of practical topics and questions of current educational interest, which has been found so profitable in years past. Teachers have come here, year after year, in increasing numbers, because they found it profitable to come here; and we propose this year to minister to their profit as well as to their pleasure. In no other way can you draw and hold a born teacher.

To topics of practical value and current interest, the session of this afternoon will, therefore, be exclusively given; and the sessions of to-morrow will include a valuable paper of a similar nature from State Superintendent Ruggles, and a significant report on the methods of promoting classical education by Principal Farr of Glens Falls.

But, as this Convocation is coincident with the one hundredth anniversary of the existence of the University of the State of New York, it has seemed fitting that much of our time be devoted to a historical survey of the work which the University of the State of New York has accomplished, and a consideration of the varied relations which it sustains to the cause of education.

Historical papers will, accordingly, be read by Dr. Steele of Elmira, and Dr. Clarke of Canandaigua, men whose names are familiar in our ears as household words. Dr. Sturgis,* of New York, will discuss the Actual and Possible Relations of the Board of Regents to Medical Education (a far more important theme than some of you, I suspect, realize); while the venerable Dr. Wilson, of Cornell University, will discuss the Relations of the University of the State of New York to the Colleges of the State — a theme whose importance none can question.

Following this paper, we are to have a conference upon Collegiate Education in the State of New York, to be opened by President Anderson, of the University of Rochester, who has filled the presidential chair for a longer period than any other man now living, and

---

* Owing to professional engagements, Dr. Sturgis was unable to be present at the Convocation.

filled it *full*. This conference, in which, it is hoped, President White, of Cornell, President Dodge, of Madison, and other educators of equal eminence will participate, will certainly be a novel, and, in all probability, a most attractive feature of the Convocation.

It is hoped, by some members of your committee, that this free conference of those especially interested in higher education, may have a practical outcome in some such association of the colleges of the State of New York, as that which is in vigorous existence and yields such beneficent results in New England. If so, the Convocation of 1884 will not have been held in vain.

Possibly the most interesting feature of the Convocation will, however, be the addresses announced for this evening and to-morrow evening by Regent Charles E. Fitch of Rochester, and Regent George William Curtis of New York; and I am sure that all the members of the Convocation will share in that satisfaction which I myself feel in view of the fact that this is not merely a Convocation held under the auspices of the Board of Regents, but one in which the Regents themselves actively participate. If political allusions were in order on such occasions as this, Mr. Chancellor, I might — as a constant reader of the Rochester *Democrat* — congratulate myself that there is still one platform on which Regent Fitch and Regent Curtis can stand in common — one cause which they can agree heartily to support.

Mr. Fitch will discuss the American College — a theme of vital importance which no man is better fitted to handle than my gifted townsman. Mr. Curtis's theme is not announced; but if the centennial oration which he has consented to pronounce is not scholarly, chaste, stimulating, felicitous — in every way worthy of the occasion — it will not be characteristic of the man.

Your committee congratulate themselves, and congratulate you, on the attractiveness of the themes — the reputation and ability of the men who have been announced for this occasion. They have occasion only to regret that the serious illness of his wife will prevent Professor Burton from reading the paper which has been announced, on "Methods of Latin Pronunciation;" and that owing to the pressure of other duties, the reading of Professor Wilder's paper on "Methods of Zoölogical and Physiological Study," must be postponed to another year.

Your committee hope, at the close of the Convocation, to be able to congratulate you on the large attendance — the prompt and regular attendance — at the sessions of this centennial assemblage.

They desire to invite freedom of discussion and frankness of utterance with reference to the various topics brought before this body; and would impress upon each member of this Convocation his personal responsibility for making the Convocation a success.

The University of the State of New York has, in past years, been subjected to somewhat severe criticism. Its right to exist, even, has by some been questioned. But I believe that it has done much (and with ample means at its disposal, would do far more) to unify and invigorate secondary education throughout the State of New York. The methods which it employs, and the plans which it forms, under the wise supervision of my genial and accomplished friend, Dr. Murray, meet, year by year, with increased approval from the most judicious educators of the State. Indeed, the opinion has, for some time, been growing in my own mind that the adverse criticism which has sometimes been visited upon the Board of Regents might more justly be directed toward those injudicious teachers and subordinate boards who abuse — instead of using — the facilities which the Board of Regents places at their disposal. I gratefully acknowledge the good which the University has accomplished in the past; but, to my mind, the University has a future before it far more glorious — far more significant — than its past has been.

All of us are, as teachers, under obligation for assistance in our work, which even the most captious and the most cynical would hardly reject — *nay*, which no one of us *can* reject, if we would; for the influence of the University permeates the entire educational system of the Empire State — its influence is felt from the primary school to the college — and its founders (albeit the ends which they had in view have hardly yet been attained) must ever be numbered among those "Dead but sceptred sovereigns, who still rule our spirits from their urns."

Let us, in recognition of the benefits which the University has conferred on us and on our children, help to make the occasion a memorial service of which the honorable gentlemen who compose the Board of Regents may well be proud.

In behalf of the Executive Committee.

J. H. GILMORE,
Chairman.

The first paper was read by J. Dorman Steele, Ph. D., of Elmira, on the Growth and Development of the Teaching of Science in the

Academies and Colleges of the State of New York. The paper was designed to show the progress of scientific teaching in the schools for advanced education, by comparing the scientific curricula, the text-books and apparatus of successive epochs with those of the present. The paper elicited an interesting discussion, which was participated in by ex-Principal Noah T. Clarke of Canandaigua, Principal Joseph E. King of Fort Edward Collegiate Institute, Principal Solomon Sias of Schoharie, Principal John E. Bradley of the Albany High School, Regent Martin I. Townsend of Troy, and Professor Cady Staley of Union College.

AFTERNOON SESSION.

Chancellor Pierson occupied the chair. The paper by Professor H. F. Burton of the University of Rochester, on "Methods of Pronouncing Latin," announced in the programme, was not presented on account of a serious illness in the family of the author.

Vice-President M. J. Kircher of Niagara University, read a paper entitled "Some Suggestions on the Study of Modern German Poets."

Professor Eugene Bouton, Institute Conductor, read a paper on "The Study of English in Academies and High Schools."

By invitation of the Chancellor, Professor W. D. Wilson of Cornell University, presided during the remainder of the session.

Professor James M. Milne of the Cortland Normal School, then read a paper on "The Limits of Normal-School Training."

An animated discussion followed this paper, which was participated in by Dr. Albert B. Watkins of the Regents' office, ex-Principal Noah T. Clarke of Canandaigua, Principal C. T. R. Smith of Lansingburgh, Professor J. M. Milne of Cortland, Principal E. A. Sheldon of the Oswego Normal School, Superintendent A. J. Robb of Cohoes, Principal Elisha Curtiss of Sodus, Principal James M. Cassety of the Albany Academy, Principal D. C. Farr of Glens Falls, Dr. N. W. Benedict of Rochester, and others.

EVENING SESSION.

Chancellor Pierson presided. Regent Charles E. Fitch of Rochester, delivered an address on "The American College."

Principal John E. Bradley, the Chairman of the Committee on Necrology, presented a partial report upon the deaths which had occurred among educators during the past year, in connection with which Professor S. B. Ward, M. D., of the Albany Medical College, read a memorial notice of Professor Jacob S. Mosher, M. D.

WEDNESDAY, JULY 9.

Morning Session.

Regent Charles E. Fitch presided. Hon. William B. Ruggles, Superintendent of Public Instruction, read a paper on "The Relations of the Public School System of the State of New York to Higher Education."

This paper was discussed at length by President Ebenezer Dodge of Madison University, Institute Conductor Eugene Bouton, Principal Cole of Troy, Superintendent A. J. Robb of Cohoes, Principal W. H. Coats of Elizabethtown, Principal S. Sias of Schoharie, Principal A. Mattice of the Seymour Smith Academy, Principal Curtiss of Sodus, President A. W. Cowles of Elmira Female College, President M. B. Anderson of the University of Rochester, Professor Wilson of Cornell University, and others.

The remainder of the Report of the Committee on Necrology was then read by Principal Bradley, the chairman. Dr. Franklin B. Hough, of Lowville, then read an abstract of a historical and statistical sketch of the work of the Board of Regents. This sketch, with accompanying statistical tables, is designed to form a second part of the present centennial publication.

Afternoon Session.

Chancellor Pierson, in calling the Convocation to order at the opening of the afternoon session, spoke as follows:

On the calendar of to-day will be found in the afternoon session the announcement of the presentation to the Board of Regents by the family of the late Chancellor J. V. L. Pruyn, his portrait, painted by Eastman Johnson. I regret to have to announce to the Convocation that the expectation of the presence of Mr. John V. L. Pruyn, the son of the Chancellor, to present this portrait, is not to be realized. When we put it in print, we had the promise of his presence, but he has not been able to come. In his place, however, we have a letter from Mrs. Pruyn to the Secretary of the Board, which the Secretary will read.

Perhaps it would be enough for me — all that would be required of me by the Convocation, as a complete discharge of my duty, if I should announce to the Convocation, that the Board on the receipt of the communication accepted the portrait of the late Chancellor and directed the officers to communicate their thanks for the kindness of Mrs. Pruyn and her family for the portrait. I hardly dare venture without an opportunity for concentration of thought and language to say more than to make the announcement, but I am sure those of you here who knew the Chancellor as we knew him — who knew his work in the Board for the years he was connected with it as we knew it, will demand no token, like this, as evidence of his beneficent influence. He planned with such sagacity and worked with such facility, that he was able to see the result in the ripe fruitage of a well-lived life. And now that we are soon to remove into the rooms prepared for us in this building, it is fitting, it is beautiful on the part of those who loved him as we respect him, that they should place in the rooms of the Board of Regents the portrait of the late Chancellor, which will now be unveiled.

Secretary Murray then read the following letter from Mrs. Pruyn:

DEAR DR. MURRAY:

Will you present to the Regents of the University of the State of New York, from my children and myself, the portrait of Mr. Pruyn, with the earnest hope that his presence in the beautiful rooms of the New Capitol may constantly recall to the honored associates he loved so well the traditions of the past, and inspire them with wisdom for the future.

Very truly yours,
ANNA PARKER PRUYN.
CLIFF LAWN ROAD, NEWPORT, R. I., *July* 5, 1884.

After the reading of this letter the portrait was unveiled to the Convocation. The following acknowledgment was sent to Mrs. Pruyn by the direction of the Board of Regents:

UNIVERSITY OF THE STATE OF NEW YORK,
OFFICE OF THE REGENTS, *July* 12, 1884.

MY DEAR MRS. PRUYN:

I am commissioned by the Board of Regents of the University of the State of New York, to convey to you its grateful acknowledgments for your noble gift of the portrait of the late Chancellor Pruyn. As an example of splendid portraiture it may appropriately take its place amid the magnificent decorations of the New Capitol. But its chief value, and that which will forever render it precious and sacred to the members of the Board, is that it will perpetually remind them of him whom for so many years they recognized not only as their official head, but by virtue of his devotion to duty, sagacity in counsel and eminent services, easily and by right their chief.

Closing as the University now does the first century of its existence and entering upon a second, its Board of Regents cannot fail to feel profoundly the impressive lessons of the past and the impending responsibilities of the future. They deem it a happy augury that at such a time there has come to look down upon them in their deliberations from this speaking canvas the familiar and benignant presence of one who by the example of his life and his noble fidelity to the trusts of his office, is at once to them a model and an inspiration.

The Board begs me to convey to you and your children who have united in this graceful and timely benefaction, its most cordial thanks, and its best wishes for your health and happiness.

Very respectfully yours,
DAVID MURRAY,
Secretary.

To Mrs. J. V. L. PRUYN.

The Chancellor then announced that the Board had come into possession of a portrait of its first Chancellor, Governor George Clinton, which is likewise destined to ornament the rooms of the Board. A historical notice of this portrait was read by Vice-Chancellor George W. Clinton, as follows:

PORTRAIT OF GOVERNOR GEORGE CLINTON,

First Chancellor of the University.

The formal presentation to the Board of Regents of the excellent portrait of John V. L. Pruyn has been made in a most admirable manner, and makes this Convocation of the University specially memorable. It is to be hoped that it foretokens the adornment of the rooms now being prepared in this noble building for the Regents of the University, with the likenesses of all the Chancellors and of other distinguished men, who, like them, have done worthy work in advocating and advancing education, and especially the higher branches of it, in the State of New York. It is probably in this hope, that I have been instructed to call your attention to this portrait of George Clinton, the first Governor of the State, and the first Chancellor of its University. Such of the Regents as have seen it, desire it for the Board. There is no reasonable doubt that it can be acquired. The members of the Convocation, who are not Regents of the University, are of the University. We are all members of the University, and all are working in somewhat various directions, for the glory of the University, on whose prosperity the safety and honor of the State so largely depends. If this Convocation should approve this portrait, express a desire for its purchase for the Board, it would, I apprehend, render its purchase by the State for the Board almost certain.

There are but few paintings of George Clinton. Investigation as to their number, histories and location has been commenced and will be pursued. Mr. Fernow finds in a collection of papers recently purchased by the State, a letter from Joseph Delaplaine to Matthias B. Tallmadge, dated August 14, 1814, containing this extract from a letter of DeWitt Clinton: "Col. Trumbull took an excellent likeness of the late Vice-President, in 1791. It is now in the collection of pictures belonging to the Corporation of New York. Mr. Ames, of Albany, has taken an approved one at a more recent period. Col. Trumbull's is vastly superior in drapery and richness of coloring. It is, I think, the best of his performances." Mr. Delaplaine adds: "One of the portraits of the late Vice-President Clinton, by Ames, is in our Academy." The original picture by Ames is in the Executive Chamber of this Capitol; the copy is in Philadelphia; the original picture by Trumbull is, I presume, in the Governor's Chamber, in the City Hall of New York.

Mr. William Taylor Hall, of Baltimore, has sent the portrait before you here for an inspection. He explains its history and his title to it as follows: John McKesson, the Secretary of the Provincial Congress of the Convention of Representation, and of the various Committees, and of the Council of Safety, and for so many years after the adoption of the State Constitution, Clerk of the Assembly, was a close friend of George Clinton; indeed I have reason to believe that the two families, the Clintons and the McKessons, were on very intimate terms. John McKesson had a sister named Maria William McKesson. A brother of John married Sarah Read, a sister of George Read, one of the signers of the Declaration of Independence. Their daughter, Maria McKesson, married Wm. Wallace Taylor of Pennsylvania; their daughter married Richard Wilmot Hall, M. D., of Maryland, and our correspondent, William Taylor Hall, is one of their children. He writes thus: "The family legend is that the picture was presented to my grandmother's aunt (Maria McKesson, born 1742), and by her handed down to my grandmother, Maria McKesson (born 1774), who brought the picture to this city (Baltimore) about 1819. I can recollect the picture fifty years and all the traditions connected with it. I can affirm that my grandmother treasured it until her death in 1858. My mother had it up to 1865 — since in my keeping."

Of course the picture will not be purchased until its authenticity and the title are satisfactorily shown.

In his speech to the Legislature of July 11, 1782, Governor George Clinton said: "In the present respite from the more severe distresses and calamities of the war, I cannot forbear suggesting to you a work which I conceive ought not to be deferred as the business of peace, the primitive encouragement of learning. Besides the general advantages arising to society from liberal science as restraining those rude passions which lead to vice and disorder, it is the peculiar duty of the government of a free State, where the highest employments are open to citizens of every rank, to endeavor, by the establishment of schools and seminaries, to diffuse that degree of literature which is necessary to the discharge of public trusts. You must be sensible that the war has occasioned a chasm in education extremely injurious to the rising generation, and this affords an additional consideration for extending our earliest care to their instruction."

In his speech of January 21, 1784, to the Legislature, he said: "Neglect of the education of youth is among the evils consequent in war. Perhaps there is scarce any thing more worthy your attention than the revival and encouragement of seminaries of learning, and nothing by which we can more satisfactorily express our gratitude to the Supreme Being for His past favors, since piety and virtue are generally the offspring of an enlightened understanding."

In his message of January 3, 1795, he wrote: "While it is evident that the general establishment and liberal endowment of academics are highly to be commended and are attended with the most beneficial consequences, yet it cannot be denied that they are principally confined to the children of the opulent, and that a great proportion of the community is excluded from their immediate advantages, the establishment of common schools throughout the State is happily calculated to remedy the inconvenience, and will therefore re-engage your early and decided consideration."

But we have evidence that, prior even to 1782, when the war was not ended, though its termination in independence seemed assured, George Clinton and many of the noblest citizens of the State were contemplating the immediate establishment of a college at Schenectady. The George Clinton papers contain the draft of a dateless proclamation by him as Governor, organizing Clinton College at Schenectady, and purporting to be issued by authority of an act of the Legislature, passed on the —— day of —— A. D., 1779, whereby it was enacted ——. The proclamation was never issued, no act authorizing it was ever passed. And it is plain that the proclamation was prepared in 1778 or 1779, in the immediate anticipation of the passage of an act which would authorize it. And it seems to me that the authors and abetters of such a project at such a dreadful time must have been worthy of and fit guardians of the liberty they won, and of all the reasonable honors we, in this age of prosperity, can pay to their memories.

The next paper was read by Dr. Noah T. Clarke of Canandaigua, entitled, "Academic Education in the State of New York One Hundred Years Ago." This was a historical paper prepared at the special request of the Committee on the Centennial Anniversary of the University. It was followed by an interesting discussion upon the history of the system of academies in the State, in which addresses were made by Principal Alonzo Flack of Claverack, Principal Joseph E. King of Fort Edward Collegiate Institute, Principal Elisha Curtiss of Sodus, Professor W. D. Wilson of Cornell University, President A. W. Cowles of Elmira Female College, and by Principal T. K. Wright of the Munro Collegiate Institute.

Announcement was made that Dr. F. R. Sturgis of New York, owing to pressing professional engagements, would not be able to be present to read his paper.

Evening Session.

The entire session was devoted to the Centennial Oration by Regent George William Curtis. This oration was prepared at the special invitation of the Board of Regents in commemoration of the Centennial Anniversary of the establishment of the University. Chancellor Pierson announced that Governor Cleveland, a member of the Board of Regents, would preside at this session, and presented him to the Convocation. Governor Cleveland spoke as follows:

Governor Cleveland's Address.

Mr. Chancellor and Ladies and Gentlemen — I certainly deem it a great honor to be permitted to preside on this occasion. It seems to me that in a State where the will of the people is absolutely the source of power, and where the people dictate so completely the course of government and the manner of its administration, that it is well for us to celebrate the centennial of the establishment of an instrumentality by the State, which is intrusted by it with the charge and direction of a higher education for its citizens. And while we thus meet in the year which marks the hundredth anniversary of the establishment of the University of the State of New York, to review what a hundred years have brought forth in the cause of education, it is fit and proper that we listen to one thoroughly identified with all the objects of the·University, and intimately connected with every thing that elevates and instructs the people. I, therefore, congratulate you, while I have the extreme pleasure to introduce to you as the orator of the evening one of the Regents of our University, Mr. George William Curtis.

After the delivery of the centennial oration by Regent Curtis, the Convocation adjourned to accept the hospitalities of Chancellor Pierson at his house.

THURSDAY, JULY 10.

Morning Session.

Dr. N. T. Clarke of Canandaigua, occupied the chair at the opening of the session, and was succeeded by the Chancellor.

Principal D. C. Farr of Glens Falls Academy, presented a report of progress from the committee appointed at the Convocation of 1883, upon the methods of promoting classical education. This report was discussed by Professor Bennett of Syracuse University, who spoke as follows:

Mr. CHAIRMAN:— It was the pleasure of this committee to appoint me its chairman one year ago. Every one knows that the duties of teachers during the school year are very pressing. We have not had opportunity for meeting and consultation as we had desired. The secretary of the committee has been very diligent in his work, and we are certainly under great obligations to him for the results which he has presented to us this morning. But we think that this subject should have further consideration. We have only made a beginning. The committee is dissatisfied with what it has done, although it has done what it could. The subject is so broad and so important that we feel that more time is needed to embody our suggestions in a paper such as would be worthy to present to a Convocation of this character and dignity, and suggest such definite points as might be discussed by this body of teachers. If it should be agreeable to this body, we would respectfully request that the committee be continued for another year, in order to complete the work it has begun.

Professor Gilmore, Chairman of the Executive Committee, spoke of the great importance of the subject; and upon his motion the committee was continued for another year, and requested to present a full report; and the Executive Committee of the next Convocation was requested to provide a place in the programme for a full discussion of the subject.

Professor W. D. Wilson of Cornell University, then read a paper on "The Relations of the University to the Colleges of the State and to Higher Education." It was afterward discussed by Principal Joseph E. King of Fort Edward, Professor Bennett of Syracuse University, Principal Flack of Claverack, Chancellor Pierson, and by the author.

College Conference.

By invitation of the Board of Regents, a conference of members of the Convocation engaged in college education was held. By special request, President M. B. Anderson of the University of Rochester, the senior college president in the State, presided and introduced the subject of discussion. He was followed by President A. D. White of Cornell University, President Ebenezer Dodge of Madison University, President Anthony of Manhattan College, General A. S. Webb, President of the College of the City of New York, President E. N. Potter of Hobart College, Warden R. B. Fairbairn of St. Stephen's College, and Brother Justin of Manhattan College.

Closing Exercises.

At the close of this conference, Chancellor Pierson in the Chair, the following resolutions offered by Dr. Joseph E. King of Fort Edward, were unanimously adopted:

Resolved, That we, the members of this Convocation, extend our hearty congratulations to the Regents of the University of New York, on this, the one hundredth anniversary of the establishment of their honorable Board, for the illustrious names that from 1784 down to our own time have adorned their annals, and blessed the Commonwealth with a wise and beneficent supervision of its academies and colleges, and especially for that progressive spirit in the Board in our own generation, which has given us the ANNUAL CONVOCATIONS and the REGENTS' ACADEMIC EXAMINATIONS ; that to Chancellor Pierson we extend our thanks for the urbanity with which he has presided over our deliberations, and that we assure him—should he extend in his person "the visitations of the Regents" to our several homes — we shall be glad to reciprocate the pleasant hospitalities he has extended to us.

Dr. Alonzo Flack of Claverack offered the following resolution:

Resolved, That the Chancellor appoint a committee of three members of this Convocation to present a paper at the next Convocation, on the subject of the conditions of granting the diplomas now granted by the Regents to their academic pupils, drawn from the experience of the colleges and universities of this country and Europe.

This resolution was adopted, and Professor William McAfee,

Principal John E. Bradley and Superintendent David Beattie were appointed the committee.

On motion of President White, the Chancellor was authorized to appoint a committee of five, to consider the plan proposed by him for the establishment of University scholarships and fellowships. The Chancellor appointed the following committee: President A. D. White, President F. A. P. Barnard, President Anthony, Professor Edward North and Professor J. H. Gilmore.

The Chancellor announced that the Board of Regents had appointed the following Executive Committee for the Convocation to be held in 1885:

Principal J. E. Bradley, Albany High School, Chairman.
President A. W. Cowles, Elmira Female College.
Vice-President M. J. Kircher, Niagara University.
Professor N. L. Andrews, Madison University.
Professor J. M. Milne, Cortland Normal School.
Principal F. J. Cheney, Kingston Free Academy.
Principal D. M. Estee, Canisteo Union School.

The Chancellor announced that the Board of Regents had conferred the following degrees:

The honorary degree of Doctor of Philosophy on Joseph Albert Lintner, State Entomologist, in recognition of his distinguished services to science by his investigations and publications in entomology.

The honorary degree of Doctor of Philosophy on Willard Parker Ward, of New York city, mining engineer and expert, for his attainments and writings in his department.

The honorary degree of Doctor of Philosophy on Sylvanus Aden Ellis, superintendent of schools in Rochester, for his services to education in his official position.

The honorary degree of Doctor of Medicine, under chapter 366 of the Laws of 1840, on the nomination of the State Homœopathic Medical Society, on S. Powell Burdick, M. D., and Timothy F. Allen, M. D., both of New York city.

The degree of Doctor of Medicine, on examination under authority of chapter 746 of the Laws of 1872, on Juan Garcia Puron, of New York city.

Chancellor Pierson in closing the Convocation spoke as follows:

Before I shall ask Dr. Fairbairn to pronounce the benediction, I wish to express, on behalf of the Board and myself, the profound pleasure which we have had in this Convocation. We offer a grateful acknowledgment to you, gentlemen, who come up hither from your hours of leisure and your hours of labor to give us such thoughts and attention as you can, and such suggestions favorable to our work, or unfavorable, as you see it, — no matter, it is in the way of rendering public good, which is all the service we have to render, and that but adorns us as persons. We thank you, we greet you with pleasure. In the coming year you will come back to us freighted with the year's experience, and ready to give it to us in full measure.

Rev. Warden Fairbairn, of St. Stephen's College, then pronounced the apostolic benediction, and the Convocation was declared adjourned.

REGISTER OF THE TWENTY-SECOND CONVOCATION.

PERMANENT OFFICERS, EX-OFFICIO.

Henry R. Pierson, Chancellor.
George W. Clinton, Vice-Chancellor.
David Murray, Secretary.
Daniel J. Pratt, Assistant Secretary.

EXECUTIVE COMMITTEE OF THE CONVOCATION FOR 1884.

Professor J. H. Gilmore, University of Rochester, Chairman.
President P. F. Dealy, St. John's College.
Professor M. Perkins, Union College.
Principal E. A. Sheldon, Oswego Normal School.
Inspector A. B. Watkins, office of the Regents.
Principal J. M. Cassety, Albany Academy.
Principal J. G. Wight, Cooperstown Union School.

COMMITTEE ON THE CENTENNIAL ANNIVERSARY OF THE UNIVERSITY.

Professor W. D. Wilson, Cornell University.
Warden R. B. Fairbairn, St. Stephen's College.
Professor Edward North, Hamilton College.
Professor C. M. O'Leary, Manhattan College.
President D. H. Cochran, Brooklyn Collegiate Institute.
Ex-Principal N. T. Clarke, Canandaigua.
Principal J. E. Bradley, Albany High School.

COMMITTEE ON NECROLOGY.

Principal J. E. Bradley, Albany High School, Chairman.
Professor Edward North, Hamilton College.
Assistant Secretary D. J. Pratt, office of the Regents.
Professor D. S. Martin, Rutgers Female College.

REGISTERED MEMBERS OF THE CONVOCATION.

Board of Regents.

Henry R. Pierson, Chancellor, Albany.

George W. Clinton, Vice-Chancellor, Buffalo.
Grover Cleveland, Governor.
William B. Ruggles, Superintendent of Public Instruction.
Elias W. Leavenworth, Syracuse.
George William Curtis, West New Brighton.
Martin I. Townsend, Troy.
Rev. Anson J. Upson, D. D., Auburn.
William L. Bostwick, Ithaca.
Charles E. Fitch, Rochester.
Rev. Orris H. Warren, D. D., Syracuse.
William H. Watson, M. D., Utica.
Henry E. Turner, Lowville.
St. Clair McKelway, Albany.
David Murray, Secretary.
Albert B. Watkins, Inspector of Teachers' Classes.
Edward I. Devlin.
Charles B. Cole.

Colleges.

Columbia College — Professor William G. Peck.

Union College — Professor John Foster, Professor W. S. Chapin, Professor Cady Staley, Professor William Wells.

Albany Medical College — Professor Willis G. Tucker, M. D.

Albany Law School — Professor Horace E. Smith, Professor H. S. McCall.

Albany College of Pharmacy — Alfred B. Huested, M. D., Secretary.

Hamilton College — Professor Edward North, Professor C. H. F. Peters, Professor F. M. Burdick, Assistant Professor George P. Bristol, Professor Oren Root, Jr., Professor A. P. Kelsey, Professor H. A. Frink.

Hobart College — President E. N. Potter.

College of the City of New York — President Alexander S. Webb.

Elmira Female College — President Augustus W. Cowles.

St. Stephen's College — President R. B. Fairbairn.

Vassar College — Professor LeRoy C. Cooley.

Manhattan College — President Brother Anthony.

Cornell University — President Andrew D. White, Professor W. D. Wilson.

Rutgers Female College — Professor Daniel S. Martin.

Syracuse University — Professor Charles W. Bennett, Trustee J. Dorman Steele.
St. Bonaventure's College — Professor Joseph Butler.
Niagara University — Vice-President Michael J. Kircher.
Canisius College — Professor Thomas S. Ashton, Professor A. Quaggenberger.
Albany Normal School — President Edward P. Waterbury, Mrs. M. A. B. Kelley, Miss Mary A. McClelland, Miss Kate Stoneman, Professor A. N. Husted.
Oswego Normal School — Principal E. A. Sheldon.
Cortland Normal School — Professor James M. Milne.
State Library — Librarians Henry A. Homes, S. B. Griswold, George R. Howell.
State Museum — Director James Hall.
State Entomologist — J. A. Lintner.

ACADEMIES.

Adams Collegiate Institute — Principals O. B. Rhodes, Mrs. A. H. Coughlan.
Albany High School — Principal John E. Bradley, Miss Mary Morgan.
Albany Public Schools — Superintendent Charles W. Cole, Principals E. A. Corbin, George H. Benjamin, J. L. Bothwell.
Auburn Academic High School — Principal George R. Cutting.
Bath-on-the-Hudson Union School, Academic Department — Principal H. B. Wilkes.
Cambridge Union School, Academic Department — Principal N. G. Kingsley.
Canandaigua Academy — Ex-Principal Noah T. Clarke.
Canisteo Academy — Principal D. M. Estee, Mrs. D. M. Estee.
Carthage Union School, Academic Department — Principal George F. Sawyer.
Catskill Free Academy — Principal James V. D. Ayers.
Claverack Academy and H. R. Institute — Principal Alonzo Flack, Professor Wm. McAfee.
Clyde High School — Principal Edward Hayward.
Cobleskill Union School, Academic Department — Principal P. F. Burke.
Cook Academy — Professor J. W. Ellis.

Crown Point Union School, Academic Department — Principal T. R. Kneil.
Delaware Academy — Principal James D. Griffin.
Delaware Literary Institute — Principal C. H. Verrill.
Egberts High School — Superintendent A. J. Robb.
Elizabethtown Union School, Academic Department — Principal W. H. Coats.
Fayetteville Union School, Academic Department — Principal C. D. Larkins.
Fort Edward Collegiate Institute — Principal Joseph E. King.
Fulton Union School, Academic Department — Principal Asa Boothby.
Glens Falls Academy — Principal D. C. Farr, Miss Anna A. Wing.
Greene Union School, Academic Department — Commissioner Clarence E. Bloodgood.
Holland Patent Union School, Academic Department — Principal C. B. Van Wie.
Hornell Free Academy — Principal Frank L. Green.
Houghton Seminary — Principals A. G. Benedict, Mrs. A. G. Benedict, N. F. Wright.
Hudson Academy — Principal C. Van T. Smith.
Jordan Free Academy — Principal John W. Chandler.
Kingston Free Academy — Principal F. J. Cheney.
Lansingburgh Academy — Principal C. T. R. Smith.
Little Falls Union School, Academic Department — Principal Leigh R. Hunt.
Mechanicville Academy — Mrs. S. E. King Ames.
Munro Collegiate Institute — Principal T. K. Wright.
Oneonta Union School, Academic Department — Principal N. N. Bull.
Oswego High School — E. J. Hamilton, Secretary of Board of Education.
Palatine Bridge Union School, Academic Department — Principal C. N. Cobb.
Pompey Academy — Principal Robert F. Sullivan.
Putnam Union School, Academic Department — Addie M. Goodwin.
Saint Mary's Catholic Institute, Amsterdam — Principal Rev. J. P. McIncrow, Prof. A. B. Haberer.

Sandy Creek Union School, Academic Department — Principal J. Edman Massee.
Schenevus Union School, Academic Department — Principal F. S. Lowell.
Schoharie Union School, Academic Department — Principal Solomon Sias.
Schuylerville Union School, Academic Department — Principal J. H. Weinmann.
Seymour Smith Academy — Principal Abraham Mattice.
Sodus Academy — Principal Elisha Curtiss.
Stamford Seminary and Union School — Principal Robert W. Hughes.
Temple Grove Seminary — President Charles F. Dowd.
Troy Female Seminary — Annie F. Woodward.
Troy High School — Superintendent David Beattie, Principal H. P. Judson.
Troy Public Schools — Principal J. W. Cole.
Ulster Academy — Principal W. E. Bunten.
Unadilla Academy — Principal E. Belknap.
Utica Free Academy — Principal G. C. Sawyer.
Walworth Academy — Principal J. C. Norris.
Waterford Union School, Academic Department. — Principal E. E. Ashley.
Waverly High School — Principal H. H. Hutton.
C. W. Bardeen, Syracuse.
Ex-Principal N. W. Benedict, Rochester.
Eugene Bouton, Department of Public Instruction.
David Burke, Mineville.
A. H. Coughlan, Adams.
Robert C. Flack, Principal Mount Hope Ladies Seminary, Tarrytown.
Adelbert Gardenier, Principal New Lebanon Union School.
M. M. Goodenough, Principal Hamilton Female Seminary.
Franklin B. Hough, M. D., Lowville.
Mrs. C. A. Ingham, Algonas, Iowa.
H. M. Paine, M. D., Albany.
Principal George H. Quay, Cohoes.
Rev. J. D. Tucker, Troy.
Superintendent Edward Wait, Lansingburgh.
Edgar S. Werner, Albany.
Charles E. West, Brooklyn.

II.

AN ADDRESS IN COMMEMORATION OF THE CENTENNIAL ANNIVERSARY OF THE ESTABLISHMENT OF THE UNIVERSITY OF THE STATE OF NEW YORK, AND THE ORGANIZATION OF THE BOARD OF REGENTS.

By Hon. GEORGE WILLIAM CURTIS, Regent of the University.

The great Puritan poet, addressing the great Puritan general, naturally recalled his famous fields of battle, but, contemplating other and different services to the State, he exclaimed:

> "While Darwent streams, with blood of Scots imbru'd,
> And Dunbar field resound thy praises loud,
> And Worcester's laureate wreath, yet much remains
> To conquer still: Peace hath her victories
> No less than those of War."

It is not the drum-beat nor the bugle-call, the proud clash of military music and the thunder of artillery, which now for many years have bidden us to the centennial commemorations of battles, that summon us to-day. Famous in war, the stately river upon whose banks we stand is not less renowned for its victories of peace. In the long contest of armed Europe during the eighteenth century for the control of the Western continent, as in the military strategy of the American Revolution, the Hudson river was still the prize. Upon the Hudson the great contest culminated and turned toward triumph. Upon the Hudson the desperate endeavor to seize by treachery what could not be gained by honorable force was foiled. Upon the Hudson the patriot army was disbanded, and from its mouth the defeated British army sailed away. But upon the banks of the Hudson, also New York one of the united colonies, constituted herself an independent State; upon the Hudson she ratified the Constitution of the United States, and upon the Hudson Washington was inaugurated and the national government began. Upon the Hudson Robert Fulton, with happy daring, freed the commerce of the world from dependence upon the fickle wind, and Dewitt Clinton drew to its bosom the harvests of the Western prairies, and made it the highway of commercial empire, as nature had made it the path of military power. Crowned and wreathed with the association of great and beneficent events, the rejoicing river, which its discoverer hoped might be a shorter passage to the spiced and golden East, flows through a region fairer than fabled Cathay, teeming with busy people, humming with various industry, its spacious valley the home of greater happiness, intelligence and prosperity than the valley of any other river in the world. It is to the shore of this historic stream, still murmuring with the music of the centennial commemoration of victories of the war, that we come to celebrate the centenary of an event not less significant, the first great victory of the peace that followed the war, the organization of the system of education in New York.

Nothing in the American Union, with all its homogeneity, is more striking than the differences of its communities, which speak the same language, share the same religious faith, cherish the same national traditions, which are welded together by every tie of blood and common interest, and which only nominal and invisible bounds divide. With all this intimate and indissoluble union, a certain individual character and spirit, a certain tone in the speech, a form of phrase, a peculiarity of temperament, a local tradition and pride, a thousand details which instantly and unerringly distinguish one community from another are as obvious as the general resemblance and the national sympathy. It is this vigor and raciness of local life which assure the united power and the common prosperity, by instinctively repelling all extreme and dangerous consolidation. Those who fear a perilous political centralization and overthrow of local rights and government by national legislation and judicial construction forget the political genius of the English race, from which we are chiefly sprung, and the tradition of the American people. Americans will never confound the necessary conditions of national union with centralized empire, and the first serious effort to change the essential basis of that union, which is local feeling and local self-government, would be the last.

Between no neighboring communities in the country is the local difference more pronounced than between New York and New England, which, practically, the Hudson river divides. It begins with the European settlement of each, and in nothing is it more striking than in the early interest in education. The most powerful motive for the foundation of a State, the desire to enjoy religious and civil liberty, was the impulse of both branches of the New England emigration. But men and women who are courageous and enduring enough to leave a tyrannical State, are not necessarily wise and persistent enough to found a free and progressive commonwealth; and the significant fact in the settlement of New England, and the key of its dominating influence upon the continent, are not only that it was effected by strong and sturdy devotees, who felt religious freedom in a savage wilderness to be more precious than the sweet and sacred charm of an ancient and historic home, but that the emigration was led by educated men. The Puritan flight from England to Amsterdam and Leyden, from Delft Haven to Plymouth, and the later voyage to Salem and Boston, was the going forth of a church and a school, a mighty march from the old world and the old age to the new world and the new age by scholars and divines; and as in the university the Reformation arose to organize modern Europe, from the university also came the creative impulse and the moral energy which have chiefly directed American civilization. It was moral energy, with a thousand limitations, indeed, but directed by educated intelligence, which planted New England, and on this happy centenary we can recall no more significant fact than that the seal of the university, that is, of highly educated leadership, is impressed upon the very beginning of our national development.

Yet that the university should have been the nursery of colonial America is not surprising. The controlling American movement sprang from the Reformation. It sought freedom of worship for itself; and as religious progress in the old world was the child of the university, it is to the university that we owe civil liberty in the new world. Wickliffe, John Huss, Jerome of Prague, and Luther; all the leaders of the new learning in England and Italy, Colet, Erasmus, Sir Thomas More — the fathers of the Reformation — spoke from the university. In the university alone could the high argument between the Roman Church and the human mind be comprehended and maintained, and there the debate between power and liberty, between alleged spiritual authority and sacred tradition, and the instinctive and inherent sovereignty of the individual mind, ended in the happy emancipation of modern civilization from medieval slavery. In America that emancipation was accomplished. The university was the school of the clergy, the clergy were the leaders of the people. Roger Williams, a clergyman, a graduate of English Cambridge, first in America and in the world, declared the fundamental principle of political and religious freedom, the principle of soul liberty, and the absolute separation of church and state. From Jonathan Mayhew's pulpit flashed the morning gun of the American Revolution. The university emancipated the human mind, and of that emancipation the triumphant American Republic is the most glorious result.

As the university was the asylum of liberty in the earlier modern epoch, so in no great modern state has the university been merely a pensioned parasite. It has been rather the well-spring of national life and the foe of tyranny. When Metternich was Austria, he suspected nothing so much as the university, and Russia quails before it to-day as a mighty masked battery of liberty. When Prussia fell at Jena, the greatest statesman of his time, Baron Stein, whom Napoleon feared more than he feared an army, founded the University of Berlin to arouse a spirit of patriotism powerful enough to revive a crushed and prostrate nation, and to stay the overwhelming Napoleonic despotism. By the enthusiasm of her people Prussia was nationally redeemed, and no redeeming impulse was more effective than that of the university. When I heard its lectures thirty years ago, it was but one of the nineteen universities of Germany, but it had a hundred and fifty professors and four thousand students, and the nineteen universities were still the nineteen most dangerous and untiring foes of monarchial reaction, and of the Holy Alliance of Despots.

The American colonial colleges were generally founded by graduates of English Cambridge and Oxford, and chiefly by Cambridge men. The larger part of the teachers were of the same universities, and the courses of study and the general discipline were the same as in the colleges of the mother institutions. The chief difference of method lay in the conferring of degrees, which at Oxford and Cambridge was the especial function of the university and not of the college. During the colonial period there were nine colleges in the country: Harvard, founded in 1636, being the oldest, and Rutgers in 1771, at the very beginning of the Revolution, the youngest. But most of them were poor and puny. William and Mary, the second in the list, and the mother of the oldest of college Greek letter societies, the Phi Beta Kappa, had no authority to grant degrees, and in 1730 it was little better than a boarding-school. One of its own fellows described it as "a college without a chapel, without a scholarship and without a statute, a library without books, a president without a fixed salary, and a burgess without electors." The young Virginia planter owed little to the Virginia college. He was taught by the domestic chaplain, or if a better education was sought, he was sent to the northern colonies or to England. It was in New England, naturally, that the most efficient colleges were found, for they all sprang from the same devoted and sturdy spirit that had established Harvard. The legend of Dartmouth, the eighth college founded in the country, was *vox clamantis in deserto*. And upon the solitary shores of the upper Connecticut in 1769, where still the wild cat cried in the thicket, and the wolf hovered about the farm, and the rigors of the climate and the exposure of the frontier were little relieved, a college devoted to the higher education might well call itself a voice crying in the wilderness. But the character that heeded the voice, the impulse which founded and sustained the college, the feeling which years afterward bred in the heart of Daniel Webster's father the purpose to send his son thither, and which nourished in the son's breast the desire to go — this loyalty to knowledge as a source of power, and to intellectual training as the means of its effective exercise — is one of the proudest instincts of human nature, and one of the vital sources of American greatness. Never was Webster manlier, never was his eloquence purer than when, in his famous argument in the Dartmouth college case, which established one of the great beacons of our jurisprudence, he said, overpowered by generous emotion, his eyes tearful, and his voice faltering, " Sir, it is a small college, but there are those that love it."

That was the spirit which the colonial colleges fostered. It was a large and liberalizing spirit, true to the historic university tradition, and naturally, therefore, the colonial colleges produced the champions and the chiefs of the political revolution. As schools of education strictly, they were as effective as the colleges of the half century after the Revolution; but they imparted a training, also, as the result proved, which conformed to Milton's familiar requirement, and to the wisdom of Wolfe, the pupil of Melancthon, that to understand Latin and Greek is not learning in itself, but the entrance hall and ante-chamber of learning. During the colonial period the number of college graduates was always small. The whole number that was graduated at Kings College, in New York, from its first commencement, in 1758, to the day when it closed its doors in the Revolution, was not more than a hundred. But a little leaven leaveneth the whole lump. The oriental tradition said that a shred of ambergris flavored the Sultan's cup for a thousand years. There were great colonial leaders who were not college-bred, for indeed, the university does not monopolize the virtues and the moral graces, nor sequester for its own children genius, and wisdom, and statesmanship, and common sense. Washington and Franklin, and Abraham Lincoln, were not college men, and greater service than theirs to their country and to mankind can no man render. Does it follow that the service of Samuel Adams and John Adams, of James Otis and James Madison, of John Jay and Alexander Hamilton, would have been greater, or as great, without the mental discipline and the wisdom which come from enlarged and illuminating knowledge of human affairs, which it is the purpose of the university to impart? Because the genius of Shakespeare asks nothing of the schools, shall the schools be closed? Because original and controlling intellectual power cannot be imparted by education, shall it not be fostered and disciplined, directed, stimulated and restrained, by the wisdom of all the ages, and the experience of mankind? Abraham Lincoln was not college bred. But Abraham Lincoln, lying before the fire of pine knots that he might read his book, was inspired by that lofty desire to lift his mind into

"An ampler ether, a diviner air,"

which is the demand for the utmost knowledge, the completest mental and moral discipline — the instinct from which the university springs.

Into this realm of the higher education New York, a trading colony with a population of various nationalities, was slow to enter, and it was not until one hundred and twenty years after the settlement that a college was founded. The chief citizens of the colony were merchants, and their sons passed from the grammar school to the counting-house and to the West India Islands. The first historian of New York, Chief Justice Smith, says that for many years he and the deputy judges were the only college graduates, except the clergy of the English church, and in 1746, the year in which a law was passed authorizing a lottery to provide money to found a college, he knew but thirteen graduates in the province, and all of them young men. The historian draws a sorrowful picture of the condition of education. He praises warmly the charms of his lovely country-women, but he admits that there is nothing that they so generally neglect as reading; that the schools are of the lowest order, the instructors wanting instruction; the common speech extremely corrupted, and bad taste everywhere evident in all public and private proceedings.

There was naturally a feeling of shame in the province that the English universities and the colleges of New England should educate the young New Yorker; and, although with evident doubt and difficulty, at length, in 1751, the money was raised, and after some vigorous discussion and opposition, lest the new institution should fall under sectarian control, the college was chartered as Kings College in 1754. It was a memorable epoch in our history. In June of that year the Albany Congress assembled, in which Dr. Franklin proposed his plan of colonial union, and in the same year the French built Fort Duquesne, upon the present site of Pittsburgh, in Pennsylvania. The next year or two, while the college president was teaching his dozen pupils, were the years of the French expulsion from Nova Scotia, of Washington's march to Fort Duquesne, and of Braddock's defeat; of the vain attack of Sir William Johnson upon Crown Point, and of the opening contest for the American continent between France and England, which was to end upon the heights of Abraham. Frederick the Great was conquering in Germany; Robert Clive was subduing and stripping India; and William Pitt, as Prime Minister of England, held the mighty thunderbolts of Britain in his hand, and every day broke with the flash and the thunder of British victory.

This was the moment when Kings College opened its modest doors in the little town of ten thousand inhabitants, at the mouth of the Hudson, and it is curious to contrast its beginning and development with the university of Göttingen in Germany, which the same King George the Second — from whom the New York college takes its name — had founded twenty years before in a smaller town in another part of his dominions. Toward the end of the century, Göttingen was the most brilliant university in Europe for the eminence of its teachers and the variety and value of its lectures. In less than a hundred years from its foundation, it counted three thousand students, eighty-nine professors, and among them some of the most famous scholars in the world; a library of three hundred thousand volumes and five thousand manuscripts, and even now the town of Göttingen has but eighteen thousand inhabitants. The American college, when it had completed its first century, in a town which had grown from ten thousand to six hundred thousand inhabitants, showed by its catalogue one hundred and forty students and six professors.

Yet such meagre figures are not the measure of its splendid service. In the twenty years from its foundation in 1754 to the beginning of the revolutionary war, as I have said, only one hundred students graduated from Kings College. But they were an army in themselves. The college in those creative days, when a great nation was to be born and great historic events to be achieved, trained men for leaders. It graduated scholars less apt to edit Greek plays than to make American history. It produced men of courage, insight and tenacity, who had learned from literature and the annals of all ages the resources of liberty and the sophistries of power. They were scholars of the world, not of the cloister. Their degrees admitted them *ad eundem* with Pym and Milton, with Eliot and John Hampden. However reactionary the officers of the college, John Jay and Robert Livingston, Gouverneur Morris and Egbert Benson, Philip Van Cortlandt and Henry Rutgers, with others of not less illustrious family names in New York, were educated Sons of Liberty, and in all the advancing life of the province they were the conspicuous leaders. And when the Tory president, Dr. Cooper, a former fellow of Oxford, entered the lists for the British government, he was vanquished by a masked antagonist from under whose visor, when it was lifted, looked the face of the marvelous boy, Alexander Hamilton, then a youth of eighteen and a freshman of the college.

Thus, as the university had guided the controlling emigration to the country, and had fostered and directed the instinct of nationality, so also it supplied the leadership for national independence. As the debate passed from sermon, and pamphlet, and argument in courts of law, from the town meeting, and the caucus, and the committee of correspondence, to the march of armies and the battle field, the colleges closed their doors indeed, but not until the statesmen of the Continental Congress and the Constitutional Convention had passed out of them. When the war ended, and the united colonies, loosely huddled in a chaotic confederation, were to be bound in a flexible, powerful and harmonious national union, once more the colleges furnished the builders of the State, and of the fifty-five members of the Constitutional Convention, thirty-three were graduates. When the Convention adjourned, Columbia and Princeton united in Hamilton, Jay and Madison to present to the country the great argument for the Constitution, and it was Alexander Hamilton, a son of

Columbia, who lifted New York into the Union, and a son of Princeton, James Madison, who placed Virginia by her side.

These are facts to be proudly remembered and emphasized upon this occasion and in this place, because there is a common and cheap depreciation of the college, as if it were a nursery of dainty feebleness or useless pedantry, from which a vigorous manhood cannot be expected to issue. Indeed, it has become a familiar sneer against every endeavor for purer politics and a higher political morality, that it is favored by college-bred men, as if trained intelligence, intellectual expansion and moral elevation were less fitted to deal with questions of the public welfare than the venal huckstering which makes politics a trade and the political ignorance which thrives upon political corruption. The remark addressed by his panegyrist to Governor Stephen Hopkins, of Rhode Island, may be truly applied to the colonial colleges: "Much might be said of your Honor's superior abilities in mathematics and natural philosophy," but above them all the panegyrist counts "your wise government of a people."

It was a just and commanding instinct which prompted the leaders of New York, when the Revolution ended, to lay the broad foundation of a system of education for the State which should tend to cherish the intelligent patriotism and public virtue which had secured American independence. Education throughout the State had been paralyzed by the war. The schools were everywhere closed. The one college was practically extinct. But, in the year after the negotiation of the treaty which recognized the final separation of the American States from Great Britain, Governor George Clinton invited the legislature to consider the question of the revival and encouragement of seminaries of learning. He was not a college-bred man, but he was a wise statesman, and one of the great Governors of New York; and in the first confused and dark hour that followed the war he felt, perhaps vaguely and remotely, but surely, the necessity of opposing to the money-making spirit, which was sure powerfully to assert its supremacy, the spirit of letters and art. It is pleasant to think of the sturdy Governor in the capital city, in whose half-charred and neglected streets the trees had been cut down and the ruined buildings had been left unrestored, and from whose shores the long-occupying and devastating foreign army had just marched away, pleading that not Tyre and Sidon, not Carthage and Capua, should be the model of the new State, but Athens, rather—

> "Athens, the eye of Greece, mother of arts
> And eloquence."

"Neglect of the education of youth"—were Clinton's memorable words in his message to the Legislature of January 21, 1784—"is among the evils consequent on war. Perhaps there is scarce any thing more worthy your attention than the revival and encouragement of seminaries of learning, and nothing by which we can more satisfactorily express our gratitude to the Supreme Being for His past favors, since piety and virtue are generally the offspring of an enlightened understanding." The Legislature did not shrink from declaring the duty which the Governor urged, of forming the minds of the youth of the State to virtue, and from this noble purpose of promoting public virtue, and consequent public usefulness, sprang the University of the State of New York.

With the English practical genius and tendency to adapt existing institutions to the actual situation, rather than to attempt a wholly new system of education, the first proposition was to revive Kings College as the nucleus of a university, to be composed of all colleges that might arise in the State, the combined institution to be governed and controlled by the Regents of the University who were created by the act. This act practically violated the charter of old Kings College, and sequestered to the State its property; nor was it improved by an amendment giving to the clergy of each denomination the right of representation in the University regency. Practically, also, it committed all the details of the management of the college to the Regents. Not only were they to employ the professors and pay their salaries, and to prescribe a system of discipline for the students, but they were to repair the college buildings, and to make the porter's lodge comfortable, and to pay the messenger £18 per annum, and to take care that the floor scrubbers were diligent, and to procure a bell for the college, and to direct the purchase of four cords of wood annually, and to defray the expense thereof from the treasury of the University. The minutes of the meetings of the Regents, in the days of this simple service, show how impracticable the scheme would become as the University developed, but the minutes have passages, also, which command attention.

On the 17th of May, 1784, a hundred years ago, the first candidate for admission to the University, in its only existing college, presented himself to the Board of Education. His name was Dewitt

Clinton. His uncle George, the Governor, was the Chancellor of the University; his father, General James Clinton, was a Regent of the University; and his son, George W. Clinton, is to-day the Vice-Chancellor of the University, honored and beloved. During the century no name is more illustrious in the annals of New York than that of Clinton—hereditary honors and hereditary esteem springing, as becomes a republic, from hereditary merit. The next two candidates who presented themselves for admission were Philip and George Livingston, sons of Philip Livingston, who came to study where their famous kinsman, Robert R. Livingston, the Chancellor of the State, studied; for then the families most conspicuous in the public service of the State and country were associated with the College and the University, while the Board of Regents itself comprised some of the most eminent men in the State. But serious defects in the law constantly disclosed themselves, and especially it was seen that it would be impossible for a single Board to have charge of the government, direction and funds of many colleges widely dispersed through the State; and on the 31st of January, 1787, a committee, of which Hamilton, Jay, Livingston, Mason, Rogers, Clarkson and Duane were members, was appointed to report upon the condition and prospects of the University. On the 16th of February, the committee submitted a report recommending fundamental changes in the organization of the University. They proposed the appointment of a distinct corporation for every college, and the establishment of a system of academies throughout the State, and that both colleges and academies should be placed under a wise and salutary subordination to the Board of Regents. On the 15th of March, Hamilton submitted a bill to be laid before the Legislature, which, on the 13th of April, 1787, by the approval of the Counsel of Revision, became a law, and is the final form of the act creating the University.

To the greatest constructive genius in our political history, that of Alexander Hamilton, New York owes the system of its higher education. But it is remarkable that when it was designed, there was but one moribund college, and no academy or public school, in the State. It is part of the prescience of genius that he knew that the one would produce the other, and six years after the passage of his act the Board of Regents recommended the establishment of primary schools, and two years afterward Governor Clinton urged the establishment of common schools throughout the State, and that vast and beneficent system of public instruction began, which fills the air from Montauk to Niagara, and from the Adirondacks to Pennsylvania, with the daily music of the free school bell, and covers imperial New York with thousands of school-houses, thronged with more than a million of scholars, maintained at an annual cost of $12,000,000; the nurseries of the general education, which is the bulwark and the defense of patriotism, liberty and law, and which, in the spirit of Hamilton's provision, which abolished all religious tests for the presidency or professorships in any college or academy under the visitation of the Regents, please God, no partisan or sectarian hand shall ever touch.

But while New York, at the close of the Revolution, was founding her system of general education under the name of the University of New York, one of the oldest and most famous schools of Europe, the University of Paris, which, in the thirteenth century, was thronged with thirty thousand students, was overwhelmed in the maelstrom of the French revolution. In 1793, the year in which the Board of Regents in New York recommended the establishment of primary schools, the schools and the University were suppressed in France; and in 1795, the year in which George Clinton impelled the Legislature to make an appropriation in aid of common schools in New York, a new school system was vainly attempted in France. In 1808, twenty years after the establishment of the University of New York, the Emperor Napoleon founded a system of secondary schools, with twenty-seven university centers in the chief towns of the country, each with its local government, and altogether forming the University of France, which absorbed the entire system of public instruction. No school was allowed to exist without its authority, no teacher could instruct except he were a graduate. In 1850, after the revolution of 1848, the exclusive privilege of the University was abolished, but its general system remained. It is, in substance, the scheme of Hamilton, carried out by a despot with immense resources and under different national circumstances. But Hamilton had the same imperial instinct. His law authorized the Regents to visit and inspect all the colleges, academies and schools which are or may be established in the State, to examine thoroughly their education and discipline, and yearly to report their condition to the Legislature. His purpose was plain and it was characteristic. Under the name of university he meant to include the whole system of education in the State, and to give it the vitality and vigor which result from local government under a strong central supremacy.

The common school system which the Regents first suggested was not committed to their direction. But its rapid growth and wide development showed how closely adapted it was to the wishes and tastes of the people of the State. In fifty years from the first act which appropriated money for the schools, there were nearly eleven thousand school districts, and more than six hundred thousand pupils, and the movement for the freedom of the schools had already begun. In the same time five colleges had been chartered, but none of them with affluent or even adequate revenues, and the Regents of the University were devoted chiefly to the care of the academies. There are now twenty-two colleges in the State, but the academies have been the chief care of the Regents. The design of Hamilton, as inferred from the act of 1787, has never been fulfilled. He conceived, doubtless, an institution which should be an active and intimate fraternity of all the colleges and academies of the State, as Oxford University is composed of the colleges in the city of Oxford. In that city —

"Ye distant spires! Ye antique towers!"

there are twenty-four colleges, each with an independent corporate organization. But there is one life, one pride, one fame, among them all. There may be Magdalen and Brazen Nose, Merton and Oriel, Christ Church and All Souls, but they are all Oxford. It is Oxford which is the school of medieval tradition; Oxford which is the fond recollection of her sons of any college; Oxford which is one of the twin scholastic glories of England. The members of every college are familiar with those of every other. Recruits from every college pull for the honor of Oxford against the picked crew of the rival university. One form of faith unites them all, and it is Oxford that sends a member to Parliament.

Is this a situation paralleled in our University? Alfred is practically as remote from St. John's, Columbia from Madison, Ingham from Cornell, as Dartmouth from Brown or Princeton from Harvard. They are separate in religious faith and academic discipline, and the fact that they are grouped together as colleges of the University of the State gives them no more essential unity of academic life than it gives them actual neighborhood. Do the boys of Columbia, of Union, of Cornell, of Hamilton, of Rochester, of Madison, of Syracuse, or Hobart, shout and sing to the glory of the University, or to that of their own *alma mater* in her own chosen melody? The Regents of the University, indeed, share with the Legislature the authority to grant charters to colleges, and to annul them whenever it shall appear that the endowment has not been legally paid; and the colleges report to the Regents their condition and the disposition of their funds. But their supervision is ceremonial and perfunctory, not vital and authoritative. The Board of Regents has no directing power over the colleges. It cannot control their instruction or discipline, and there is little community or life, or interest, or association, among the colleges themselves. How many of them have adopted even the modest suggestion of the late Chancellor Benedict, that they should place a head-line on the title pages of their catalogues, stating that they were colleges of the University? Each prescribes its own course of study, and confers its own degrees, without reference to the University. They are friends, indeed, inspired by a generous emulation. In the convocation, each college bears its part with ability, and courtesy, and grace. But each is conscious that it is a law to itself, that there is no supreme, superior authority, to which it must defer. The convocation is the arena of delightful and valuable discussion. But it is a confederation of sovereigns, not a national union.

Hamilton, however, no more designed a scholastic than a political confederation, and undoubtedly the University of New York is not what he foresaw. It is but a pleasant and unnecessary fiction, that it is a kind of American Oxford. It is a fiction because there is no vital resemblance between the institutions. It is pleasant because of the association with the venerable English school. It is unnecessary, because the University of New York has a distinct, and dignified, and beneficent character and function of its own. That function, during the century, has been two-fold — it has been both direct and representative. The foundation of the University marks the establishment of a system of education extending from the common schools to the colleges, and in this system it has fulfilled an illustrious part as the official intermediary of the secondary or higher schools, chartering academies and colleges, receiving their reports, providing for the teaching of teachers, conducting a vast and progressive scheme of examinations to determine a suitable grade of academic studies, and to adjust the ratio in which the bounty of the State shall be distributed, and finally, responsibly supervising the State library, now of more than one hundred and twenty thousand volumes, and the State Museum of Natural History, renowned for its paleontological treasures. This is a service of complex and infinite detail, requiring incessant attention, the utmost promptness and accuracy, signal administrative ability, and a wise and comprehensive direction. It is, therefore, with just pride that the Regents may truly say, upon their first centenary, that this ancient and most important trust of the service of the State has been discharged with a fidelity, an efficiency, and an economy, which I will not say are unequaled, but which are certainly unsurpassed in any department of the State government. The annual appropriation for the Regents is but $9,000. There are no salaries paid except for those of the office, for actual work, and every dollar of the Regents' appropriation stands for a full hundred cents' worth of effective service. Modest, unostentatious, in the best sense conservative, and devoted to a lofty and ennobling duty, it is not without reason that the members of the Board of Regents are selected for their unpaid service with an impressive and dignified ceremonial, and that the State chooses to appoint her representatives and guardians of the interests of higher education in the Commonwealth with the same solemnity with which she selects her Senators in the national Legislature. It was with the same sense of fitness that some of the Regents, in days somewhat more formal than these, caused the church bells to be rung to announce their entrance into a town to visit the academy, that the mind of youth might be impressed with a due sense of the dignity of these representatives of the State interest in academic education. The praise of the efficient work that I have described belongs mainly to the administrative officers of the Board at the capital of the State, of whom the Secretary is the executive agent, and in nothing is the State of New York more fortunate than in the character and ability of the eleven gentlemen who, during the century, have held the office of Secretary and Assistant Secretary of the Board of Regents of the University. Had every office in the State been filled with the same single regard to personal character and especial fitness, the annals of New York would seem to be those of Sir Thomas More's well-ordered Utopia, or Plato's ideal republic.

This is the first of the great services of the Board of Regents of the University, and of this service there has been no intelligent denial. The poet Halleck, indeed, in some good-natured verses long ago gently derided the disproportion between the pomp of the appointment of the Regents and the nature of their duty, of which, however, he knew little; and there have been suggestions in the Legislature, and especially in the Constitutional Convention of 1867, that the relations of the State to education should be intrusted to a single direction, and not divided, as now, between the Board of Regents and the Department of Public Instruction. But to this view, however correct it might be in theory, as also to the other proposition, that the Department of Public Instruction in the Common Schools should be a bureau in the University Board, or the counter suggestion that the trust of the University Board should be transferred to the Common School Department, it has been always strongly objected that nothing could be more unwise than to change a traditional system which is at once so effective and so economical. This reply has seemed to be so reasonable in itself, and the light of more general and intimate knowledge of the services of the Board, that this ancient institution was never more firmly fixed in the public confidence and regard than it is to-day upon the happy completion of its centennial anniversary.

The second great service of the University is not measurable like the first, by statistics and details. It is a service of moral influence, of intellectual elevation. For the University of the State of New York is the perpetual witness of the imperial Commonwealth to the profound truth of George Clinton's words, that "piety and virtue are generally the offspring of an enlightened understanding." It is the continuing declaration of the State that the higher education promotes a higher national and local life, that colleges and academies are not roots of feebleness but sources of strength, and that there is no more insidious enemy of free, popular institutions, than the man who derides trained and educated intelligence. If in other countries, what the State honors the people honor, because they are accustomed to be led by the government, in this country, what the State honors the people honor because they are the government. They know that neither the college, the academy, nor the common school, the counting-room, the work-shop, or the caucus, can do more than inspire, develop and regulate innate powers and disposition. But they have learned, for their own history teaches, that the youth who earnestly desire the knowledge and the training which the college supplies, are those who become men that the country wants; and they plainly see and gladly own that no community can serve its own best and highest interest more effectively than by providing, amply and worthily, for the utmost possible development and discipline of the moral and intellectual powers with which it is endowed.

This loyalty to the mere name of the higher education is one of the most significant facts in our national life. President Barnard, of Columbia College, an authority on the subject without a superior, five years ago estimated the whole number of colleges in the country to be four hundred and twenty-five, or one to a little more than one hundred thousand of the population. The whole number of students he computed to be one to twenty-five hundred of the population, while half a century ago it was about one student to two thousand inhabitants. Many of these colleges are but enterprises of private speculation, many are but little more than well-meaning high schools, and very few of them can be called in any true sense universities. But they show the instinctive loyalty of the people to the idea of a liberal and comprehensive education. They attest the national consciousness that the word "college" stands for a great and noble public influence. Take from the country the educated force, in all its degrees, which these institutions represent — reduce the standard of education to reading, writing and the elementary rules of arithmetic — banish the literature of England, Germany, France, Italy, of Greece and Rome, their philosophy, their art, the story of their political and social development, and the record of the progressive march of liberty through different ages and in widely-varying institutions — seal up again the marvelous arcana of science with which modern genius has so bountifully blessed the world — assume that the common school, fundamental and beneficent, and indispensable as it is, furnishes all that the American citizen needs to know, and implant, if you can, in the American mind, profound distrust of the counsels of highly-educated men — would you have blessed or cursed the land? Would you have given the national mind higher moral elevation or greater practical power? Would the national character be purer, stronger, better? It is the inestimable blessing of this annual commencement season that it summons us from the absorbing and unsparing competitions of trade, from the furious passions of political controversy, from the heat and fret and toil of daily life, up, up, to the mount of vision, to meditate the divine decrees, and to behold clearly the truth that it is not riches, nor empire, nor enterprise, nor any form whatever of material prosperity, but unbending fidelity to the moral law written upon the consciousness of every citizen, which is the sure foundation of great and enduring States, and which, while it remains unshaken and supreme, will forever renew the American republic as the celestial order of nature renews the glory of midsummer.

Mr. Chancellor, the men of a hundred years ago, from whose hands we have received the great trust which we administer, long since have passed away, and our descending footsteps follow theirs. The exigencies of those times, not less than of ours, demanded wisdom, abounding knowledge, devoted patriotism, moral energy, and from the desire and purpose to provide and perpetuate these primary social forces this institution sprang. So, likewise, those who follow us, and who, a hundred years hence, as now we recall our predecessors, shall recall us — let us hope not altogether as unfaithful — will find that the same spirit and influence and power which moulded and marshalled the controlling American emigration — which conducted the prodigious colonial debate with Great Britain — which fostered in the American heart the demand, and secured from the British crown the acknowledgment of national independence — which raised the States from the shifting sands of confederation to the eternal rock of national union — and which, in subsequent days, dealing with tremendous national controversies as they arose, gave the land peace with freedom, are the forces which alone can cope successfully with the vast questions that are arising before us, the humane and supreme forces of intellectual training, of copious knowledge, and of inflexible morality, which are represented by the University of the State of New York.

III.

THE AMERICAN COLLEGE.

By Hon. CHARLES E. FITCH, Regent of the University.

GENTLEMEN OF THE CONVOCATION : —I find my theme in the leading of this centennial occasion. I wish to speak of the American College, emphasizing in the treatment both adjective and noun of the *American College*, with its native inspiration and its distinctive functions. An outworn theme, perchance, you will say, frayed and made threadbare at thousands of literary festivals, torn into shreds from hundreds of commencement stages. Nay! it is a pertinent and a persuasive theme, whilst there are graduates of American colleges to confess their filial obligations, a vital and an exigent theme whilst the American system is assailed by so many and by such various foes, by empirics who, in the name of the new education, would perplex and confuse it by multiform and incongruous elective courses ; by radicals who, in the name of reform, would revolutionize it; and by iconoclasts who, in the name of the universities they would build, by State and national largess on its ruins, would first destroy it. I bring to the discussion no special gifts of scholarship ; for the men of my profession, much as they sometimes vaunt themselves upon their superior wisdom, are, at the best, superficial in their attainments, glancing at a subject and then forsaking and forgetting it, rarely probing deeply or searching exhaustively. I do, however, bring to my theme the prompting of my early New England training, long residence in two New York college towns, with some cognizance of and slight official connection with the workings of the system in this State; and, as thence arising, a reluctance to essay new educational departures, unless I can see very clearly that the new ways are better than the old. The restless explorer is not necessarily the intelligent discoverer. The critic is not uniformly — indeed, he is rarely — the constructor. Change, merely for the sake of change, is, of all things, least desirable. Possibly, from my point of observation, I may make some suggestions upon the subject in hand, which might not occur to either the technical scholar or the professional educator.

I shall certainly try to present a practical view of the American College as related to the American State, and to the evolution of American citizenship. I do not expect the assent of all who hear me in the opinions I shall advance; but, as I hold freedom of discussion to be one of the chief advantages of this Convocation, and that, from such discussion, wise conclusions will be reached, I trust I may have credit for the honesty of my convictions, if not for the strength of my positions.

We are in the din of a fierce educational debate. There are the clamor of theories and the claims of elective courses, which have not yet attained the dignity of experiments. There are censures upon existing modes of teaching and schemes innumerable for modifying, if not for improving them There are demands for larger freedom in the choice and for wider latitude in the range of studies. There are sneers at the poverty and jibes at the inefficiency of the smaller American colleges. It is urged that, by their numbers, they lower the standards, and, by their importunities, curtail the revenues, that should belong to a few favored institutions. Certain colleges do, indeed, fairly provoke ridicule by adopting the sounding title of universities, when they have nothing in common with universities; but it may be said, in passing, that none regret more keenly this foolishness of ambition than do some who are responsible for the instruction and government of these colleges, but not for their inapt naming. State foundations are exalted in comparison with colleges sustained by patronage and benefaction, and those under denominational auspices are specially assailed, as narrow in their limitations, as cramping mental expansion and as inharmonious with the American polity and the spirit of the age. Culture is deified and discipline is derided; and as a resultant, there is the strange jumble of the high school and the university in one — a kind of spiritual alembic for the instant transmutation of Kaspar Hauser into "admirable" Crichton, a patent furnace which, at a single heating, will convert the coarsest clay into the finest Dresden china. With all this clangor of controversy, these evidences of unrest, these pretensions of sciolism, how stands the American college? What is its place in the comprehensive scheme of education? What is its object? What warrant is there in its history for its perpetuity?

The place of the college in the American educational system is defined accurately in the inaugural address of President Carter of Williams, as, under his administration, it has been illustrated admirably. In brief, it is in advance of the gymnasium; it is antecedent to, although in much of its practical significance, independent of the university. It is in no sense a professional school, but is a preparatory school for all the professions. It has a fixed curriculum, formulated from the experience of the wisest educators, not flexible to the whims of callow striplings. It pursues no branches of study to their furthest outreach, but it suggests the purpose and stimulates the passion of all who would seek, along special lines, the ultimates of human knowledge. As Warden Fairbairn of St. Stephen's College says: "Its work is to develop the intellect, to draw out into conscious operation all the powers and capacities with which the mind of man is endowed, to whet and sharpen the mental faculties, so that we can make use of them in the affairs of life.' The college must also, in the words of President Carter, "regard the development of character as embraced within its functions;" and again, "it is the cultivation of the *whole* nature, in the years when every faculty is responsive, that is aimed at in the true college." And here comes in the value of that personal influence of the educator over the pupil, which has had such important and salutary bearing upon the formation of American civilization, and which cannot be insisted upon too strongly as a factor in the solution of the problem of American education. Without, therefore, detracting from the dignity of the American college, but rather in its exaltation, we may say that in the scheme of education, its province is wholly preparatory — preparatory to the higher departments of study that obtain in the university, preparatory to the professions, and above all, preparatory to manhood and to citizenship, in this view justifying Milton's conception of "a complete and generous education, that fits a man to perform justly, skillfully and magnanimously all the offices, both private and public, of peace and war."

In this view also, the American college is conformed to the fundamental American principle — its democratic diffusion, and it is thus conformed mainly, as it should be wholly, upon the voluntary plan. The State erects the common school at every cross-road, and over hill and dale its bells ring out their invitation to the rich and poor alike. De Tocqueville observes the fact, and Buckle, in commenting upon it, insinuates something of reproach, in that "the stock of American knowledge is small, but it is spread through all classes." We may claim that the reflection of the publicist, however pertinent it may have been fifty years ago, has lost much of its force, and that America, as well as Europe, has laid the foundations upon which will be built the most exact and elegant scholarship; but if we were driven to the choice between the highest culture for the few and the fair education of the many, it would not be difficult to declare our preference. Better citizens than savans; better common schools than universities; better the dissemination than the concentration of knowledge. Where the State does, or, at least, should stop, the voluntary system begins, and bears in its strong arms the American college. Whilst we are called upon justly — in a spirit, not of pessimism, but of patriotism — to deplore the unbridled sway and license of wealth in this country; the fictitious social distinctions it ordains, its baleful prominence in politics, its demoralizing display of extravagance in living, and its open employment of the agencies of corruption, we may as justly offset these pernicious outcomes by that splendid liberality, which has been the prince-bountiful of education, here founding a college, there establishing a seminary, here endowing a professorship, and there constructing a laboratory or an observatory, going up and down this imperial domain of ours, as a farmer treads his April field, scattering to the right and to the left the seeds of intelligence, virtue and religion, from the increase of which the golden harvests are being gathered. But not alone to conspicuous benefactors, like Lawrence and Vassar and Rich and Wells and Morgan and Litchfield and Deane is the American college indebted. All honor to those who have given of their abundance. Honor also to those who have given of their slender means, and whose offerings are redolent with the sweet savor of personal sacrifice. One hundred and eighty-four years ago, ten New England clergymen met at Branford, each with a bundle of books under his arm, which he gave for the founding of a college in the colony of Connecticut, and, in this humble way, Yale College had its origin. In the years that have intervened, the same missionary zeal, following in the track of the pioneer, from Plymouth Rock to Puget Sound, has, with much of self-denial and in spite of many obstacles, but always with unfaltering faith, dotted every State and Territory, along the lines of settlement, with institutions of higher learning.

But we are told that there are too many of these institutions; that they cumber the ground; that beneficence, as related to them, has been too indiscriminate, if not too lavish. In truth, they are fewer proportionately to our population, to say nothing of area, than is the lyceum to France, or the gymnasium to Germany. Don't let us be misled by a wrong use of terms, which confuses the college with the university, and ignores the true comparison. But the raid upon the American college proceeds, after a most un-American fashion. The colleges of Ohio, of which, as you know, there are a goodly number, have especially fallen under the ban of captious criticism, and have been inveighed against and ridiculed, the plea for their extinction having been intimated unmistakably, if not urged specifically. The purport of the argument reveals itself in the objections preferred. This college has an insufficient philosophical apparatus. Therefore, it should not be. That college has not a telescope of as many diameters as the one at Harvard; this has not a library as large as that at Yale; and still another has not been able to endow a chair in Sanskrit. Therefore, none of them should be. Level them all to the dust, with their excellencies, as well as their defects. Nay, not so! says an enlightened American conservatism.' These institutions are not, indeed, perfect. They have their general and their individual deficiencies. Some of them still feel the stress of poverty, and some are hampered by dogmatic councils, but all are doing more or less good work — work which would not be done, except for them. They are something, and that is better than nothing. They are many lights in many places, and this is better than a single light, though it be placed upon the mountain top. They attract to themselves many students who would, without them, have no advantages of higher education and they elevate and clarify the communities in which they are located. Thus they serve a dual purpose in the economy of citizenship, which is not to be lightly regarded nor recklessly depreciated. The Puritan civilization which a century ago pushed through the wilderness to occupy the banks of the Ohio, and a little later began to till the fertile acres of the Western Reserve, made no mistake when it took with it the college, as well as the plow, the spelling-book and the Bible. Let the State which has so small a percentage of illiteracy among its citizens of American birth, keep Kenyon and Denison and Oberlin and Urbana and Antioch and Hiram, even if she has Adelbert.

You will not consider me as making any invidious discrimination if, in this connection, I refer to an institution with which, from my own residence, I am acquainted, and concerning which I deem myself somewhat competent to speak. Thirty years ago, a Baptist college was established in a city of Western New York — a little college, but one which its sons love. Its classes have never averaged forty members. Until recently it has had pecuniary embarrassments to contend with, and, notwithstanding some late benefactions, is still comparatively poor. It has had, however, at its head one of the first educators in the land — a man of superb intellectual endowments and of immense stores of knowledge serviceable to his use, a man, too, of a rare quality of personal magnetism, which has drawn his pupils toward him to receive his impress, as the men of Rugby received that of Arnold, or those of Williams that of Hopkins. The faculty has been well equipped for its work, embracing such eminent teachers as Dewey and Kendrick and Lattimore, with others of like stamp, and the standard of scholarship has been high; but the controlling mind — the energizing force has been that of Anderson, who has supplemented the curriculum by earnest presentation of the duties which educated young men owe to the State, finding his theses in the onward sweep of events, and for whom his students have that rapt admiration with which Mrs. Browning apostrophises his Swedish namesake, "a man of men." Under him the college has, in addition to students from abroad, instructed many of the youth of the city who, without its presence, would have had neither the means nor the inclination to pursue their studies beyond the grammar school and the free academy; and, better still, many of these have not thought it beneath them to dedicate a generous scholarship to business avocations, so that the city is peculiarly distinguished for the number of liberally educated men who are serving their day as merchants and manufacturers, and even as clerks, as well as lawyers and doctors. A few weeks since Rochester celebrated the semi-centennial of its existence as a municipality, and, amid the festivities, there was no influence that received more cordial recognition than that which this little college has exerted upon the community in promoting its mental progress, in elevating its social tone, and in moulding an exceptionally pure order of morality. Would you deliberately extinguish such a light? Nor may I fail to notice how another city, with which I was long identified, has responded to the quickening and the refining influence of the college, which was there established some twelve years ago. Syracuse University may never justify its pretentious title, but it already justifies the purpose of its being.

But it is said that the American college is under denominational control. Waiving in the argument the fact that the sectarian bias is not nearly so pronounced as it is represented, and that there is a much larger measure of religious freedom than the critics concede, we say unhesitatingly that the American college should be under denominational control. The reason for the being of sectarian colleges is a republican reason, and here we are in direct issue with the advocates of State institutions. Slowly and painfully, but none the less surely, has the principle of the utter divorce of church and State, as essential to the purity of the one and to the integrity of the other, sought assertion. It is becoming established as the dominant American idea. Not yet, indeed, has it received its full and undisputed expression, for there are still odious features to be eliminated from State constitutions, and practices which custom sanctions in spite of law, to be abrogated; but the tread of the best thought is in the right direction, with no backward steps being taken, and statutory and organic law is defining the metes and bounds of the secular State and the spiritual church, independent each of the other. The secular State has no legitimate relation to education beyond its elementary stages. Higher education must be conducted on the voluntary system, and, therefore, by the various sects, as the only proper and practicable agencies in the premises. This is *not* a Christian nation. This *is* a Christian people. Observe the distinction, for it is one too often neglected. We do not write God in the Federal Constitution, but we engrave His name upon the tablets of our hearts. Individual benefactions and associated effort, for the elevation and the amelioration of the race, asylums, hospitals, colleges, therefore, take Christian expression, and the emulation and the attrition of the sects thus produced are not to be deplored. They are among the best outcomes of our national being — the very flower of our liberties. We are not ashamed of our colleges, although it is assumed — and this is the merest assumption — that they have come to a dead halt, decrepid, useless, incapable of further progress. They must yield to State institutions, which alone can stride vigorously onward. Before we give up our colleges, we want two things proved — two things which cannot be proved. The first is that their methods are radically defective, and the second is that sectarianism is incompatible with higher education. It is, on the contrary, in complete accord with it. The thirty-nine articles have played a pretty important part in the history of Cambridge and of Oxford, and yet no one will venture to assert that they have obscured the classic effulgence that glorifies the Isis and the Cam.

In one regard, especially, the character of the hostility to denominational colleges is irrational, for the demand for State interference with higher education comes, in large measure, from those who assume to be the most strenuous champions of the secular State. I honor them for their fealty to the secular State, for their opposition to religious exercises in the public schools, to the exemption of church property from taxation, to Sabbatarian laws as such and for their adherence to other reforms that the secular State involves; and I should be surprised, if I could be surprised at any emanation of contradictory human nature, that they can be, in any particular, untrue to their own premises; but as I have also seen men, who base their religious conditions upon pure reason, swing into vagaries of superstition, I regret, rather than marvel at, the eccentricity. But into what absurdities are these sticklers for State education betrayed. It is certain that, when education has passed the elementary — at least, the secondary — stage, it must receive, in one form or another, a sectarian inclination. I know it is claimed that the theological element can be eliminated from higher education — that there can be an impartial survey of history, a purely technical study of science, without reference to speculative thought or spiritual inquiries, which it seems necessarily to embrace, a colorless teaching, like that of the three R's, extended through the infinite of investigation. To use this theory is as fatuous in conception as it is impossible of application. Here are courses of lectures in French history, in which are portrayed the statesmanship of Mazarin, the controversies of the Gallican church with the see of Rome, the gilded selfishness of the *Ancien Regime*, the atrocities of the Reign of Terror. Here is the progress of the English nation, from Plantagenet to Guelph, including the secession from the papacy, the rebellion from the tyranny of Charles Stuart and the revolution of 1688, to be traced. Here are the researches of physical science to be unfolded, the deductions of philosophy to be enforced, the postulates of political economy to be inculcated. Can you explore the stars, or delve among the rocks, or follow the course of nations, without trenching on the domain of theology, without engaging in disputes that have vexed the centuries and deluged the continents with blood? These are fair questions, entitled to respectful consideration and candid answers, before the issue of State control as against denominational supervision of the college system is to be regarded as determined.

Nor are higher institutions of learning relieved of the feature of sectarianism, because that sectarianism is of the inclusive, rather than of the exclusive, type. To harbor all beliefs may be as sectarian as to harbor one belief. Pantheism is sectarianism. Atheism is sectarianism. Agnosticism is sectarianism. The all embracing faith of Abbott and of Weiss, appropriating truth from Brahma and Confucius and Moses and Mahomet and Christ is also sectarian, or if terms which sound less harsh are preferred, has the theological bias just as certainly as the Nicene creed or the Westminster catechism. Therefore, an institution which, either in catholicity or in indifference, welcomes to its chapel Roman Catholic priest and Jewish rabbi, Congregationalist preacher and Baptist elder, is a medium through which religious instruction is conveyed, just as surely as is the college, the chapel of which would be profaned, if any one spoke therein who wore not surplice, and was not of the apostolic succession. These affirmations may appear bigoted and severe to those who, in the pride of their opinion, claim to have emancipated themselves from the thraldom of sect; but they are true, nevertheless, and are conclusive as to the proposition that higher education is connected with theology by a bond as enduring as that which united Chang and Eng and which, like that, cannot be dissevered, whilst both have being. In devout recognition of this fact, upon the persuasion of duty, in constantly increasing appreciation of the distinct functions of the church and of the State, with more and more of robust independence, higher education in this country has been mainly within control of the various religious denominations, and, under these, the record of what the American college has wrought must cause the heart of every patriot to swell with pride, the heart of every Christian to lift itself in thanksgiving. Its work is in our statesmanship and in our heroism. We trace its luminous impress in every phase of our national development. It has stood for the right. It has led the national advancement. It has drafted constitutions. It has framed laws. It wrote the declaration. It sealed the national redemption with the blood of its sons. It has graced the pulpit. It has expounded statutes. Through the press, it has made and moulded public opinion. It has kept pace with the march of science. It has given us a scholarship sound, but not finical — a scholarship also comprehending all possibilities of research.

It may possibly occur to you that positions thus pronounced, concerning the relations of the State to higher education, are inconsistent with upholding the functions which the body, the centennial of whose creation we now commemorate, derives from the State and, with its consent, exercises through appropriations from its treasury. I cannot so regard them. The inconsistency is more apparent than real. The Board of Regents has some supervision, but little control, over the colleges of the State. Its province is chiefly advisory. It may suggest, but it does not command. It may grant charters upon certain prescribed conditions, and may refuse the same when they are not complied with. It has the right of visitation, but does not assume to interfere with the internal polity of the institutions under its care. The theory upon which it was originally constituted, that of a central authority supreme over separate and independent colleges, like the governing corporation of an English university, was found impracticable, not to say inconsistent with the American scheme of education and, by successive modifications of the laws, it has been restricted to its present powers. It were easy, indeed, to repel the insinuation, which is too often preferred by the unthinking, that the board is a merely ornamental appendage to State administration, and perpetuates a tradition, rather than exemplifies a vital force. I might were it not more properly within the scope of other papers, and especially within the purview of the distinguished gentleman who is to deliver the principal address, enlarge upon the work that has been accomplished by the university within the century, to which the yearly gatherings of this Convocation bear ample witness, which abundantly justifies its being; but, in this connection, I am dealing with its limitations, rather than with its prerogatives, and would emphasize its harmony with the freedom of the college from both the dictation and the bounty of the State. In these respects, certainly, our educational system is in gratifying contrast to that of some of the newer States where the college, on a public foundation, is subject to the changes and the caprices of the ballot-box, and where, by the arts of the politician, various sects and interests strive for supremacy in its management. I do not, of course, fail to give such weight, as is its due, to the plea that in the newer communities, there may be greater need for State interference than in the older, wealthier and more populous commonwealths, but I believe that educational progress is best served by the non-interference of the State, and that such progress has been best illustrated where the voluntary system has had freest play, as it thus has play, to-day, in the colleges of New York, through the protection and supervision, but not through the control, of the Board of Regents.

What test shall be applied as to the value of the American college? Obviously, there is but one practical test and that is found in the record of what its graduates have achieved in after life, the walks they have led, the summits they have climbed. There can be no record of drawing-room culture or of sybaritic dalliance with books. If there could be, it would be worthless. It is from the busy world, where mind contends with mind for the mastery, that we must deduce our estimates. The proportion of college-bred men who have made their mark in the professions and in public life is very large, and let me add, that to the names of few of these has any taint of the scandal which has smirched the names of so many others been attached. They seem to have had an immunity from reproach, or rather they have not suffered reproach, because they have not deserved it; because, by their education, they were fortified against temptation. Until about fifty years ago, college graduation was the certificate of an aristocratic caste, the only aristocracy which is worth a moment's deference, the aristocracy of letters. With the multiplication and the diffusion of college privileges, such caste no longer obtains, and it is probably well that it does not, but college-bred men remain the leaders in all that is worthiest in public affairs — the clean men, as well as the able men; and it is a notable circumstance in the comparison, that the smaller colleges have considerably the better of the larger and more pretentious ones. I will not weary you with statistics, but you will pardon an allusion to my own *alma mater*, where I stood the other day upon the ground which the footsteps of ninety classes of ingenuous youth have pressed, near the hallowed spot which was trodden by those who carried the torch of Christianity into the darkness of heathendom, and led the way in the evangelization of the world. In the quality of the influence which Williams has exercised, her sons may well cherish a commendable pride. Let me collate a few figures of the decade with which I am most familiar, that from 1850 to 1860, when the best beloved and most persuasive of American college presidents was at the meridian of his usefulness, and in the full vigor of his physical as well as of his mental powers, to whom his disciples yet returning, bring their offerings of love and of reverence, the frankincense and myrrh of grateful hearts, thankful that he is permitted to descend the vale of years, with his faculties undimmed, and that their acknowledgments may precede his apotheosis. During the period indicated, four hundred and seventy-four persons were graduated. Of these, one hundred and forty-seven entered the gospel ministry and thirty-five have received the degree of doctor of divinity. Twenty-five have been professors in colleges and professional schools, and six college presidents. One hundred and thirty-four have been admitted to the bar, and six have been judges of courts having appellate jurisdiction. Forty-five have practiced the healing art, and ten or twelve have become widely and favorably known as medical teachers or as specialists. Of the large number who enlisted in the war of the rebellion, five rose to the rank of brigadier or major-general, many were commissioned officers of various grades, and several died for their country, either in the shock of the battle or by wasting wounds or disease. The list of authors and scientists is a very considerable one, and the roll of those who have achieved distinction in public life, in State Legislatures and in executive trusts, is a long one. There have been three Representatives in Congress, and two United States Senators, and, above all, there was that illustrious one, whose life began in poverty and was nurtured in privation, which grew in strength, as grows the oak from the buffeting of the blast, who overcame the impediments of birth and fortune, loved learning for learning's sake, applied himself to those studies which afterward enabled him so worthily to exalt American scholarship, as well as to adorn American statesmanship, and who

> "Moving up from high to higher,
> Became on fortune's crowning slope
> The pillar of a people's hope,
> The centre of a world's desire."

You will, of course, understand that no invidious reference is intended in this allusion to a single period, and that it is introduced simply by way of illustration. The proportion might be cited over and over again from other periods and from other institutions. The influence of the American college upon American life is the fact to be emphasized.

When, therefore, we think of what the American college has accomplished, we may be pardoned for that conservatism which clings to it upon substantially the established basis, and refuses to sanction empirical modifications; at the behest of that restlessness which permeates the entire current of our American life, and cries for the new, like a baby for the moon, merely because it is the new. We are not yet convinced that it is wise to substitute university eclecticism for a rigid curriculum, and we are especially sceptical of its wisdom as proposed to immature minds, which have neither the capacity for selection nor the perseverance for pursuit. We do not yet believe that the university and the college can be welded into one, although the former may well be superinduced upon the latter. We have a profound respect for scientific investigation, but we cannot quite sympathize with that scientific craze which rejects all, save science, as either trivial or useless, and sneers at the study of the classics as superfluous, when it is apparent that they must precede it in orderly sequence, as confessedly they furnish it with its terminology. It was when Louis Agassiz stood at the head of American scientists that he said : " The longer I live and study, the less confidence I have in the scientific investigations of specialists or men who know but one thing." The college is depreciated as neglectful of the sciences, but we remember that it was the Christian college that first gave them greeting, and that their truths were first intelligently and systematically unfolded by Christian teachers, such as Dewey, Silliman, Hitchcock, and their compeers. We have an admiration for what is called, in modern parlance, culture, embracing, in its wide sweep, the sunflower of Oscar Wilde and the microscope of M. Pasteur, but we still have the thought that culture, even at its best, may be superficial, and that there are impediments of time and of memory which suggest the reflection whether discipline of the faculties, within a limited range, may not be more serviceable than the heterogeneous acquisition of knowledge that may be as distracting as it is likely to be evanescent.

And this brings us to the crucial issue between the friends of the new and of the old education — the value of the classics as disciplinary agents, and the significance of discipline as an educational force. You will not expect me, at this stage of an address already lengthened, to enter upon a discussion which has been elaborated fully by the most competent educators. Without reiterating the grounds for it, I accept the conclusion of President Porter, that " not only have the colleges judged rightly, in giving to the study of languages the prominence which it receives, and that the Greek and Latin deserve the pre-eminence which has been assigned them, but that there are peculiar reasons why they should be even more thoroughly and earnestly cultivated than they have been." There is, however, within the range of the discussion, one suggestion that seems to me exceedingly pertinent — and that is that the assault upon the classics is made ignorantly by two classes of critics — by those who have never studied them, and by those who, having studied them more or less, fail to appreciate, or at least to confess, the benefits they have thereby derived. The first class needs no attention at our hands. They cannot speak with authority. They only assert, out of a dense stupidity, something about which they know nothing. There is another class, however, which, having gotten bone and sinew and muscle from classic breast, turn, let us charitably say in ignorance rather than in malice, to pierce the heart of the mother that nourished them. Many graduates — and I am one — learned "little Latin and less Greek" during their college residence and went straightway into the world, and forgot even the little they had learned; but who shall say that nothing of this was incorporated into their mental entity by a process of absorption, or who shall assume to minimize its effect upon the structure of their thought, their capacity for exertion, the lucidity of their style, or the success of their lives? Who can doubt that the trenchant blade, with which Charles Francis Adams struck at the deficiencies of classic training, was forged and tempered, thirty years before, in the heat and glow of his Harvard work-shop? As President Porter again says: "Let it be conceded that some studies are chiefly disciplinary, and it by no means follows, because the graduates of colleges are not distinctly aware of the value of the course by which they have been trained, that the course was not the best conceivable for the very persons who are the least sensible of what it has done for them." In his eulogy upon Matthew H. Carpenter, before the Supreme Court of the United States, after describing his superlative gifts of speech, Judge Black says: "I have sometimes wondered where he got this curious felicity of diction. He knew no language but his mother-tongue. The Latin and Greek, which he learned in his boyhood, faded entirely out of his memory before he became a full-grown man. At West Point, he was taught French and spoke it fluently; in a few years afterward he forgot every word of it. But, perhaps, it was not lost; a language, though forgotten, enriches the mind, as a crop of clover plowed down fertilizes the soil." Nay! it was not forgotten. It never is quite forgotten. It may change its form, but not its entity. Permit me here to modify statements which otherwise might seem to be too dogmatic. I have no doubt that the rudiments of science may be as naturally, as advantageously acquired at a very early age. There is force in the apothegm of Herbert Spencer that "our lessons ought to start from the concrete and end in the abstract." Botany is to be learned in the fields, geology among the rocks, astronomy from the welkin, bright with stars. Nor do I doubt that something of freedom in elective courses may be allowed during the last two years of the college curriculum. This is now generally admitted and acted upon; but, in the main, there should be no change, certainly no sweeping change, and the curriculum should remain substantially as it has heretofore been prescribed.

To sum up: the integrity of the college system should be maintained. It is the best for practical results, for preparation for higher learning and for preparation for citizenship. No really intelligent friend of the university will assail the college. I am fortunate in having received a letter from President Gilman, of John Hopkins University, which is a university in fact, as well as in name, in which he says: "I believe in sustaining at Williams, Amherst, Rutgers, Hamilton, Marietta, Kenyon and many other places the American college, and, in a few places, endeavoring to build up universities." Yes, we add, the university is the cap-stone of the American educational system — its foundations laid in the common schools, its walls fair and sightly in their proportions, the college, and, crowning all, as the mighty dome rests upon the massive structure of St. Peter's, the university. We who are conservative concerning the American college are quite as anxious that the university shall be established as are they who are constantly planning it, but who would not build it on solid foundations, either placing it in the shifting sands or springing it as an arch, in mid-air, without supporting piers.

Just as truly as these, do we desire to see in America, as in Germany, a guild of scholars who shall pursue the track of science to the outermost fields of discovery — philologists of the nicest discrimination and the most extended repute, philosophic historians, omniverous students. And we shall have them. We need not fear that we shall lack elegant scholarship. That will take care of itself, as "the old red sandstone" sharpened the wits of "the stone-mason of Cromarty," and the sparks from his anvil fired the brain of Elihu Burritt. In metropolitan centres our universities will surely arise — they are arising. The queenly city, within our own borders, which fringes with splendor the blue expanse whereon the navies of the world may ride, which is yet to control the commerce of the continents, and is to be the most populous, as well as the most magnificent, of marts, where ring the hammers of industry and where wealth ministers, not only to luxury, but also to art and letters and to all that truly enriches and ennobles humanity, is to be the seat of such a university — a university which, embracing all facilities for instruction and research, shall attract to itself the flower of American youth — those who, in the rapt ardor of scholarship, shall dedicate themselves to the solution of its most abstruse problems and honor by their discoveries the select fellowship in which they will be enrolled — a university which shall resolve the metropolis with a lettered fane reviving, in more than their ancient lustre, the glories which clustered about that of Padua or of Verona. It will more than fulfill our loftiest ideal and satisfy our most exalting ambition. As a loyal son of New York, proud of her commercial supremacy in the sisterhood of States, anxious for her supremacy in the higher realm of thought, I hail with joy the fitting coronal of her educational system; but I hail it as a crown and a consummation of what has already been wrought, not as implicating in its exaltation the abasement of a single course, the displacement of a single stone, which has been laid in her temple of learning. In harmony with, not in hostility to, the American college, is the American university to achieve the grandest results for American scholarship.

IV.
ACADEMIC EDUCATION IN THE STATE OF NEW YORK ONE HUNDRED YEARS AGO.

By NOAH P. CLARKE, Ph. D.

Mr. CHANCELLOR, AND LADIES AND GENTLEMEN OF THE CONVOCATION: — I am to speak to-day of the history of academic education in this State one hundred years ago.

Let me first say a few words of the State itself. New York was in swaddling clothes one hundred years ago. She was born at White Plains, Westchester county, on the 10th day of July, 1776, and was consequently eight years old — one hundred years ago to-morrow; and as the age of States is reckoned by centuries and not by years, she was only an infant in arms, but yet of remarkable strength for her age. The evidence of her birth is found in the resolution of the Legislature of the Colony assembled at White Plains, "that the Provincial Congress of the Colony of New York be changed to the Convention of the Representatives of the State of New York."

The State then comprised fourteen counties, Kings, Queens and Suffolk, on Long Island; Richmond, New York, Westchester, Dutchess and Charlotte, now Washington, east of the Hudson; Ulster, Orange, Albany and Tryon set off from Albany in 1772, west of the Hudson, with Cumberland and Gloucester, now in Vermont.

Tryon county, changed to Montgomery in 1784, embraced all the territory of the State west of a meridian running through the centre of what is now Schoharie county, which was cut off from Albany in 1785. In all this western stretch of Washington county to a meridian running through the westerly bend of Lake Ontario, with the exception of here and there an Indian village or trading post, there was but a single settlement at Whitestown, where Hugh White, from Middleton, Ct., in 1784, had planted himself and family in the very heart of the interminable forest, stretching from the Hudson to the Pacific. The same year James Dean pushed out a little further and built him a hut near Rome, on lands given him for his services as an interpreter. Three years later, Joseph Blackmer, afterward the pioneer of Monroe county, located still further west. In 1788, Major Asa Danforth and Comfort Tyler, going by water, for want of roads, landed at the mouth of Onondaga creek. Here Danforth built a log tavern, which, for years after, was the "wayside inn," for the bold men who were pushing their way into the great western door of the "long house" of the Iroquois. Here Danforth and Tyler discovered the saline waters of Onondaga valley and at once entered upon the manufacture of salt, of which in 1792 they were making sixteen bushels a day. The same year John Hardenbergh got on to Hardenbergh Corners, now Auburn. In 1789 Oliver Phelps of Suffield, Ct., having, in company with Nathaniel Gorham, of Boston, purchased of the State of Massachusetts all the territory of the State west of the old pre-emption line or west of Seneca lake, comprising what is now Ontario county, and the fourteen counties of which she is the mother, came to the Indian village of Canandauguay, Canandaigua, and began the settlement of the "Genesee country." During 1789 and 1790, one hundred and seventy-nine families settled upon this magnificent domain, making a population of one thousand and eighty-four — seven hundred and twenty-eight males, three hundred and forty females, seven free blacks and nine slaves.

From such facts, which might be greatly multiplied, it is evident that all there was practically of the State of New York and its institutions in 1784, was confined to its fourteen counties, and to such portions of them as were washed by the waters of the Hudson and of the ocean and Long Island sound, which at that time contained a population of some two hundred thousand souls.

It should be borne in mind that the long struggle of the Revolution had but just closed; that conflicting land claims, especially in reference to the territory of Vermont, were embittering the spirit of the people to such a degree as to threaten the public peace; and that the whole social fabric of society was very much broken and disturbed, growing out of the poverty resulting from the war, making the time very inopportune for entering upon any great movement of organization or reorganization of a system of public education. Hence it seems to us at this day remarkable that, under circumstances so discouraging, a movement of such magnitude as the legislative creation of the University of the State of New York, and a Board of Regents of the same should be made.

The patriotic impulse that prompted the change of the charter and the name of Kings College to Columbia College, of Tryon county to Montgomery, and of Charlotte to Washington, was as natural as it was commendable, but the creation of a body to care for and nurture the colleges, academies and schools of the State, before there was scarcely any such in existence, was a bold and magnificent step in advance, and was the beginning of a work which has outgrown the wildest conception of its founders, and is to-day the glory of our great State.

In the act creating the University of the State of New York, it is recited " that it shall, and may be lawful to and for the said Regents, and they are hereby authorized and required to visit and inspect all colleges, academies and schools which are or may be established in this State, examine into the state and system of education and discipline therein, and make a yearly report thereof to the Legislature."

I refer to this remarkable language to show the almost prophetic vision of this body of legislators, as there was not at that time an incorporated academy in the State, no system of common schools, and only one feeble college which was bitterly complaining of its crippled condition, its want of funds and of a library and mathematical apparatus by the means of which it could induce young men to finish their education at home rather than at colleges in the other States.

Soon after the creation of the University, on the 17th of November, 1787, a day ever memorable in the history of academic institutions in this State — two academies, both of Long Island, which had for some time been waiting, knocked at the Regents' door and asked to be admitted as the first-born children of the University of the State of New York. These academies were Clinton (named for Governor Clinton), at East Hampton, Suffolk county, and Erasmus Hall (named for Desiderius Erasmus, the great German scholar of the sixteenth century), at Flatbush, Kings county.

It will strike one as somewhat remarkable that the first academies incorporated by the Regents were not in the large and populous counties of New York and Albany, but in the sparsely settled counties of Long Island. There was no city of Brooklyn then, and Kings county was the least in population in the State, sending only two representatives to the Legislature of seventy members, while New York sent nine, Albany ten, and Suffolk five.

In their first report to the Legislature in 1788, the Regents say: "We find that Erasmus Hall contains twenty-six students under the tuition of Mr. Brandt Schuyler Lupton. Rev. John H. Livingston, D. D., has been appointed principal, who with the trustees have determined to maintain two departments — the classical and the

English — the former to comprise the Latin and Greek languages with geography and the outlines of ancient and modern history; the latter, the English language, reading, writing, arithmetic and book-keeping; French is taught to all who desire it, and elocution is taught in both departments. The institution is without funds, but the scholars give encouraging proofs of diligence and proficiency.

"Clinton Academy has fifty-three students; twelve in Latin, Greek, logic, natural philosophy, mathematics and geography; seventeen in English grammar, writing, arithmetic and accountantship, and such of them as choose the French language. The common school or class have reading, writing, and arithmetic; speaking and reading in public form a part of the education of all.

"The tutors appear attentive to the instruction and morals of their pupils, who on their part appear attentive to their studies.

"The academy has no funds and the tutors are supported by the pay received for tuition."

The committee making the report regret that the University they represent is likewise destitute of funds, not having the means of providing for necessary contingent expenses.

In their second report of these academies, made in December of the same year, the Regents note with great satisfaction an increase in the number of students, the ability and excellence of the teachers, and the commendable diligence and proficiency of the pupils; but serious evils, arising from a total lack of funds in the hands of the Regents, are referred to, as threatening to render the duration of these institutions limited or precarious, and they respectfully suggest that the lands belonging to the State, at Crown Point, Ticonderoga, and Fort George, be set apart by the Legislature, so that in some way an income might accrue to the University, which could be used, from time to time, in sustaining the infant academies then existing, and those which should be erected in every part of the State.

I refer to these two pioneer academies in detail, in order to call attention to the original idea of the academy, its position in an educational system, and the principle of its foundation. There were in the thirteen States, at the close of the war, ten colleges — Harvard, Dartmouth, Yale and Rhode Island College, now Brown University, in New England; Columbia in New York; the College of New Jersey, now Princeton, and Queens, now Rutgers, in New Jersey; William and Mary and Hampden Sidney, in Virginia, and the University of Pennsylvania, in Pennsylvania.

The design of the college was to educate young men in classical and English literature, mathematics and philosophy after the manner of the English and German universities from which they were modeled.

There was as yet no system of common schools in the State, and elementary instruction was carried on, mainly, by voluntary schools or by private teachers. The young were fitted for college by the minister of the parish, by private tutors, or by some classical school maintained by a few who had sons to educate. The academy was created to furnish, primarily, instruction in the Latin and Greek languages, mathematics and history, as a preparation for college, secondarily, instruction in the common English branches as a preparation for business life; the primal idea being that of a classical school. Hence the language of many of the academy charters, borrowed largely from the act incorporating the Board of Regents, that they were founded "for the instruction of youth in the languages and other branches of useful learning," was very significant.

The foundations of these early academies are worthy of notice: they were not appropriations made by the State, nor moneys raised by taxation of the people at large, but were the free-will offerings of noble men and women who desired such an institution located in their midst, whose benefits might be extended to every youth in the range of their influence. The founders recognized their personal duty, not to the youth of their own generation only, but of the generations to come to train and educate them for true Christian citizenship, and so, out of their scanty means, they set apart and consecrated forever, what they could to this work, and there is no more conclusive and gratifying testimony to the recognition of this obligation on the part of every true citizen of our great Commonwealth, from that day to this, than is seen in these voluntary foundations of our secondary schools, amounting now to more than six millions of dollars.

The relation of the University to the infant academies and to such as thereafter should be created, as understood by the first Board of Regents, is of interest. While the recognized duty of the Regents was primarily that of superintendence over all literary establishments that might be formed, they were also to afford timely assistance to such schools as needed it, and to make appropriations, as they might be able, of money, for the purpose of promoting science and literature. The relation was not that of paternity strictly, but that of carrying out the obligations resting upon the State to encourage by substantial aid those institutions which were created by the State "for the purpose of securing to the youth that education, culture and character requisite for the defense of freedom and rational government."

Up to the year 1800, or during the first sixteen years of the life of the University, there were incorporated by the Regents nineteen academies. In 1787, two — Clinton, Suffolk county, Erasmus Hall, Kings county. In 1790, two — North Salem, Westchester county, Farmers' Hall, Orange county. In 1791, two — Washington, Washington county, Montgomery, Orange county. In 1792, two — Union Hall, Queens county, Dutchess, Poughkeepsie. In 1793, two — Hamilton, Oneida county, Schenectady, Schenectady county. The former merged in Hamilton College in 1812; the latter in Union College in 1795. In 1794, two — Johnstown, Montgomery county, Oxford, Chenango county. In 1795, three — Kingston, Ulster county, Canandaigua, Ontario county, and Union, Stone Arabia, Montgomery county. In 1796, three — Cherry Valley and Otsego, Otsego county, Lansingburgh, Rensselaer county. In 1791, one — Columbia, at Kinderhook, Columbia county.

I shall in this paper regard these academies as the academies of one hundred years ago, and shall confine myself in what I have to say mainly to them, for if they were not all existing in fact they were in conception and were only waiting for favorable circumstances to bring them into being and give them a local habitation and a name. First, as to their origin.

There comes a time in the development of any great, successful movement when it begins to claim for itself public regard and public help; but the initial steps are often far back and out of sight of the world at large. The academies of our time can be created to-day, and with splendid buildings and all appliances of apparatus can to-morrow start off with the *eclat* and demonstration of a well-established and successful school. Not so the old academies. They were a new thing — an untried mechanism. The people, especially the uneducated classes, looked upon them with incredulity and suspicion. They thought there was an aristocratic flavor to them which smacked a little too much of the mother country, from which we had just swung loose, therefore their first years were years of struggle, poverty, and of small results. We have not the histories of all these institutions at hand, and have only glimpses at the best, but probably what is true of one is true of all, with variations in detail according to the influences amidst which they came to exist;

and being more familiar with ten of these institutions than with the others, we shall be obliged to use them as typical of the academies of their day.

The Academy of Kingston, Ulster county, as far as we can learn, is the oldest in the State, its origin dating back to 1774. It was founded by "the trustees of the Freeholders and Commonalty of the town of Kingston, for the instruction of youth in the learned languages and other branches of useful knowledge." In suitable buildings provided by the trustees the academy prospered till 1777, when it was burned, with the village, by the British army under Clinton when on their way to effect a junction with Burgoyne at Saratoga. Another building of stone was soon after erected and opened for pupils in 1792. The academy was incorporated in 1795.

Erasmus Hall was organized by a few gentlemen of Flatbush. In 1786 a larger and commodious building was erected and a school opened, which was incorporated in 1787.

In 1819 there died at Argyle, Washington county, at the age of eighty-four years, Rev. John Watson, a Scotchman, and an accomplished scholar. Suffering under the severe affliction that had befallen him in the death of his young wife and only daughter, he left his home and came to this country, hoping to escape his sorrow by the new cares and labors that might be found in a forest home. He came to this city of Albany, went northward to the very frontier of civilization, purchased wild land and began to clear away the forest and prepare his fields for agriculture. One day, while out hunting, he became lost in the dense swamp-woods, was overtaken by night, but finally in a frozen condition found his way to the hut of an Indian who, with the kindness characteristic of his race, nursed him with the tenderest care and watched over him like a father for many days. The shock to his system was so great as to throw him into a fit of sickness. One of his frozen limbs was amputated and his physical condition very much shattered and broken. After a long sickness he recovered sufficiently to think of entering again upon some service. In his crippled condition he could no longer go on with agricultural work, and so after some consultation with the minister of the church in the adjoining settlement, also an educated Scotchman, he was led to open a classical school, that he might train up some young men for the service of the church and of the State. Thereupon a house of logs was built by his neighbors; seats and a table of logs were made, constituting all the furniture of the house; and then, in 1780, on the frontier of this great State, with no school or settlement north or west of him, upon those rough benches of hewn logs began *Washington Academy*, which has just now come to her one hundred and fourth birthday, covered all over with the glory of her century's work, none of which has been grander than that of the first ten years of her life, when she was but a log academy, but during which time she sent out men equal in educational power and influence to any that followed in after years — " Scholars that could stand before kings." This classical school, as soon as possible after the organization of the Board of Regents, took steps for an Act of Incorporation, which was accomplished in 1791.

After his graduation from Yale College in 1778, Noah Webster received from his father an eight dollar continental bill, worth about fifty per cent, with the comforting remark that "thenceforth he must rely upon himself for support." As the country was then engaged in a fearful, and to some minds, a doubtful conflict, there seemed no opening for educated young men, except the law, teaching the young idea how to shoot, or buckling on their armor and going to the front to shoot for themselves. Whether there was any lack of patriotic devotion or not, Mr. Webster, after some time spent in legal studies and in teaching private schools, went to Goshen, Orange county, and opened there a classical school, which was the first step in the subsequent foundation of Farmers' Hall, an academy which, in 1784, was well known out of Orange county and drew its pupils from a considerable distance.

In the good old town of Claverack, settled by families from Holland, there came, about 1776, one John Gabriel Gebhard, a clergyman of scholarly attainments and love for classical learning. Being the minister of the parish, and father of the proverbial Dutch family, he opened a school for instructing his own seven sons, with those of some of the "best families" of his parish, in the ancient languages. This parochial school soon led to the establishment, in 1779, of the Washington Seminary, which for twenty-five years was conducted with great success, preparing for college and for subsequent distinguished service in the church and in the State an unusual number of men. Upon the death of Dr. Gebhard, the school relapsed and was changed for a time into a common school. The life of the true Claverack Academy, baptized into another name, had not yet begun. The time and the man for that work had not yet appeared. They were reserved for our own day.

I refer to but one more.

Canandaigua Academy was largely the realization of the conception of Oliver Phelps of Suffield, Ct., the purchaser, with Nathaniel Gorham, of the "Genesee Country." Mr. Phelps was a native of Windsor, Ct., a poor boy and early thrown upon his own resources. His schooling was very limited and of ordinary quality. His first money was made by buying and selling a brush fence. Being a Connecticut boy he naturally enough took up peddling, and when he subsequently ran for Congress in Ontario county, his political enemies sneered at him as the "wooden nutmeg peddler," but he went to Congress, notwithstanding. After the war, in which he took an active part, he moved to Suffield, and engaged in business, acquiring considerable property and honored with many important trusts by his fellow-men, while at Suffield he made a will in which he set apart a considerable sum of money to found an academy *for poor young men*, for whom he had great sympathy. When he came on to begin the settlement of the new country, he brought the idea of the academy for poor young men with him, and so, almost his first act, after extinguishing the Indian title to their lands by fair and upright negotiation, was to give by deed four thousand acres of land for himself and two thousand acres for his friend, Mr. Gorham, for the founding of an academy "for the instruction of youth in the languages and other branches of useful learning." This deed of gift bears date January 28, 1791. In this deed it was specified that part of the lands conveyed should be exclusively appropriated to the purpose of promoting in the minds of the youth to be educated in said academy, an ardent attachment to national liberty and the just rights of man, and, therefore, there should be set apart yearly the sum of $20 as a premium to be given to that youth, being a student of said academy, who shall compose, and deliver at the yearly commencement, *the best oration* on the excellence of a republican government, or, in the mellifluous language of the deeds, "the transcendent excellence of a genuine representative republican government, effectually securing equal liberty founded on the rights of man."

Another portion of the land was set apart "to be applied toward educating in said academy such young as, having bright intellects and amiable dispositions, bid fair to be useful members of the community, but, from the incompetency of their resources, are unable, without assistance from the fund hereby appropriated, to acquire a suitable share of literary information to enable them to do extensive good to their fellow-men." All of which provisions have gone on with the years, carried out in letter and in spirit from that day to this. The academy was incorporated in 1795. Immediately thereafter, a building — excellent for the time, fifty feet square and three stories high — was erected, which building forms a part of the present academical structure, and has been used without interruption, (save one year given to its enlargement in 1833), or accident from fire or flood for ninety-one years in well-directed and successful educational labor. In the enlargement and reconstruction of the building, the old academy was inclosed by the brick walls of the new, the old corner posts being still visible.

Organization.

The plan of the old academy was very simple, usually having but a single department, and that under the care of the principal, who was clothed with all powers of superintendence, instruction and discipline. The academy building usually contained but one schoolroom, and the sexes were educated together. The number and range of studies was very limited, and assistants were employed only as the school prospered. In Canandaigua Academy the girls were early separated from the boys, and occupied a room for study by themselves, under the care of a lady, which room was set off from the main room by a thin board partition, which soon came to look like a ventilating arrangement, or like the rear end of a pistol gallery.

The salaries of teachers were small, varying from $300 to $500. The first teacher of the Canandaigua Academy, Mr. Dudley Saltonstall, was employed at $400 and the tuition amounted to $319. His statement of the first year's work is of interest and is as follows:

For the first two quarters — average attendance, 20.
Latin scholars, 10 at $3.75 per quarter $75
Other scholars, 10 at $2.75 per quarter 55
—— $130

For second two quarters — average attendance, 30.
Latin scholars, 12 at $3.75 per quarter $90
Other scholars, 18 at $2.75 per quarter............... 99
—— 189

Total receipts.................................. $319

Mr. Saltonstall brought in his bill for the balance, $81, against the trustees, but willingly renewed his engagement as principal, with a compensation consisting of the tuition alone. The salary of Principal Treadwell Smith, of Kingston Academy, in 1797, was £170 — $423. It is very probable that the salaries of the academy principals rarely reached at that time $500.

Text-Books.

Like the Christian Church the academies, grammar schools, colleges and universities of this and of all lands have for centuries been studying the same text-books in all their classical work. The Cæsar, Livy, Cicero, Sallust and Virgil, the Xenophon and Homer of the schools of to-day, are the same precisely as when the first students, ages ago, read their story or scanned their exquisite measure. What editions of these ancient classics, or what grammars were used in these early academies, we do not certainly know; though in the course of study of one of the classical schools of Boston, in 1785, the following text-books are named:

Cheever's Latin Accidence.
Ward's Latin Grammar.
Nomenclator.
Clarke's Introduction to the Latin Language.
Garretson's Exercise.
Moore's Greek Grammar.
Priest's Greek Delectus — a book "intended not for a display of knowledge, but to render the introduction to the Greek language as easy as possible, and to assist beginners only."

Of other books, both English and American, previous to the spelling-book, grammar and reader of Noah Webster, published in 1783-5, the only reading books were the Bible, the Psalter, and the New England Primer. The spelling-books were Fenning's, Moore's, Delworth's and Perry's, all of which were superseded by Webster's, which were the first of the kind published in the United States. The first English grammar used in the Boston schools was the Young Ladies' Accidence, published by Caleb Bingham — intended for his female pupils — whose full title was "The Young Ladies' Accidence, or a short and easy introduction to English Grammar, designed principally for the use of young learners, more especially those of the Fair Sex, though proper for either." This, with Webster's, which was published two years before, gradually gave way to Murray's Grammar and Abridgement, which came into use about the beginning of this century and became a standard of authority, as did Daboll's Arithmetic, for more than fifty years.

After the Revolution the principal reading books were Webster's Third Part, The Colombian Orator, The Brief Remarker, The American Preceptor, Morse's Geography, and Murray's English Reader. The American Preceptor and Colombian Orator were the work of Caleb Bingham. The selections were more lively than those of Webster's readers, and so took a stronger hold on the public taste and held their place long after Webster's had disappeared.

The charm of these books of Bingham was their original dialogues. Who wrote them is not certainly known; but some of the fascinating poems in The Colombian Orator were written by David Everett, a Dartmouth graduate, who afterward became the publisher of a Boston paper.

That famous poem which contains much rhyme, but little poetry, beginning —

"You'd scarce expect one of my age," etc.,

was written by him for sport; yet ere he was aware of it, he had an immortality scarcely second to that of the author of the wonderful rhymes of Mother Goose, for there is no poem-speech extant that has been spoken by so many orators in aprons and short clothes as this. It has held the same place among the little fellows that Patrick Henry's "Give me liberty or give me death" has among aspirants for academic honors.

It seems like recalling the joyous days of our early boyhood, as we remember how from a little closet we used to come out into the capacious kitchen of our old home, and there, after our proper bow to the select audience, drawing ourself up to the height of the occasion, we "spoke" those immortal words.

> 'You'd scarce expect one of my age,
> To speak in public on the stage
> And if I chance to fall below —
> Demosthenes or Cicero;
> Don't view me with a critic's eye,
> But pass my imperfections by." etc.

It was as real to us as the fact of our existence, and the plea for a kind judgment on our performance was urged in all sincerity; and though we had no idea of Demosthenes or Cicero, whether they were gods or men, we always felt, after the effort, that we stood immeasurably below them.

In the mathematics the early books were Dilworth's, Pike's, Adam's, Colburn's and Daboll's Arithmetics, Playfair's Euclid,

Colburn's Algebra and Jesse's Surveying. Other books were Morse's Geography, Goldsmith's small Histories, Watts on the Mind, and Paley's Theology.

In a list published in 1804, of text-books used in the schools of this country previous to that date, there were thirteen spellers, twenty-eight readers, sixteen grammars, fourteen arithmetics, three dictionaries, four works on book-keeping, four histories, two surveyings, one composition, one mental philosophy, one moral philosophy, none of which are now found in the academies of this State, as appears from the latest Regents' Report.

In the report of the Superintendent of Common Schools in 1830, it appears that there were in the common schools in the State one hundred and twenty-five different kinds of school books, of which the following were largely in excess of others: Murray's English Reader, Murray's English Grammar, Webster's Spelling Book, Daboll's Arithmetic, The New Testament, Woodbridge's Geography, Watkins' Dictionary.

Apparatus.

Of apparatus there was but little and that of the simplest and most inexpensive kind. In the better schools there were usually a small air pump, a bell-glass receiver, and hemispheres, a cylindrical electrical machine, a Leyden jar, dancing image plates, and electrical bells, some mechanical forms of levers and pulleys, possibly an Atwood machine and whirling tables, an Archimedes' screw, a Barker's mill, a common pump, a magnet, a surveyor's compass, a prism, a lens, a mirror, a siphon, a thermometer, and a box of mathematical instruments; but as far as I know there was no blackboard, lead pencils, ruled paper, engraved copy-books for writing, metallic pens or clear flowing ink. In Canandaigua Academy no blackboard was seen or known previous to the advent of Mr. Henry Howe, in 1828, who, soon after becoming principal of the school, introduced the blackboard, which by his efforts was soon after put into many of the common school-houses of the country. It is within our own recollection that our writing-books were homemade of unruled foolscap, doubled and stitched together and ruled for writing with lead plummets of our own make. Our slate pencils were also made from the soft clay stones from our gullies which every boy whittled out for himself and for the girls who used them for the double purpose of ciphering and to eat.

If any work was done in chemistry — and there was but little at the best, for chemistry and her sister sciences, geology and mineralogy were hardly born in those days — there would be found a few glass retorts and bottles, a blow-pipe and a tin lamp, a quantity of lead pipe and a pot of white lead to cement cracks and joints, a pneumatic cistern improvised from a wash tub with a perforated shelf on which an iron pail inserted would serve as a gas holder, an oxygen apparatus, consisting of a capacious sheet-iron furnace, and iron bottles capable of holding five or ten pounds of saltpetre, these bottles having long gun-barrel necks to which the tubing could be attached.

The making of oxygen then was a work of no mean magnitude. The furnace into which the iron retort filled with saltpetre was placed, was seven times heated like Nebuchadnezzar's furnace, and after several hours of patient waiting and watching, bubbles of gas would be heard coming through the water from the end of the pipe into the holder of the pneumatic cistern, or passing into the bladder-bag more commonly used; and if a couple of gallons of gas could be obtained in half a day's time, a most successful work had been done, and the two gallons of gas would answer for the illustrations of a term. There was not much taught or learned of chemistry, but enough to show a class that water was composed of two gases, one of which would burn and the other would not; and that air was composed of two gases, one of which would support life and the other would not, which a distinguished graduate of Yale College once told me was about all the chemistry he remembered of his college course.

Libraries.

It is probably true that libraries are found in all the old academies, as I believe it was one of the conditions of their incorporation. The very first effort often in the foundation of a school was a collection of books to establish a library as in the beginning of Yale College. These libraries were not always made up of such books as young men and young women liked most to read. They were often the gifts of clergymen and scholars whose reading most likely had been of a deep and theological character, with such books as might be found, that had come down from former years, and which had long lain among the rubbish of the household, so that their libraries were often not unlike some "missionary boxes" sent by well to do churches of the east to the self-denying laborers on the outposts of civilization.

In a recent letter from a student of Canandaigua Academy, of 1812, Mr. Albert H. Porter of Niagara Falls, he says: "The library was in the south-west corner of the building and contained from twelve to fifteen hundred volumes, notably several ponderous volumes of Baxter's works, twenty-four volumes of Mavor's Universal History, Rollin's Ancient History, Hume's England, Shakespeare and other works of the English poets and prose writers. Among the novels were Tom Jones, Gil Blas, Don Quixote, The Scottish Chiefs and Thaddeus of Warsaw. I do not remember a single American author in the collection. Prescott, Bancroft, Irving, Bryant and Cooper, whose works now abound, were not then known, and periodical literature was then in its infancy.

On my first acquaintance with the academy in 1837, I found a good circulating library of several hundred volumes used by the students, also a teachers' library of two hundred volumes used as a reference library, which was probably established about 1830, when the academies, under the appointment of the State, entered upon the work of educating teachers for the common schools.

Instruction.

Of the methods and character of the instruction in the first academies we know but little.

The principals were generally, if not always, college graduates and often clergymen — men of thorough education and of an active and outspoken piety, who regarded the education of youth next to the work of the Christian ministry. It is, therefore, fair to assume that the work of those teachers was one of conscience as well as of ability, and was carried on with a singleness of purpose that secured the best results.

It was eminently a personal service. The teacher came into close relations to the pupil. The smallness of the classes and the limited range of subjects of study allowed full time for the most thorough work. There was no clamoring world outside calling for the boys and girls for the public service. The colleges did not want the boys until they were of good age and well fitted for their higher work, so that the academies were happily relieved of much that tends in our day to produce an education which is at once superficial and unsatisfactory.

The books were few, and hence much of the instruction was memoriter. The old teacher had great faith in "the form of sound words," hence a good memory often outranked with him all other qualities. The rules and definitions of German, Latin, Greek and English, with the declensions of nouns and adjectives, the conjugations of the verbs, the lists of adverbs, conjunctions and prepositions were generally thoroughly committed, and so fixed in the memory that they held their place to old age, like the incidents of early youth. Often the texts of Virgil and Homer, the orations of Cicero and the songs of the Bucolics, were not only committed to memory, but were spoken from the stage after the manner of declamations or recitations.

The spelling book was learned by heart, and every good speller knew just where in any table the hard words were to be found.

In arithmetic the definitions and rules were committed, and the "sums" ciphered out. There were usually no recitations, but each scholar worked on his own line, getting an affirmative response to his question, "Please, sir, show me how to do a sum?" when the case appeared to be one of dire necessity. Sometimes the teacher had his arithmetic all in manuscript; and when the pupils worked their examples, the teacher would compare them with the manuscript, and if they varied in the least they were pronounced wrong, and the pupil must do the work over. The story is told of one Master Tileston of the Boston school who, having given out a sum from his manuscript, was soon asked by the boy to whom he gave it to examine his work as he had finished it. The old teacher took down his manuscript, compared the slate with it and pronounced it wrong. The boy went to his seat, reviewed his work, but finding no error in it returned to the desk and asked the teacher to be good enough to examine the work, for he could find no error in it. This was too much to ask of him. He growled, as his habit was when displeased, but he compared the sums again and at last, with a triumphant smile, exclaimed: "See here, you *nasty* wretch, you've got it, 'If four tons of hay cost so much, what will seven tons cost?' when it should be 'If four tons of *English* hay cost so and so.'"

There was little time spent in those days discussing methods of teaching, but each teacher went on in his own way, and in his own manner, and did good, solid, honest work.

Again, the teacher never lost his individuality by aping the habits or manners or methods of others; hence every school had its own characteristics and peculiarities. The school was the school of the teacher and not of the educational board. He gave to it its character; he was its life, its spirit, its inspiration, and he wrought his own individuality into the minds and hearts of his pupils.

The styles of teaching were as various as the teachers themselves. Of Mr. James Stevenson, a very successful principal of Washington Academy from 1810 to 1817, and of Canandaigua from 1818 to 1822, Professor Tayler Lewis, one of his pupils at the former, says: "He taught us Moore's Greek Grammar by making tunes of the paradigms of the verbs and adjectives and then causing us to sing them, while he kept time with his long rod and stamped his foot vehemently at every breath. I never had a better teacher." And the now old men who were his pupils at the latter academy, are full of the stories of his teaching and of his quaint and striking illustrations.

One of his well-remembered illustrations was what he called the story of the "big dog and little dog," to illustrate the grammatical relation of double subjects in sentences like this: "He who soweth sparingly shall reap sparingly." He would say, "If you throw two pieces of meat to two dogs, the big dog will snatch the piece nearest to him, and the little dog will be obliged to take the piece left." Now he would say, in this sentence, the dogs are "he" and "who," and the pieces of meat are "soweth" and "shall reap." The big dog "who" seizes the piece of meat "soweth" *nearest* to him, and so the little dog "he" must take the piece that is left," shall reap; " therefore, "who" is the subject of "soweth," and "he" is the subject of "shall reap."

Discipline.

The discipline of those schools was stern and perhaps severe. The unquestioned authority of the teacher, the supremacy of the established laws, and the implied obedience of the pupil were the fundamental doctrines of school government. Sin was wicked and deserved punishment; disobedience was sin, disrespect was sin, laziness was sin, and, as such, they must take the penalty of violated law, yet with such compassion on the part of the good teacher that the sinner saw no personal vindictiveness, but, on the contrary, the kindest regard for his welfare.

If the teachers of those days were severe beyond what we might think proper and right, it was due both to the age in which they lived, and to their strong convictions of right and wrong. The age demanded more deference on the part of the pupil and more authority on the part of the teacher, and, while it is not claimed that they were wiser or better than good teachers of our time, they did a work which challenges the admiration of the world, and to which we owe much of the educational power of our day.

It is in the secondary schools, more than in the colleges, where the foundations of scholarship and of character are laid — where the discipline which controls the life is secured. The academy gets hold of the pupil at a more tender age, when he has seen less of the temptations, sins and vices of the world, and before the Christian influences of home are weakened, so that the beneficent work of our generation is largely the product of the secondary education of the generation preceding.

In the Washington Academy, to which I have already alluded, in the distinguished faculty of which, Mr. Chancellor, you once held an honorable place, there were, in an early day, men of elegant scholarship who, in after years, became eminent in their several callings. Such men as Rev. Dr. Alexander Proudfit, Rev. Dr. George W. Bethune, Prof. Taylor Lewis and others, who, in their day and *our* day, stood not behind the men of any age in all that pertains to the highest type of Christian scholarship. And what is true of this academy is doubtless true of every academy which is old enough to have a history, and will continue to be true, as long as genuine and faithful academic work shall be carried on.

The number of students sent to college by the old academies was probably greater in proportion to the number taught than now. In the letter of Mr. Porter, already referred to, relating to Canandaigua Academy, he says: " Among the college men here previous to 1812 were Thomas Morris, Nathaniel N. Howell, Dr. Williams, Peter B. Porter, Dudley Saltonstall, John Ewing, John C. Spencer and Rev. Wm. F. Torrey. Of my acquaintances at school two entered college in 1815, three in 1816, and four in 1817. How many were sent to college from this academy from that time to 1853 is not known, but from 1853 to 1882, over two hundred and fifty were fitted and sent to college or to higher professional schools." During the first century of Washington Academy two hundred young men were sent to Union College alone.

The academies never came to their best work until after the organization of the common-school system under the efficient labors of the late Gideon Hawley. Under this system the common school was planted in every district in the State, and systematic, elementary work began. These schools soon became the feeders of the academies, as the academies of the colleges, forming a system admirably adapted to their work and their age. The number of academies began to multiply to meet the demand for higher education in every part of the State, so that in the next twenty-five years from the organization of the common-school system, there were incorporated by the Regents and the Legislature one hundred and seventy-two academies.

In this admirable system, running through half a century, the common school was placed near the homes of the people, with facilities for furnishing, at trifling expense, elementary instruction to every child. The academy, founded by private liberality, more removed but centrally located, received from the common schools such as desired to so far extend their studies as to fit them for college or for professional or business life. The colleges were interested in the prosperity of the academies, as the academies were in that of the common schools. The common schools began to look to the academies for their teachers, as the academies did to the colleges for theirs; so the interest of each was in the prosperity of all, and under this system the educational power of the State was greatly increased. The masses of the children in the common schools were well instructed. The academies furnished good men for the colleges, and the colleges in turn, sent out thoroughly finished men; and it may be questioned whether, after their last thirty years of educational experimenting, the needs of the masses, outside of the cities and villages, have been better met than they were under the old system.

Some, perhaps most, of the old academies have thought it wise, under the pressure of the competition of free schools, to give up their charters and become the higher departments of union free schools; and by doing so, have doubtless brought the higher education to a larger number, even if they have lost something of the characteristics of the old academies. It is certain that some of them are, by this arrangement, doing a better work than ever before; but it is a natural feeling that I have, which has grown up within me during an unbroken period of more than forty years of true academic service, which leads me to love and venerate the old academies. The academies that have been able to hold on their way in their proper, legitimate work — that have been spared the contentions and jars of political school boards and groanings over the heavy burdens of taxes for their support, I honor them for the great work they have done — for the educated men and women they have furnished, and for the impulse they have given to the educational progress of our age. They are eminently worthy of a more liberal aid on the part of our legislators, and of the continued confidence of you, gentlemen of the Board of Regents, who were created to care for them, that they may be for the future, as some of them have been in the past, the truest models of our secondary school.

The relation of the academy to the instruction of teachers is one of great interest, but time will not allow of its discussion here. The academy, as a source of educational power, is often overlooked in estimates of its value. Wherever located it becomes an educational centre from which radiate untold influences for good. The influence of a single educated Christian man, or of a faculty of devoted teachers in a community is soon felt, not only among the few, but among the masses. And there soon spring up desires for better opportunities and a better life. The wonderful temple of fame in the old Webster's spelling book, has stirred many a youth to an effort to scale those rugged heights and enter that temple; and so the presence and influence of a single educated man in a town have quickened the impulses and energies of young men and young women, and lifted them into a higher and a grander life.

When I was a mere lad, the young minister of the parish brought his new bride to our old home to live until the parsonage should be made ready for them. He was a graduate of Williams College, and the only college man in town, and we lads — two of us — felt a little afraid of him — as the combination of education and gospel in one man was a power, the outcome of which we were by no means certain of. But before we were aware of it we found our fears had all given place to admiration and respect, as he took part with us in our little work and seemed so handy about the farm; for aught we could see he could mow as handsome a swarth and rake as fine a winrow as the best of the men.

One day he said to us, I want you to go with me to-day and help me to measure the east hill or "Hatch hill," as it was known. We knew the hill was steep and difficult to climb, and pretty high, but we did not doubt his ability to measure it if he said he could.

He soon appeared ready for the work. He had in his hand a queer-shaped thing — a quarter circle cut from a pine board, a plumb-line hanging from the square corner, a couple of tin sights on one edge, and a handle of leather on the side. This thing, he said, was a quadrant, by means of which he was to measure the mountain. We started across the flats for the mountain; borrowed a two-rod chain of a surveyor on the way; and soon reached the field of operation. We drove a stake, and our minister friend stood over it and, through the tin sights, looked at the top of the pine tree that marked the top of the mountain, and said he was taking the angle of elevation. What that was we did not know; but he let us take it, and the plumb-line showed the same angle. We then measured toward the mountain, drove another stake, and repeated the operation of angle-taking. The whole operation was repeated in order to see if any mistake had been made. We were then informed that the work was all done, except a little figuring, which he could do at home. After dinner he called us out, and said he had found the height of the mountain to be one thousand one hundred and eighty feet. But how? He did not measure it, but only measured a short line on the level land and took some angles at each end of it. We knew nothing of triangles—that the sides of a plane triangle are to each other as the sines of the opposite angles, or that radius is to sine of the acute angle as hypothenuse is to side opposite—and so this whole work was to us a profound mystery — a mystery which he could not explain to us — and we saw it. But we saw and felt much more — that he had created in us a desire and a determination to know more than we then knew; and I feel to-day that that forenoon's experience had more influence on me as an educational force, than any other that I can recall. I have taken scores of young men through the same steps since, but never without thinking how I was started in my early life. We had no academy then in that town, but the soul and power of the academy we had in that *noble teacher; and his study for several years after was a true academy, where quite a number of boys got a good send-off in their educational work.

These centres of power and influence you, gentlemen of the Regents and the law-makers over you, have placed in more than six hundred different localities in this broad State, some of which indeed have disappeared, but not until they had done good service in the educational field.

The academy has exerted a great influence upon the question of the higher education of woman.

In most of the academies, early and late, the sexes have been educated together. But the academic course to the young man and the young woman had a vastly different aspect; to the one it was a stepping-stone to higher privileges and rewards, to the other it was often the sad end of educational opportunities, and the young

---

* Rev. John C. Morgan.

woman leaving the academy had only before, at the best, the life of a partly educated woman. It was not, therefore, to be wondered at that the friends of female education looked anxiously for a deliverance from this state of things. The colleges were closed against women. The professional schools did not want them, and even some of the academies would not allow them to study the higher mathematics or the ancient languages.

Up to 1830 there had been incorporated by the Regents several female seminaries, notably among which the Waterford Seminary and the Ontario Female Seminary, under the care, respectively, of Mrs. Emma Willard and Miss Hannah Upham. Mrs. Willard soon removed her school to Troy, where she established the Troy Female Seminary.

These noble women, with Mary Lyon, who was laying the foundation of the Holyoke Seminary, saw the work of the education of woman from a higher stand-point than those who had gone before them. Differing greatly in their special gifts, and so giving to their schools a decidedly individual character, they began the work of a truly higher culture of their sex.

The first object in these schools seems to have been to train up teachers for the higher schools, and then to furnish for all the broadest culture and training they could secure. In this work they spent their lives, and the teachers from their schools took their places over the land as the principals of such seminaries, or as the heads of the ladies' departments in mixed schools. The results of their efforts soon began to appear in the establishment of seminaries of a higher order such as the Packer Institute, the long-honored lady principal of which was a daughter of the Ontario Female Seminary, the Elmira Female College, Vassar College, Wells College, Ingham University, and others.

It is not yet a settled question whether the co-education of the sexes is a desirable end to be attained, but it is clear that an education for women equal in all respects to that provided by our best colleges for men is practicable and will surely come. To this end has the influence of the academies for the century past been tending, and if such a consummation shall ever be reached it will be largely due to the noble life labor of Mrs. Emma Willard, who was once introduced to the New York State Teachers' Association, at Rochester, by the late Professor Charles Davie, "as the mother of us all."

A word in conclusion: About the year 1824, two young men —

HISTORY OF ACADEMIC INSTITUTIONS.   79

one from under the shadow of that fine academy at East Hampton, the other from Shoreham, Vermont; the former a graduate of Hamilton, the latter of Middlebury — came to Onondaga county in this State; the one taking charge of Onondaga Valley Academy, and the other of Pompey Academy, the two academies first organized in that county. After a short service the one was, in 1830, called to the Cortland Academy, at Homer; and the other, in 1828, to the Canandaigua Academy. In these new fields these men began the great work of their lives. They were very similar in their scholarly habits and tastes, of elegant classical attainments and intensely interested in all the practical questions of the day; they created in the minds of the youth under their influence an enthusiastic desire for the advantages which the academies afford to their students. They traveled through the counties, lecturing upon philosophy and chemistry, illustrated by experiments with such apparatus as could be obtained, and allured young men and women to a higher education. These two academies, under their instruction and guidance, became the great educational centres of Western New York, to which students came from this State and from all the States of the then opening west. For twenty-two years the one labored in Homer, when, after a work which should satisfy the highest ambition of a Christian scholar and teacher, he took charge for four years of the Normal School of this city, and then became the efficient and beloved Secretary of this august Board of Regents, which work he continued till nearly the close of his life. The other kept on his work for twenty-three years, when with impaired health he retired to a farm, where he lived for seventeen years with the benedictions of thousands of young men, whom he had educated, resting upon his head — Samuel B. Woolworth, Henry Howe — noble men, true and devoted teachers. They wrought a great work — their work remains. Such men give us a beautiful and striking illustration of the grand product of true academic work.

REMARKS OF PRINCIPAL ALONZO FLACK, PH. D.

Mr. CHANCELLOR, GENTLEMEN AND LADIES OF THE CONVOCATION: — The letter from the Regents, that brings me before you, says that "as a veteran, we expect something historical and prospective of you." In the few minutes that I detain you, I will take these three points in the order that the letter calls for them. My own idea of a veteran is one that is worn out in the service, his head white, his limbs trembling, and his face wrinkled, and is unfit for further service. A friend of mine who lisped, said: "They thay I lithp, but I don't perthieve it mythelf;" and on this definition of a veteran I must say, I do not perceive it myself, and therefore how I come here under authority as a veteran must be explained in some other way. I entered an academy under the Regents, with Principal Larkin of the Argyle Academy in 1840. I taught there in 1845, as assistant in science and mathematics under Principal McCracken; hence I claim an antiquity of thirty-nine years since I commenced service as an academic teacher in this State. I took charge of the New York Conference Seminary in Charlotteville, in 1850, and have been consecutively a teacher from that time till to-day. To be sure I had not made a mistake, I looked up the report of that first year of the New York Conference Seminary. There were six hundred and seventy-four pupils registered, and in the report of 1854–1855 I find that one thousand two hundred and fifty-three pupils were reported, and that seven hundred and forty-nine drew public money as higher English or classical scholars. No student under sixteen years of age could be admitted. Having been a long time teaching, I may be a veteran in that respect. I am, perhaps, among the old ones here; but I have other testimony as to my age in this respect. I was invited to a wedding in this city within two years, where a very learned and distinguished professional gentleman of the city of Albany was present, who had been a member of the New York Conference Seminary when I was principal in 1851, and knew at that time Mrs. Flack, then a pupil. He took her to supper and sat next to me. He told her of his experience at the New York Conference Seminary in 1851, when she was a pupil with her husband's venerable father, who was a very stern schoolmaster of his day. When I visited the Wells College, for which the Hon. E. B. Morgan had done so much, he greeted me in the parlor, and shaking my hands long, said he knew "a score or more of young men who were educated there between 1850 and 1855 by my venerable father. I have had this sort of experience running all along through my life, which makes me think I may be older than I look.

Now as to the history. I can go back only one-third of a century with any degree of accuracy. I commenced consecutive work in 1850, by taking charge of the Conference Seminary at Charlotteville, *fifty-five miles west of Albany by the stage*. In order to carry out the intentions of the letter calling me here, I must contrast the work of the Board of Regents in my early experience with that of

HISTORY OF ACADEMIC INSTITUTIONS. 81

the present. I intrusted my first report of the six hundred and seventy-four students to the President of the Board of Trustees, Mr. Thomas La Mont of Charlotteville, with instructions to deliver it to the Secretary, Dr. T. R. Beck, with great care. The report of 1854 and 1855 (a document on which I expected to draw fourteen or fifteen hundred dollars of public money, and which I thought, perhaps, I could get discounted by the honorable Secretary, and take the money back with me), containing the record of one thousand two hundred and fifty-three pupils, was too valuable to trust with a merchant, so I took the stage, with the document close to my heart and came down to Albany myself. While riding through old Schoharie on that jolting stage, I mused on my reception by the honorable Secretary. I had heard that he belonged to the *nobility* of Albany. I thought many principals might present reports who wore finer clothes than I did, but not one in whose bosom beat a heart that felt itself worthy of more praise for good work done than in mine. No pilgrim ever went to Rome expecting a richer blessing than I expected at Albany. I thought of the nobleman in Scriptures who went into a far country to receive a kingdom, who gave his ten servants ten pounds to occupy till he came; who said to the one who gained ten pounds, "well done thou good servant, because thou hast been faithful in little, have thou authority over ten cities;" and I expected certainly I would be given authority over the little village of Charlotteville, and be greeted with a smile and a bow; but imagine my astonishment when I came into the office of the honorable Secretary of the Regents. He did not look up from a manuscript he was examining until I commenced the little speech I had prepared to make on my entrance, and which I did not get off as well as I expected. I stood very straight with the consciousness of being a good and faithful servant, and with a reasonable expectation of an approving word at least.

I said with a somewhat tremulous voice, "Honorable Mr. Beck, Secretary of the Regents, I have brought you my annual report, claiming seven hundred and forty-nine higher English and classical pupils, and a registry of one thousand two hundred and fifty-three during the year," and I handed him the ponderous document (it was written in a plain, coarse hand and was weighty). The trustees' report was placed inside the principal's schedule as of little importance compared with the schedule, and Mr. Beck took the document with a firm, knit brow, and when he perceived that the schedule and report were not "annexed" as the law requires, he held up the principal's schedule in one hand and the trustees' report in the other, and with an awful look said, "young man, do you ever expect to get to heaven after *swearing* these two are *annexed?* There you see they are *separate.*" I turned paler than the eclectric light of the present day. I saw as distinctly written on the walls of the Secretary's office as old Belshazer did, " mené, mené, tekel, upharsin." You are weighed in the balances and are found wanting. It was a minute before I recovered myself enough to realize that the principal who brought that weighty report was not to be put down without a reply.

I said firmly, Mr. Beck, don't annex mean to join, to unite ? "Yes," he replied. Well then, when we clergymen unite and join in holy matrimony man and wife, we do not take a needle and thread. They are joined and united enough to stand forever. He looked a little confused and said, "very well, you are excused." I returned to Charlotteville not feeling nearly as happy as in coming. I do not mention this fact to condemn the dead, but to illustrate the progress made in the Regents' office during the third of a century.

Severity in that period was characteristic of our profession. A neighbor and friend of mine, who commenced teaching private pupils in New York city sixty-four years ago, flogged the sons of many of the first families in New York for failing to get a lesson, the son of John Jacob Astor included. The preacher and the teacher dwelt more on God's justice in those days than to-day, and I refer to this event only as a matter of history.

We feel that we live in an advanced age when we contrast the past with the polite, benevolent reception every one received from the late Secretary Woolworth and his assistants, and now from his worthy successor and his board of assistants. I only wish the spirit of our firm Mr. Beck could look in the Regents' office now with its preliminary and higher examination — reports, etc., etc.

Now I turn to the future. The future of the Regents is indicated in what they have accomplished in the past. *The preliminary certificate* (an institution in itself), *the intermediate certificate, the English diploma, the Latin diploma*, each bearing a high value over the whole country, is an inspiration to those in charge of higher education in every State in the Union. From the popularity and usefulness of the examinations that entitle pupils to these testimonials, there will come a State examination in every public school in the State — examinations and papers adapted to the capacity and age of the pupils to be examined — four or five papers of different grades of advancement in arithmetic—three in English grammar, two in geography, etc.—so that the Superintendent of Public Instruction can know the work done by teachers in the public schools of the State. The law of progress in education is so certain that it can be affirmed as a certainty, that the Regents will see in the near future their system of examinations, in some form, adopted in all the schools of the State.

In the future the Regents will, I have no doubt, grant to the pupils in the academies another *diploma*, combining all now in the two *diplomas*, and adding more English subjects and French and German. The Regents in the future will also grant examinations sufficient to entitle those passing them to the degree of Bachelor of Science, Bachelor of Philosophy and Bachelor of Arts. If the Regents do not themselves confer these degrees in the future, as I think they should, they will recommend colleges to confer them on those having cards in subjects prescribed by them to have such degrees. This will make the courses of instruction more thorough in the academies and academic departments in union schools, and improve both them and their *instructors*.

This course will add to the number in existing colleges rather than diminish, and more than quadruple the number of degrees conferred in the State and require more discipline to get the degree. This Board of Regents has a right to be proud that it has instituted and sustained a system of examinations that will permeate every school of the State, from the academies of the State, to the cities, and to the public schools, and to the schools of other States, until we shall have it reported to us as a fact that New York is the nucleus and centre of a system of thorough examinations that is nowhere else found. I took a vacation last October for a couple of months, and passing through the edge of Canada and west as far Dakota and Nebraska, I went to many of the high schools. I found very many of the principals graduates of the colleges of our State. I told the students of these examinations. The principals asked for the papers and said it would be a good thing to establish such examinations in their schools. I believe the Regents are to have, in the future, a grand day that will not be longer delayed than their one hundred and twenty-fifth anniversary, when the prophecies of these few words of mine will be history.

Remarks of Principal Joseph E. King, D. D.

Mr. Chairman :—If I had known just what ground the learned Dr. Clarke would take in presenting his paper on the History of the Academic Institutions of the State of New York, I would have attempted by a paper to supplement it; but I did not know that. I have been charmed with his paper, and the literature of the subject he has handled admirably. I have known for forty-one years the academies in the State of New York. I meant to prepare for college in one of them. Providentially, however, my college preparation I found in the Giddings and Garfield district, Ohio. The vocation of the academy for the last half century has been three-fold, each of which might have had its history written : In the first place, to prepare and send to college on an average annually one, two, three or four boys or young men, rarely over six, scarcely ever ten. The dignity and importance of this work has been appreciated by the colleges. If these supplies had been taken from them they would have a very different history themselves. The colleges are to the academies of our State what the lower Hudson is to the upper Hudson. There must be an upper Hudson or there could be no lower, and unless there are mountain rills there would be no streams to float the commerce down. To supply this demand of the colleges by preparing students has been the missionary work of all the academies; it has never been financially remunerative. But the academies have found their compensation for doing this work in the increased respect they have enjoyed in the community. The demand for college preparatory work has necessitated the employment of a bright man, college-bred, sometimes a couple of them, at the head of the academy. This has given tone and character to academies. Many a man of very choice character and culture has lingered in charge of these academies and has gone to his profession better equipped than he could have otherwise been. Many successful public men have acknowledged their experience in these academies to have been the effective foundation of their success. The second vocation has been to teach the common branches in and beyond their elements, and something of algebra, something of the history of the United States, always accompanied with required essays, to a great multitude of intending teachers, and of youth that have not been content with the common schools; who have lingered one, two, three or four terms at the academies and gone out with its impress more effective workers, better in the aggregate, and exerting a beneficial influence that it would require the calculus to measure. The third and the main vocation of the academy has been to do academic work for the choicest young men and young women from the villages or hamlets of our whole State — those most ambitious, most enterprising; to take them under its tuition and keep them some years — not a few of them coming without that purpose, but being induced to prepare for college. The great majority, perhaps anywhere from fifteen to thirty-five per cent of the real academic students who pursue the common branches, go on to algebra and geometry and almost always Latin and rhetoric and general history and several of the sciences, scarcely ever less than two, sometimes up to five. These academic students, by the thousand in the aggregate, have gone out to professions, to teaching, to business, to life with no mean scholarly preparation. They have received the outlines and something of the substance of college culture. I have read with more than the interest of curiosity the red books of the Legislature. I have looked up the little outline of the lives of the men who are at the front, and I have noticed this : where one man refers to a college as having educated him, three, four or five refer to the common schools, and ten, twelve or more refer to the academies. The preparation of these youths for their work of life has been the great vocation of the academy. These academies have sent out young men and women to their work who have been able "to give a reason." It is a peculiarity of all the successful academies that they have maintained such an institution as the lyceum. In these academic lyceums parliamentary orators have been made. It is adapted to quicken their faculties, to stimulate them. It has taught them parliamentary rules, and the average academicians, to use that big term, have gone out to the world capable of thinking while standing on their feet, capable of meeting bright men and vanquishing them in square debate, and this they learned in the academic lyceum. I have noticed in not a few of the stronger academies another characteristic feature. Together with imparting something of the substance of a collegiate education and the advantages of the lyceum, it has been their aim to send out their students trained in manners and in address. The academy has been their home. They have been subject to the friendly criticism of the teachers day after day, and they go out qualified to act their part in society or in the church, as well as in the councils of the State. As was intimated in the paper of Dr. Clarke, in those academies which have had a long lease of life, by which they have maintained their vitality, the rule is, there has been a man at the head; his personality has dominated, and that man was almost inevitably one who was a pronounced Christian man who did not apologize for the Bible or for the faith, but assumed them to be first truths that were to have reverence and reception. And this quite substantial crown of culture has been the characteristic of academic life and work. And you will find, sir, if you mark these academic students, if you follow them they take their places with their fathers in the church. They know how to pray as well as they know how to speak. You will find when they come here to the Legislature they know how to do committee work; they know how to make a point of order; they know how to express themselves on their feet.

I might also say a word or two about what has been done toward the quiet solution of the problem of co-education: Both sides of the house for the last fifty years have been represented in the academy and have demonstrated several things: That the girls, as a rule, can get a lesson more rapidly than the boys in all the studies of the course with a single exception — in which they do not desire to excel, because there is but little motive for it — the department of mathematics. Their success is only exceptional in algebra and geometry. In the languages they lead; in rhetoric and history they lead; in the sciences they are not behind; and the wholesome effect on the other side of the house as to the manners and the deportment of young men and boys is most obvious. The young men have behaved themselves; the young men are not cruel; they do not engage in hazing; they are respectful to women; they are gallant; they are her champions. The women themselves are better mannered; they are not hoidenish; they are not screaming girls; they are women. We have found *that* to be true of co-education. When we leave the secondary school, other arguments come in. They are of maturer age. I am not so sure about that, but, so far as co-education in the secondary schools is concerned, it has come here to stay. These academies have found the Regents' examinations a tonic. They bring a good deal of work. There are busy brains here in Albany who send the questions to us in good form. There is a salutary stimulus about it. It kindles the ambition of the youths. We do good work and we are helped by it every time. I won't detain you any further.

REMARKS OF PRINCIPAL ELISHA CURTISS.

Mr. CHAIRMAN:— It was not expected that I should speak on this subject when the executive committee first announced the programme; but when I arrived here in Albany I was invited by the chairman to make a few remarks — something about the history of academics and academic institutions of this State. When Dr. Clarke went back a hundred years I had to respectfully bow, because I know little about the academies of a hundred years ago. In the western part of the State, from which I come, there were no academies at that time, hardly any fifty years ago. But speaking of academies as they now exist in the State, in nearly every county, we find them presided over by normal school or college graduates, who, beyond doubt, are doing excellent work in their way. It is that department that demands men of intelligence and culture — men furnished, almost exclusively furnished, by colleges or normal schools, who labor in the academies in these localities and educate those who seek a higher education. It seems to me, at the present time, it is the great duty of the academy to educate, or give a start, in the higher branches of education, to those pupils who, perhaps, could not attend college, or who would be but ill prepared to attend college. Here they can be brought up at home without the temptations that would surround them should they go from home. Under the guidance of their fathers and mothers, and the teachers who preside over the schools, they can obtain a limited education. I am very glad that the Albany Normal School, and I suppose nearly all the colleges of our State, accept a preliminary academic certificate in lieu of an examination in arithmetic, grammar and geography and other preliminary branches. Years ago when we went to college we went with fear and dread. I can realize now it must have been a great labor for the college faculties to examine all these pupils, and it must have been at a great expense. If we send students from our part of the State to Cornell, we know what to expect. If we conform to certain regulations they pass an examination; they have letters of credit, certified to by the Regents of the University of the State of New York; they will be admitted without examination. I believe the Albany Normal School sends out a circular, stating that those who have passed a preliminary examination will be admitted without examination, and those who have an intermediate certificate will be admitted to the second year without examination. Well, in every county there are those who never go to college, and who do not attend a normal school, and still it is within their range to attend an academy and join the teachers' class, and the reports show that nearly one-half of the teachers of the State have been members of teachers' classes. As I suggested, almost every academy has either college or normal school graduates in its faculty, and they are training the teachers of the common schools of the State of New York — fitting them well to teach school, perhaps even in the highest school. Graduating from an academy, they could not expect to be principals of the large village and union schools of the State, but there is a class of schools numbering from ten to thirty-six scholars, and sometimes fifty to sixty, that normal school and college graduates seldom have attempted to teach. They seek higher places, or places where they can afford to give more wages, and for these small places — the common schools, the people's colleges — students instructed in academies furnish teachers. Fitted and prepared by the academies of to-day as they are, those teachers do good work. Of course all their work is not confined to that. I remind you we prepare a few for college ; I doubt not every academy in the State of New York sends at least one or two every year to some college. Of course it has not been my pleasure, teaching only just a little portion of the time, commencing twenty years ago and being consecutively principal of the same school during that time, to have a very wide range of knowledge with reference to academies of the State. I have been teaching ever since the Regents' examinations were instituted. We like to compliment the Regents on the questions they send out. We complain most, by the way, when the fewest pass. If they pass, all is well; if they do not, we say the Regents are not reasonable in the questions they ask. If they pass we say they were just the questions, and they met our expectations exactly. It is a little owing to the class of students we have to pass. These examinations on the whole, the preliminary examinations of the State of New York, have been getting better each year since their first inception. They are as good as they can be ; more systematic, perhaps, than formerly. Still the old examinations tended to give an impulse to the student, and were an incentive to the teachers. This marks the progress of every academy in the State of New York. It is perhaps a little to be regretted that they seek to measure the teaching qualities of an academy by the number that have passed the Regents' examination, still there must be some criterion. I do not know as it will ever be the case that these examinations will extend to the common schools of the whole State, and that they will send their papers here to Albany. I am not a prophet like Dr. Flack. Had I known the subject, and the wishes of the executive committee I would have prepared myself. I certainly apologize to the principals present for making any remarks at all on a subject that should command the learned consideration and the great experience of those men who have been teaching twenty, thirty, forty, or as Dr. Clarke, fifty years or more. At least they say he is the Nestor of the teachers of the State of New York; and as I have been to this University Convocation for twenty consecutive years, with one exception, I remember, I looked up to him as a sort of father twenty years ago.

Dr. WILSON in the Chair: — If the Convocation will allow me I will make a remark which has grown out of my own observation and knowledge in reference to what Dr. King has just said. In Cornell University, it is known we have students of both sexes — the females are usually from one-eighth to one-tenth. None of them of course are taking the courses that require the higher mathematics as in engineering, the mechanical arts, and various branches dependent upon and absolutely requiring a knowledge of mathematics. Now set those aside and the ladies who select mathematics as a matter of choice will be a larger proportion than the men. And not only that, some of the very best mathematicians we have ever had were ladies who chose it for pleasure. One of our best mathematicians is a lady in the senior class, and she takes mathematics as a matter of choice. And as a general thing the lady students stand fully as high in mathematics as the gentlemen.

REMARKS OF PRESIDENT A. W. COWLES, D. D.

Mr. CHAIRMAN :— May I be allowed to add my testimony, having had charge of a college for young women for twenty-eight years? I can emphatically confirm the statement of Dr. Wilson. I believe there is no appreciable difference between young women and young men in their capability for the study of mathematics or for any thing else. I believe, indeed, they are specially capable of continued confinement to study; being accustomed to being in the house and to sedentary habits, they can do more work in a day than the boys can. We have had in the Elmira College, a full college mathematical course through spherical trigonometry and analytical geometry with elective calculus, and mathematical astronomy with the use of the observatory and instruments. Their enthusiasm is in these studies very great, and I think we ought to have that impression removed entirely from our minds, that there is any difference in capacity or taste for mathematics, arising from what is sometimes called sex in mind.

Remarks of Principal T. K. Wright.

Mr. Chairman :— I have not been accustomed to speak before the teachers annually gathered in this place, although I have been the principal of three academies of the State during the last thirty-seven years — six years in Pompey Academy, five in Jordan Academy, and twenty-six in the Munro Collegiate Institute at Elbridge. I have, therefore, been engaged in the business of teaching forty-six solid years — nine in New England and thirty-seven in New York — two in district schools and forty-four in academies. I have also attended these Convocations from the start, with one or two exceptions. Still I speak with some reluctance, it being the first time I have attempted to say a few words before my fellow teachers. It may be the last. Most present probably are more gifted in speech and have more of a desire to be heard than I have. I prefer to listen to others. Touching the subject just discussed, my experience as a teacher confirms me in the belief that there is no marked difference in the capacities of ladies and gentlemen in acquiring the different branches of knowledge. I have observed that the gravest opinions on this subject are generally given by those who have had the least experience as teachers. Girls learn to spell, read and write as readily as boys. They get a knowledge of the higher branches just as readily. Grouped together in the same class, the girls keep well up with the boys, whether in algebra, geometry, trigonometry, the calculus, the sciences, or the dead languages. Such has been my experience.

I wish to say a few words upon another subject. I feel quite proud that I am a member of the Empire State. I have done some work for it ; it has done much more for me. Although it has taxed my property and the property of us all, it has doubtless done it for a good purpose. By looking around, we readily see where some of that which was once our property has been invested. From time to time the Legislature has seen fit to call for an additional million of dollars, in order to push on the work of the Capitol to completion. How many more millions will be called for we do not know. We wish the building to be finished. It is a grand structure and we are willing to put some more of our means into it.

Thirty-eight years ago I settled in Onondaga county, at Pompey

Hill. There I taught six years; from thence I went to Jordan, where I taught five years; from thence to Elbridge, where I have taught twenty-six years. Should any one ask why I have stuck to the business of teaching so long, I could reply, because I had a family of children on my hands to be educated, uniform good health, and a love for my profession.

In the academies mentioned above, many were prepared for college, took a full college course, and entered upon their professions. After thirty years have passed, it is natural that the teacher should look back and see if he can gather up any trophies of success. Some of those students have been sent to Albany, to assist in making laws for the State. Some have been sent to Washington, to help make laws for the Nation. Others stand high in the clerical profession I will name but three — Hiram Haden of Cleveland, Ohio, Henry Duguid of Syracuse, N. Y., and Frank Hiscock of Syracuse, N. Y. They all had their send-off from Pompey Hill. Frank Hiscock did not take a college course. Having good natural abilities, and not a superabundance of means, he chose to enter upon his profession with only the education an academy could give. Most of us know what he has accomplished. I, for one, feel proud of him. So I do of all those, my former students, who have taken an advanced standing in society and given a good account of themselves. Occasionally one says, " you made a man of me." I take only a part of the credit to myself. Good material is required out of which to carve a beautiful statue. So, also, fair abilities at least are needed on which to build an efficient man.

The colleges of the State are doing a great work, but I verily believe that the academies and the higher departments of union schools are doing a still greater. The student shapes his course toward a higher life, or it is shaped for him, more in the academy than in the college. During the late war of the Rebellion more students enlisted from the academies of this State than from the colleges. Forty-seven from the Munro Collegiate Institute transferred their names from the daily roll-call of the academy to the roll-call of the muster station. They went to the front; thirty-seven only returned; ten laid down their lives for their country. Without doubt many of the academies of the State sent as many or more to the war. Such, then, are the trophies that the academies can show.

I chanced to fall in with a gentleman at Chancellor Benedict's reception, three or four years ago, here at Albany. After introducing each to the other, he inquired from what part of the State I came.

I replied, from the Munro Collegiate Institute, Elbridge. I am acquainted with the school, said he. How? By the examination papers sent to the Secretary of the Regents. So it is. The academies are better known by the examination papers, sent from the several academies from term to term, than by the principals who present themselves here at the Convocation yearly. For much of the best teaching is done by those assistant teachers who are seldom seen at the Convocation.

On the other hand, the Regents, their Secretary and his assistants are better known to the principals of the academies by their work and by the letters exchanged between them during the year, than by the casual greetings at the Convocation, although these are always very cordial. We are pleased also with the promptness with which our letters are answered, when making inquiries of any kind of the Secretary of the Regents.

We notice changes in the Regents' Report from time to time for the better, also in the blanks sent for our annual report. All these things indicate advancement and improvement in the cause of education. I have sometimes thought I would like to return to this world one hundred years from now and see what progress shall have been made in the various departments of human action. During the past hundred years certainly the progress in the cause of education has been great; we have every reason to believe that in the next century it will be still greater.

V.

THE HISTORY AND CONDITION OF SCIENCE-TEACHING IN THE ACADEMIES OF THIS STATE, AND SOME REFLECTIONS THEREON.

By JOEL DORMAN STEELE, Ph. D.

In the limited time allowed me for the preparation of this article I have been able to make only what, in days now happily past, we learned to call a *reconnaissance*. What little I have discovered I submit, hoping that my meagre report may possibly be of service to some one who shall hereafter occupy the field in force.

"A century ago" in science seems to us an age. The phlogistic theory was then scarcely overthrown, and Lavoisier was still busy in laying the foundations of chemistry. Count Rumford, or, as we should know him by his plain American name, Benjamin Thompson, had not yet proved that "heat is a mode of motion." Humboldt was still to take mankind by the hand, as Virgil took Dante, and lead the way through the Cosmos. The asteroids wandered unknown in space. Galvani's frogs were sporting in their native ponds. The very latest chemical news was that one Cavendish had proved water to be composed of two gases — hydrogen and oxygen.

Fascinated by the vast strides of recent science we are sometimes disposed to underrate the triumphs of the elders. The nineteenth century philosophers stand in the foreground and fill the whole angle of vision. Physics without Young, Arago, Ampère, Faraday, Kirchhoff or Henry; chemistry without Dalton, Gay-Lussac, Davy, Liebig, Bunsen or Draper; physical geography and geology without Humboldt, Buckland, Lyell, Agassiz, Hitchcock, Dana, Guyot, Hall, Winchell or Dawson; biology without Lamark, Cuvier or Darwin; and astronomy without John Herschel, Leverrier, Lockyer, Young, Langley or Newcomb — all look so barren that we are half inclined to wonder why our fathers ever studied science.

With such thoughts in mind, I have found it a very pleasant task to examine some of the scientific school books used in the academies during the last generation.

The oldest text-book I have been able to find is BLAIR'S EASY GRAMMAR OF NATURAL PHILOSOPHY, printed in England (1804) and republished in this country. It is a tiny, well written, and neatly illustrated work. There are chapters on matter and its properties, motion, mechanics, pneumatics, acoustics, optics, electricity and magnetism, and a brief section on astronomy.

But far more popular, in the early part of the century, was MRS. MARCET'S CONVERSATIONS ON NATURAL PHILOSOPHY. This author also wrote similar works on chemistry and political economy. Of the latter, Macaulay says: "Any girl who has read Mrs. Marcet's book could teach Montague or Walpole many lessons on finance." Martineau's biographical sketches speak of Mrs. Marcet in glowing terms. In England, there were numerous editions of her conversations, and they were reprinted in this country. Mr. Blake, a Boston teacher, edited the edition of 1824, adding questions at the bottom of the page after the good old fashion. In the language of the Yankee publisher, "Mrs. Marcet's treatise on natural philosophy has probably contributed more to excite, in the minds of the young, a fondness for studying the science, than all other works together." Let me quote from the table of contents. There are chapters on the general properties of bodies; the attraction of gravity; the laws of motion — simple and compound; the mechanical powers; hydrostatics; springs, fountains, etc.; pneumatics; wind and sound; optics, etc. Notice that the divisions are very like those now used, but that electricity is omitted. The topics follow one another naturally, the style is pleasant, while many of the examples are familiar to us. Strangely enough, in the centre of the work, is interpolated a treatise on astronomy, containing four chapters on the earth, the planets, the moon, and the tides. In the edition before me, printed at Boston in 1831, I am surprised at the classic beauty of the illustrations; they are not pictures, but drawings of practical value.

The next step in the progress of scientific instruction is chronicled in the preface of COMSTOCK'S SYSTEM OF NATURAL PHILOSOPHY, published at Hartford in 1832. The following extract is very suggestive:

"Mrs. Marcet's Conversations on Natural Philosophy, a foreign work now extensively used in our schools, though beautifully written, and often highly interesting, is considered by most instructors as exceedingly deficient — particularly in wanting such a method in its explanations as to convey to the minds of the pupil precise and definite ideas.

"It is also doubted by many instructors, whether Conversations is the best form for a book of instruction, and particularly on the several subjects embraced in a system of natural philosophy. Indeed, those who have had most experience as teachers, are decidedly of the opinion that it is not; and hence we learn, that in those parts of Europe where the subject of education has received the most attention, and consequently where the best methods of conveying instruction are supposed to have been adopted, school books in the form of conversations are at present entirely out of use."

A leaf of recommendations follows the preface. I give a specimen in full. It shows that the phrases even of our fathers survive in our speech and writing. This letter is from John Griscom, LL. D., then principal of the New York High School, and one of the best science teachers of his day:

NEW YORK, *June* 19, 1830.

ESTEEMED FRIEND — I have received and examined thy book on natural philosophy, with much satisfaction. I have no hesitation in saying, that I consider it better adapted to the purposes of school instruction than any of the manuals hitherto in use with which I am acquainted. The amiable author of the Conversations threw a charm over the different subjects which she has treated of by the interlocutory style which she adopted, and thus rendered the private study of those sciences more attractive; but this style of manner, being necessarily diffuse, is not so well adapted to the didactic forms of instruction pursued in schools. Hence, also, more matter can be introduced within the same compass, and I find, on comparing thy volume with either of the editions of the Conversations now in use, that the former is much better entitled to the appellation of a system of natural philosophy, than the latter. The addition also of electricity, and magnetism is by no means unimportant in a course of instruction in the physical sciences.

I am, with great respect,
JOHN GRISCOM.

P. S. — I have recommended thy book to all the pupils of our high school, who attend to natural philosophy, and it is the only book which we shall now use as a class-book.

This very excellent philosophy is doubtless familiar to many present. Indeed, the copy I have was put in my hands as a text-book just forty years since. How familiar, and yet how strange the work appears. Familiar cuts, illustrations of principles, definitions and statements occur on every page; and yet it seems strange to look over a natural philosophy with no reference to heat, galvanism, thermo-electricity, spectrum analysis, or conservation of energy; that assigns only four pages to magnetism, and thirteen to electricity; and that speaks of light as "composed of exceedingly minute particles of matter," of the sun as "the largest body in the universe," and gravely remarks that "perhaps from a high mountain a cannon-ball might be thrown five or six miles." Here again, as in Mrs. Marcet's book, astronomy is sandwiched in as a separate chapter, but occupying seventy-five of the two hundred and ninety-five pages of the entire book. Wind, also, appears as a topic under acoustics. The connection in this case is so slight, it is interesting to find the classification adopted by different authors.

Arnott's Elements of Natural Philosophy was published in England, in 1827; was translated into nearly all the European languages and was extensively used in this country. Professor Youmans says that "a generation ago it was the leading text-book." It contained a wealth of illustration expressed in exceedingly happy language. Here the term "natural philosophy" was made to cover a treatise in astronomy, and another on physiology. The title of one chapter carried the thought back to other days. It is this: "The Imponderables — Caloric, Light, Electricity and Magnetism."

In both these works we find the great principles of physics so carefully defined and illustrated, that one cannot but be impressed with the idea that, after all, the old preponderates over the new. Because the new is fresh, and we are all eager to keep abreast with the times, the recently-discovered truth often takes the precedence of long-established principles, that, on account of their age, have lost their novelty, but are still, as before, the basis of the subject. It would surprise one to see how much the pupil thoroughly grounded in these old books would know, and how little he would have to unlearn.

In chemistry, as in physics, there were conversations, and then the didactic text-book. The older teachers will remember the best, perhaps, of the latter kind — COMSTOCK's ELEMENTS OF CHEMISTRY (1831). This was, in part, based on the larger work of Dr. Turner, published in London, 1827. In his preface, Comstock remarks: "Of all the sciences, chemistry is the most complete in respect to its language, the order of its arrangement, the succession of its subjects, and hence in the facility with which it may be learned." How easy it all seemed fifty years ago! The phlogistic theory had been swept away; an admirable and systematic nomenclature had been adopted; the atomic theory, with the law of definite proportions and equivalents, had given a basis of philosophy and invested the composition of bodies with a new interest; while the brilliant experiments of Davy had attracted universal attention. Happy day! The intricacies of the new nomenclature were yet far in the future. The conceptions of unitary structures, of quantivalence, of organic radicals, of substitution, were unknown. Imagine the look that would have come over the face of a student of Comstock, who should have been asked to give the chemical constitution of, for example, ethyl — amyl — phenyl — ammonium iodide.

Following Comstock, came the profound work by Silliman, and the popularization of the subject by Youmans. To how many of us Professor Youmans' charming lectures were like the opening of a great gate letting us into a new realm of thought of which we had never dreamed.

Geology is a science almost of yesterday. When Silliman began to lecture at Yale (1804), "most of the rocks were without a name, and classification of the strata was quite unknown." In 1820, Professor Eaton and Dr. Lewis Beck, made a geological survey of Albany county, and ten years later, Professor Eaton published his geological text-book, with a colored map of New York geology. The survey of New York State, commenced in 1836, by Vanuxem, Emmons, Mather, Torrey, Lewis Beck, DeKay, and him whom we are proud to have in our midst to-day — James Hall, opened a new era in the study, and by classifying the palæozoic rocks made our geologic fields classic ground for all time. HITCHCOCK's ELEMENTARY GEOLOGY, published in 1840, passed through thirty editions in twenty years, and did much to popularize the subject. It specially served, in part, to allay the violent prejudice that had arisen in many minds because of the supposed anti-biblical tendency of geologic teachings. The instructor of to-day knows little of the bitter opposition the teacher of twenty-five years ago often experienced from his patrons if he ventured to insinuate that the earth was not created in six days, of twenty-four hours each. What Huxley so aptly termed, in his Chickering Hall lecture, the Miltonian Hypothesis was then only too currently insisted upon, as many of us found to our cost.

Cleaveland's Treatise of Mineralogy appeared in 1816, and fostered the growing taste for this study. The Edinburgh Review, in those days when it was praise indeed to speak well of an American book, said that Cleaveland's was the "most useful work on mineralogy in the language," and advised its republication in Great Britain. Dana's Mineralogy came out in 1837, and soon became, what it is to-day, the standard authority.

Astronomy is the oldest of the sciences, yet in the early part of the century it seems to have been considered in school work, as we have seen, a sort of addendum to physics. The oldest American academic text-book I have been able to find is the NEW AMERICAN GRAMMAR OF THE ELEMENTS OF ASTRONOMY, on an improved plan, by James Ryan; it was published in New York, and copyrighted in 1825. Herschel's Outlines, afterward so popular, appeared in 1849. OLMSTEAD'S LETTERS ON ASTRONOMY, printed in 1840, were addressed, as the author tells us in his preface to the revised edition, to a female friend (then no more) whose exalted and pure image was continually present in the composition of the work. The eminence of Professor Olmstead and the richness of his diction gave these Letters a wide circulation. The appearance of BURRITT'S GEOGRAPHY OF THE HEAVENS, especially when revised by Mattison, formed an epoch in astronomical teaching in our schools. Many of us recall the feeling we experienced when we first opened those beautiful charts and realized that then we could teach the subject as never before. It is not strange that at one time this work was adopted in our academies almost exclusively.

Did time and space permit I should like to name many other academic text-books used by our fathers and by us in our first attempts at teaching, such as Lincoln's Botany, Comstock's Physiology, Bonnycastle's Introduction to Astronomy, Mrs. Phelps' Philosophy, Robinson's Philosophy, Euler's Letters to a German Princess, Comstock's Geology, Parker's Philosophy, Potter's Science and Arts of Industry, Smith's Philosophy, and many others. But ere I leave this subject, I must make a suggestive quotation from "An Address to the Public, particularly to the Members of the Legislature of New York," by Emma Willard, published in 1819. This remarkable educator here sketched her idea of a female seminary. Among the studies to be pursued she recommends that of "natural philosophy, which," she says, "*has not often been taught to our sex*. Yet why should we be kept in ignorance of the great machinery of nature, and left to the vulgar notion that nothing is curious but what deviates from her common course. * * * In some of the sciences proper for our sex, the books written for the other would need alteration; because, in some they *presuppose more knowledge than female pupils would possess;* in others, they have parts not particularly interesting to our sex, and omit subjects immediately pertaining to their pursuits." From this we might suppose that a publisher's prospectus of the time would have run somewhat after this style: " A natural philosophy reduced to the comprehension of the female mind," and " A chemistry expurgated and revised so as to include only those subjects that pertain to the pursuits of women." What would good Miss Willard have thought if she could have seen the thorough course of laboratory work pursued by the young men and women of Cornell, or the comprehensive schedule of study at Syracuse, Vassar and Elmira?

Let us now pass on to notice the apparatus formerly used in our schools.

A century since, experimental science was just developing. It should be chronicled as a matter of history that, at this early period, during the dark days of poverty that followed the Revolution, the Regents of the University encouraged its growth in a practical manner. Within a month after the organization of the Board, in 1784, it authorized its foreign agent " to purchase such a philosophical apparatus for Columbia College as Dr. Franklin, Mr. Adams and Mr. Jefferson, ministers of the United States, advise." This measure seems, however, to have failed, for the minutes contain several allusions to the need of apparatus, until, in 1786, it was voted to pay £200 to Dr. Bard, then professor of natural philosophy in the Medical School, for the apparatus he had secured under the direction of the Board. In 1790 the sum of £750 was appropriated to the purchase of books and apparatus; one-half to Columbia College, and one-half to the four academies then under the care of the Regents (viz.: Clinton, North Salem, Goshen and Flatbush), the apparatus, etc., to belong to the Board and to remain in these institutions at its pleasure. In 1793 there was a similar appropriation, and in 1794 another of £1,500; the latter sum, however, to be divided between the purchase of books and apparatus, and the support of "youths of genius, whose parents were too poor to pay for their education."

Frequently, too, when special appropriations were made by the Legislature to particular academies, there was a clause inserted requiring the authorities of the institution to secure an apparatus.

Thus, for example, in 1826, an act for the relief of Jamestown Academy provided that before receiving "the said sum of $1,600 the trustees shall give security for the faithful application of said sum to the erection of a suitable building for said academy, and to the *purchase of a library and chemical apparatus*." The act of 1834 prescribed that the excess of the literature fund over $12,000 should be assigned by the Regents to the schools under their visitation for "the purchase of text-books, maps, globes, philosophical or chemical apparatus" to the amount of not over $250 per year; but, with a nice discrimination, specifies that such school must first have applied an equal sum to the same object. The act of 1838 directed that "no academy shall participate in the annual distribution of the literature fund until the Regents shall be satisfied that such academy is provided with a suitable library and apparatus." The act of 1857 fixed the amount to be applied by the Regents to the purchase of apparatus, etc., at $3,000.

This seems like a small sum, it is true, for a great State to apply to such an object, but its influence has been most marked. From our own knowledge, we can testify of academies that, through the fear of losing their share of the literature fund, have provided themselves with "a suitable library and apparatus;" and of teachers who, struggling to procure proper facilities for work, have found the assurance of the Secretary that their contributions would be doubled by the Regents, just the lever needed to encourage their patrons to do what otherwise they would never have attempted. All honor and thanks to the men who devised and carried out this beneficent scheme. Many a school owes its library and apparatus entirely to the stimulus of this appropriation.

As to the general character of the apparatus used in the early times, I have been able to secure little information. In 1835, the Regents voted an appropriation to buy apparatus for Fairfield, Canandaigua, St. Lawrence, Kinderhook, Middlebury and Montgomery academies. Nearly all the lists are alike; I append the one furnished Fairfield, as a specimen:

Orrery	$20 00
Globes	12 00
Numerical frame and geometrical solids	2 50
Movable planisphere	1 50
Tide dial	3 00
Optical apparatus	10 00

Mechanical powers	$12 00
Hydrostatic apparatus	10 00
Pneumatic apparatus	35 00
Chemical apparatus	25 00
One hundred specimens of mineralogy	10 00
Electrical machine	12 00
Instruments to teach surveying	80 00
Map of United States	8 00
Map of New York	8 00
Atlas	5 00
Telescope	40 00
Quadrant	15 00
Total	$309 00

Notice that the Regents were thus instrumental in distributing among the schools small mineralogical cabinets, a year before the geological survey of the State began.

Those whose memory dates back three or four decades will recall the standard apparatus of that time — the table air-pump, the cylinder, electrical machine, Barker's Mill, the frame with the mechanical powers, a trough battery, Hare's compound blow-pipe, etc.

It is not very long since physical laboratories for students' use were unknown; instruments of precision were unthought of; chemistry was relegated chiefly to the physician or the druggist; while the apparatus used in school was largely for the illustration of the principles of natural philosophy. Astronomy boasted of an orrery, an instrument invented by Dr. Rittenhouse, of Philadelphia, about 1768. Occasionally an academy possessed a movable telescope. But within the memory of some present there was not an observatory on this continent. So late as 1825, President Adams, in his first message, declared that "it is with no feeling of pride as an American that the remark may be made that on the comparatively small territorial surface of Europe there are existing upward of one hundred and thirty of these light-houses of the skies; while throughout the whole American hemisphere there is not one." The president's rhetoric was not equal to his aspirations for scientific advancement. Not only did his plan for an observatory in connection with a national university come to naught, but, worst of all, his conceit of calling an observatory "a light-house of the skies," excited such universal ridicule that the subject became obnoxious for years. To arouse a roar of laughter at the president's expense, it was necessary only to allude to his so-called plan of "finding a light-house in the skies."

Repeatedly afterward, Adams and others advocated the scheme of a national observatory, but it was long delayed, and the building was not opened until 1844. Meanwhile, the first telescope, above a portable size, was set up at Yale College in 1830; the first observatory was established at Williams College in 1836; and the United States Observatory at West Point in 1839 was the fourth in order. Others followed apace so that the Dudley Observatory, incorporated in 1853, was the twenty-second; and Hamilton College Observatory — since so famous under the directorship of its noted planet-finder Dr. Peters — was the twenty-third.

As to the date of introducing and the number of schools teaching science, my inquiries lead me to believe that more academies formerly pursued this branch of study, at least through physics, than is generally supposed. The appropriations by the Regents for the purchase of apparatus, the early reports of these schools to the Regents, and the personal statements made by teachers who distinctly remember classes of fifty years ago — all tend to the same conclusion.

Chemistry and physics were taught first in Union College (1797), and next in Columbia College (1802), though in the medical school of the latter institution they were pursued long before.

The academy record, so far as I have been able to collect it, is as follows:

Name.	No. of pupils in natural philosophy.	Date.
Clinton Academy	12	1788
Kingston Academy	6	1804
Union Hall Academy	23	1804
Oyster Bay Academy	3	1804
Catskill Academy	6	1804
Cayuga Academy	1	1805
Fairfield Academy	10	1806
Hamilton Oneida Academy	3	1806
Erasmus Hall	9	1807
Lansingburgh Academy	5	1807
Hudson Academy	....	1813
North Salem Academy	....	1813
Ballston Academy	....	1813

History of Science-Teaching in the Academies.

Name.	No. of pupils in natural philosophy.	Date.
Dutchess Academy	....	1813
Onondaga Academy	....	1813
Hartwick Seminary	....	1815
Clinton Grammar School	....	1830
Gouverneur Wesleyan Seminary	....	1830
Delaware (Delhi) Academy	....	1830

(Some of the above academies are extinct, or merged into later institutions, but the full record is given as a matter of history.)

From the Regents' report of *fifty years* ago (1834), which includes sixty-seven academies, I have compiled the following table:

Name of study.	No. of schools in which said study was taught.
Natural philosophy	62
Chemistry	44
Geology	....
Natural history	9
Botany	18
Mineralogy	1
Anatomy	1
Physiology	....

The latest Regents' report (1884) includes two hundred and fifty-seven academies and academical departments. I have compiled from it the following table:

Name of study.	No. of schools in which said study was taught in the following years: 1873.	1883.
Physics	131	208
Chemistry	69	146
Astronomy	58	138
Zoölogy	4	51
Geology	46	106
Physiology	102	208
Botany	126	143

The greatest change that appears in the later table is the introduction of geology and physiology, which were not taught fifty years ago. Instruction was given in geology first at Jefferson Academy in 1834—

1835, Comstock's text-book being used; during the following year, the study was pursued at Jefferson, Washington and Bridgewater Academies. It is a source of great gratification to notice that, *during the past decade* (1873-1883), *the number of science-classes taught in the academies of the State has very nearly doubled.*

It is easy to imagine the method of science-teaching employed in the early days. In education, as in geology, there are retrospective types. As the garpike explains the ancient Devonian fishes, and the nautilus reveals the structure of the ammonite, so enough old-fashioned pedagogues have survived to furnish a key to the paleozoic age of education.

How vividly the ancient method comes to mind as we recall our own school days. Occasional lectures were given on pneumatics, hydrostatics, etc. The apparatus was brought out of the case; the dust of the preceding year was brushed off; a withered apple was made plump, and a frightened-half-to-death mouse was scientifically exterminated under the receiver of the old table air-pump; a boy was put on the insulated stool and his hair caused to stand up like "quills upon the fretful porcupine;" next, the class, taking each other's hands, formed a ring and received the shock of a Leyden jar. So, the hour passed all too quickly, with much fun and little science, and then the apparatus was carefully put away for the next yearly exhibition.

For class-work, the book was placed in the hands of the pupil; a lesson was assigned, which he was expected to "learn by heart" and then recite verbatim. Practically, however, the book being kindly provided with questions at the bottom of the page, we inclosed with brackets such portions of the lesson as we thought would be required for the answers. Happy was the boy who had an old book marked by a brother or sister who had gone over the ground before. He could commit exactly what was needed, and was saved all trouble of reading over the rest of the text. Neither pupil nor teacher ever thought of making any appeal to the object described. No one could identify in real life the thing he had read about in his book. As Agassiz so well-remarked, "The pupil studies Nature in the schoolroom, and when he goes out-doors he cannot find her." In fact, he never looked for her.

Since that time there has been an entire revolution in method. I do not think that this change occurred at any fixed date. Professor Silliman, in his address at the grave of Priestly, commemorating the centennial of the discovery of oxygen in 1774, said: "The year

1845 marks the beginning of a new era in the scientific life of America." I cannot accept the doctrine of educational catastrophism. It is more probable that there has been, through many years, a gradual evolution of better ways of teaching.

Numerous causes have conspired to bring about this result. By the close of the first half-century from the formation of our government under its new constitution, enormous changes had taken place; the number of States had doubled; the population had reached seventeen millions; the great west was growing with marvelous rapidity; the railroad system was fairly inaugurated and our immense treasures of coal and iron were being developed. Then came the conquest of Mexico, and the discovery of gold in California, laying open the untold resources of a vast region to the skill and enterprise of an already highly-stimulated people. Science was, even before this, making rapid strides. Grand generalizations thrilled the pulse of the world. Applications of principles to common life brought the subject within the comprehension of practical men. Every one who had a daguerreotype taken by the process initiated by our own Dr. Draper, felt a dawning respect for the wonders of science. The triumphs of steam and electricity were patent to all. Men saw the "labor of a year shrinking into the compass of a day; the travel of a day into the compass of an hour; and the thought of man outstripping the velocity of light." They demanded to know something of the new forces that were shaking the nations. The call arose on all sides for a wider curriculum and more practical methods of study in the schools. Out of such an environment grew up the new education. Technological schools were established, the first of which was our own Rensselaer Polytechnic Institute, founded so far back as 1824. The colleges gradually yielded to the unwelcome necessity. Laboratories were erected. The modern methods of science-teaching were introduced. Students came back into the academies equipped with the recent views of education.

The change that has been wrought during the last twenty-five or thirty years is marvelous. The colleges can now demand for entrance a better knowledge of science than they themselves gave in their regular course a quarter of a century ago; many a country academy and city high school can boast a finer apparatus than the college then afforded; and in not a few secondary schools, competent teachers (they are worthy of the name of professor), in their laboratories and in the open field, are bringing their pupils face to face with nature.

I cannot join in the fashion, at present very common among a certain class of specialists, of pointing the finger of contempt at the average academic science-teacher. Cram is not the goddess of the academy alone. She sometimes lives and reigns in institutions of loftier name. The "birds whisper in the air," of indifferent professors who lock up their cabinets, or go through listless laboratory work that is only the ghost of the new education; and, of pupils who repeat, parrot-like, the names of fossils and compounds they never saw, describe abstruse theories they never applied, and read off from their closely-written cuffs and collars the formulæ they are too lazy to commit and too ignorant to grasp. Such exceptions prove nothing against one class of institutions more than another. The average school is as good as the people want, and far better than they are willing to pay for. The over-burdened teacher, occupied with his regular recitations every hour in the day; required to teach, besides the whole sweep of the sciences, perhaps half a dozen branches of study, ranging from arithmetic to the Iliad; with no time to prepare experiments or to clean up after them, except in precious hours stated, at the cost of health, from his meals, rest and exercise; having no money, save what he takes from his own scantily-filled purse, to pay for chemicals, and the expense of working and repairing the apparatus provided, as well as for making the simple instruments he would like; unable to purchase books and too weary to read them were they his; knowing that science is constantly advancing, yet shut in, by a necessity he cannot overcome, from every source of information,—is it any wonder if, too often, in sheer despair, he takes refuge in the old-fashioned method, and teaches chemistry as he does Greek—from the book!

Permit me, in closing, to offer a few reflections:

1. The error is sometimes made of trying to turn an academy into a college. The science-teacher mistakes his own growth for that of his pupils. Because he understands a subject more fully and easily, and can talk about it better than formerly, by that *transference of quality*, so natural to us, he conceives that his pupils are more advanced, and can digest stronger food than those of a few years before. He accordingly attempts to teach the most abstruse theories to mere boys and girls. While claiming a place for science among the more elementary studies, because it employs and cultivates the powers of observation, he yet seeks to elaborate formulæ as difficult as any grammatical analysis. Years will be required for those child-minds to expand sufficiently to grasp such comprehensive views, or

to gather in enough material for their application. Now, a theory is only a thread on which to string the isolated beads of fact, but if one have no beads, of what use is the thread? Time and again, patrons and pupils complain of this tendency, and remark of their teacher, " he is growing too learned for us; he ought to be in a college." The effect of such teaching is to destroy the interest naturally felt in scientific pursuits; to render them dull and unattractive; and to send the pupil out into life with no incentive to, or love for, further study.

2. The progressive, studious teacher delights in the newest discoveries of science. They fill his mind, and stir his blood. Fired with their wonders, he is liable to dwell upon them to the exclusion of that which is old, and hence "flat, stale, and unprofitable" to *him*, but new, interesting, and absolutely necessary for his *pupil*. Secondary classes need principally the elementary facts and laws, and very little indeed of scientific gossip. They should be well grounded in truths, most of which our fathers knew almost as well as we do.

3. To be intelligent now-a-days demands a general acquaintance with many branches. Even to read a metropolitan newspaper understandingly requires some information concerning science, history, art, literature, geography — a not mean range of scholarship. With a certain class of people this kind of universal knowledge is stigmatized as superficial. How often do we hear the maxim quoted, " A little knowledge is a dangerous thing." "A very dangerous adage it is," says Huxley. "If knowledge is real and genuine, I do not believe it is other than a very valuable possession, however infinitessimal its quantity. Indeed, if a little knowledge is dangerous, where is the man who has so much as to be out of danger."

It needs a life-time to become profoundly learned in any branch. But because one does not wish to calculate an eclipse, may he not learn enough of astronomy to understand the law of gravitation, to trace the constellations, to see the planets with a telescopic eye, to appreciate the splendid triumphs of celestial physics, and to make the heavens a source of joy for his life-time? Because one does not care to name every timber and brace and rafter of the "house he lives in," may he not learn enough of physiology and hygiene to understand the laws of his own being, and to conserve the highest working energy of his mind and body? Because one does not desire to make an analysis of an ore, may he not learn enough of chemistry to understand its common applications to his every-day life, and to the arts and sciences?

Such knowledge may seem very superficial to the astronomer, the physician, and the chemist, yet it makes one intelligent in society and business, opens up new avenues for study and thought, and is useful in manifold ways. To obtain the exact knowledge of anatomy required to be a surgeon, would be almost useless for one who does not intend to follow that profession, while the details, not being daily recalled to mind, would soon escape his memory. It would be far better for him to spend his time in gaining a general acquaintance with these branches that would give him that broad culture which forms so valuable a possession for a well-read man of the world. Moreover, "the little knowledge" that is dangerous, is that of the man with a hobby, who knows only one thing, who did not lay a broad foundation before he began to build up the specialty of his life's work. The narrowness of his view, the nearness of his horizon, the lack of all notion of the interrelation and interdependence of ideas, make his knowledge a source of peril to himself and others.

This general acquaintance with science should be "real and genuine" so far as it goes. Thoroughness is a quality applicable to a little, as well as to much, knowledge. One term's work may be just as far from superficiality, be just as true to the scientific spirit, and be just as perfect of its kind, as a year's labor. Accuracy, definiteness of conception, and readiness in the application of principles, will be best attained, not by an elaboration of the profundities of a subject, nor by a familiarity with its rare details, but by the mastery of its general laws, its characteristic ideas, its most commonly-observed facts; in a word, by getting into its spirit and becoming able to *reason after its manner.*

4. Are we not liable to overestimate the value of a written examination as a test of attainment in science and a basis of advancement in grade? The demand in elementary science is not a smattering of every principle, but a positive grip of the leading truths and their related facts. The test of progress is one's mastery of the scientific method. The new education requires the pupil to see accurately, to judge for himself and to apply principles intelligently. We teach him how to use apparatus, how to seek out his own illustrations, and how to improvise simple instruments for proving or explaining his statements. We expect him to weigh, to measure, to scan, to analyze, to combine. We make much of exactness and neat-

ness of manipulation. We show how investigations are made, and, when the pupil is sufficiently advanced to warrant it, we encourage him to venture upon little excursions of his own. Now, nearly all this work *with* nature, instead of *about* nature, and hence the most valuable part of the science-teaching, lies outside the reach of a written examination. A few problems and queries may be propounded, but the haste and excitement of an examination by no means favor that calm, judicial clearness of thought with which one should always study a query that nature presents for his solution.

Both teacher and pupil realize, when preparing for such an examination, that the result will be likely to hinge upon the remembrance of details. "They accordingly work," says Huxley, "to pass, not to know; but outraged science takes its revenge. They do pass, but they don't know." Now, in all this the delicate aroma of fine teaching entirely exhales.

5. The path of the beginner is not the path of the investigator. At first, the pupil must take things upon authority. It is a mere waste of time to set him at work to discover and prove for himself. He is ignorant of scientific laws and processes; he cannot rely upon his own reasoning and he ought not to; he knows neither the limits of, nor the errors incident to, examination; he cannot interpret results; he does not understand how to manipulate apparatus; and his crude work may disprove the very thing he ought to prove. The idea of turning a tyro into a laboratory, and thinking that, because he is learning how to bend a glass tube, or to make oxygen gas, he is therefore on the high road to discover every secret of nature, is as absurd as it is injurious. A wonderful power of manipulation may be acquired without gaining a single philosophical idea.

A certain amount of thorough elementary study, accompanied by lecture-table illustrations from the teacher, and a gradual introduction into the use of apparatus, the methods of experimentation, the properties of matter, and the broad scope and application of natural law, should, in general, precede any laboratory work, either physical or chemical.

6. Oral instruction, or better, *oral assistance*, is invaluable as a help in science-teaching. It supplements the deficiencies of every book; it gives freshness and vivacity to the recitation. But when a little excitement in class is substituted for the steady drill and toil of the individual mind ; when the teacher does all the winnowing and screening of the subject for the pupil, and feeds him only the "bolted flour;" when the youthful, immature pedagogue

proposes to make, off-hand, a better book than the trained author with the experience of a life-time; and when dry skeletons of thought and scraps of facts are presented on the black-board, to take the place of the rounded periods, the clear analysis, and the vivid illustrations of a modern text-book, — then, I say, give me back the paleozoic teacher and the educational methods of a former age! Knowledge not born of the travail of the soul is useless. The report of the committee on science-teaching that was given before the American Association for the Advancement of Science, at the session of 1880, well reads: " Where it is all talk and no work, and text-books are filtered through the imperfect medium of the ordinary teacher's mind, and the pupil has nothing to do but to be instructed, every sound principle of education is violated, and science is only made ridiculous."

7. " Science," says Professor Cooke, " is noble, because it considers the noblest truth." The grand conceptions with which the physicist deals have, aside from their scientific interest, an immense educational value. It is a far nobler work to form character than to impart knowledge; hence the thoughtful teacher watches every opportunity to exercise this rarest function of his office. To the discerning eye, the physical in nature constantly presses up against the spiritual. How full of meaning is the law of gravitation, the mutual sympathy of sounds and motions, the change of food into flesh, the conservation of energy, the adaptation of the eye to light, and the whole range of related facts.

When the pupil first discovers that the flavor of an apple reveals the nature of the tiny bud that was put into the stem twenty years before; when he beholds a lily — fair as the white robes of a saint — growing from the black mud of the swamp; when he sees a solid crystal building itself up out of a transparent liquid, in exact accordance with the principles of molecular architecture; when he finds that he cannot succeed in an experiment so long as he varies a hair's breadth from the line of an invisible law; when he realizes that the force which pulls his arrow to the ground, rounds the orbit of the planet,— how naturally, at such pregnant moments, may the thought of pupil and teacher detect the infinite presence, and the mystery of matter culminate in the mystery of God.

Remarks of Noah T. Clarke, Ph. D.

Mr. Chancellor: — I desire to express the great pleasure with which I have listened to the paper by Dr. Steele, and I also wish to say a few words upon one or two points suggested by it.

History of Science-Teaching in the Academies. 111

When we studied science fifty years ago we learned it from the text-books and from the mouth of the teacher, as it is largely learned to-day, but we, more than now, implicitly believed all that was printed and all that was told us, though a good deal of it we have come to know is neither true in theory nor in fact. We occasionally had a little illustration given of some philosophical law, with a nice explanation by the teacher.

I remember a Barker's centrifugal mill (involving the principle of the turbine wheel), which consisted of a perpendicular cylindrical tube, crossed at the bottom by a horizontal tube, whose arms had near the end orifices opening on opposite sides, so that when the tube was filled with water the wheel would move in a direction opposite the outflowing jet, which motion was explained by the book (Comstock's) by saying that the jets striking against the air were, by the reaction of the air, pushed around. It seemed to us then to be a good enough explanation, although it seems to us now to be very absurd.

But the teacher could not be wise above what was in the book, and he usually knew only what the book told him, and so a great deal of the science of those times was truly science *falsely so called*. Later we studied Comstock's Chemistry, often committing the experiments to memory and accepting all the theories and explanations, with but little idea of chemical facts or laws or principles. We studied the law of affinities, single, elective and double, the gases that loved and the gases that hated, and those that neither loved nor hated, and we thought we understood pretty well the ground principle on which the worlds were made. We studied astronomy and learned that if the plane of the earth's equator and that of the ecliptic ever coincided, as they would in all probability in a hundred thousand years, the seasons would not occur and the earth would cease to be a habitable globe, but we were comforted by the remark of the author, that this sad event would not occur until long after the present generation should be dead and beyond the reach of such a catastrophe.

We studied the laws of heat and the methods of its production, and we thought we knew what we meant when we said it was largely produced by oxidation; but we are told to-day that we were all wrong in our notions of this mysterious agency. We knew that the old phlogistic theory which controlled the thought of the scientific world for a hundred years had given place to this theory of oxidation. And now we are told that heat is only a mode of motion;

that motion and force are convertible into heat, and the temperature depends upon the amount of molecular motion, etc. And so we are led to ask where are we to-day and where shall we be one hundred years hence in the field of scientific inquiry? Are we sure of the teachings of science to-day? Are we sure we have at last reached the true explanation of things and can say positively this or that *is so?* We know more about the properties of matter, the play of forces, but do we know much more about the real nature of these forces, or material likes and dislikes? We know much more of the power of steam than we did when the first steamboat cut the waters of the Hudson; we know it has been harnessed to nearly every contrivance for labor, and that to-day it is doing half of the world's work, but that mysterious agency still baffles our inquiry as completely as does electricity, gravitation or light. The teachers of science to-day, therefore, need to be careful in their work, as doubtless much that is held to be true, of theory especially, will have its day only to give way to something new, as others have done, which have attempted the explanation of what belongs to the hidden and the profound. We know that science is having a wonderful development in our day. The developments of the last ten years in the one field of mineral oil have astounded the world. In the great International Exposition at Philadelphia in 1876, there was exhibited in a single case some eighty bottles of extracts, some liquid, some solid, obtained from mineral oil, most, if not all, of which have a fixed value in commerce and the arts. Alcohol has been derived from the marsh gas series and without any saccharine matter whatever. Oil of mustard is manufactured on a large scale from oxalic acid and glycerine. These and like facts are wonderful — almost beyond comprehension — and while we can receive them as such, it seems to me we shall never be able to see fully how God works through all these invisible and remarkable agencies. I am content, therefore, to take the facts as they are; accept them and make the most of them, remembering that the facts are of God, but the explanations are of man.

Remarks of Principal Joseph E. King, D. D.

Mr. Chancellor:— I think this paper is admirable, not only for what it says, but for what it does not say, as a representative specimen for us to follow, holding to the subject and leaving surplus matters out — an admirable method, it seems to me, in which the writer has imitated his own style in the making of text-books; considering them for elementary instruction, admirable for what they do not say, as well as what they do; limiting to the characteristic facts, the basis, the outline given. It seems to me the doctor's skillful attempt to portray the growth and development of the teaching of science is an admirable paper for what it says and does not say. We have had a supplement from Dr. Clarke. I have only to say this thing with reference to the assertions of the paper and the omissions of the text-books of the author in distinction from other text-books. The author in his new editions begins too commonly to put in supplementary observations running out after curious things and presently it breaks down and it becomes useless as a text-book. When he has attained his object he should not spoil it by going out so.

The other remark I was going to make was one by way of apology for "the paleozoic age." I must protest that the teacher referred to by the doctor as not showing where nature was, or not inducing the boys to look for her at all, was not the teacher who gave me instruction. We were chuck full of human nature and all out of doors was legitimate stamping ground for us, and we were keen-eyed and could invent apparatus. There was no lack of nature out-doors or in these early times, and it was utilized too.

Remarks of Principal Solomon Sias.

Dr. King, I believe, has struck one point that is valuable to us, and I have questioned repeatedly whether the multiplicity of apparatus was not injurious to our scholars. Our intricate pieces, illustrating the more intricate topics, give an idea of the mystery and unapproachableness of the operations of nature, and the children are no longer keen-eyed and inventive, no longer manufacturing something. If it is not furnished by the school they stop. They think it cannot be done. They do not study up means and ways. They do not look around and find something to illustrate, explain or apply the principles. As to the tidal instrument Dr. Steele referred to, it was a valuable thing in those old times, and I am not sure it would not be a good thing, with a little improvement, to be brought into our school-room again. If I remember right, it was from fourteen to sixteen inches square and worked with a key on the back which turned the painted disk of the earth around. Behind this disk was an elliptical one representing the tides which swept around as the moon moved along in its path, so that the tidal wave kept very nearly under the moon, and although it turned in the same direction as the earth it was kept perfectly independent by means of a cross band on the back of the instrument. Bye and bye came the shadow of the moon and gave the idea of an eclipse as it swept across the painted disk representing the earth. The shadow of the earth went off the opposite side of the board before it came to a point, and, therefore, extended out into space, nobody knew where. We used to ask that question sometimes.

REMARKS OF PRINCIPAL JOHN E. BRADLEY, PH. D.

I listened to the paper of Dr. Steele with a great deal of satisfaction; and I am glad to express that satisfaction, not only on account of the paper, but also in view of the remarkable progress which it shows us has been made in scientific instruction and in the appliances at hand at the present as compared with a generation or two ago. I am not prepared to add any thing on the historical aspects of the subject and merely rise to indorse and emphasize, if I can by a remark or two, one of the points which was made by the reader of the paper. It is that in teaching science, the instruction should be adapted to the age and grade of the scholar. All teaching should do this, but I think teachers of natural science and physical science often make this mistake, of not adapting their work to the capacity of their classes and, as we say, shooting over their heads. There is a constant temptation to the teacher, especially if he has made a special study of a subject to try to give his scholars that which is curious, that which is profound, that which is in one sense fundamental, but which their youthful minds cannot yet receive. Such instruction, instead of creating an interest in the subject and attracting pupils to it, only drives them from the study. They soon grow weary of what they do not comprehend. I have often seen this illustrated within my own observation. Now we should advance gradually in our teaching and seek to bring the study down to the comprehension of the class. While we should be logical and philosophical in our development of a subject, we should constantly guard against introducing facts which are too difficult for the class to comprehend. Science is full of such facts and they often seem very interesting and important to the teacher, especially if he has made special study of the subject. But if he allows such facts to divert him from the more elementary instruction which he should give, he not only wastes his time but confuses his scholars. The nature of the mind is to grasp facts one by one. We learn by observation. The experiments of to-day are compared with those of yesterday, and the process is carried through a long series of observations. We thus learn some fundamental law, some grand principle of science which is valuable and suggestive to the man, but which, if laid down prematurely as is often done, as a first principle, is meaningless to the child. A sound method in teaching, the natural method, leads the pupil up, step by step, to the point where he can comprehend the great laws of the science. The teacher who begins with what are sometimes called first principles makes a great mistake. Men of science have reached these conclusions by long investigation; they are the result of grand generalizations and inductions. The child is expected to grasp them at the very outset. He cannot do it, and hence conceives a dislike for the study. He should be led up to them through experiments and illustrations that will enable him to see their significance. This is the work of the high school and academy, and not to teach the more profound and intricate matters growing out of many of the sciences.

I wish also to make another suggestion. The wide extent of the field of study, and especially of scientific study, has been referred to. We cannot include in the school curriculum a tithe of all we would be glad to teach our scholars. There is a partial remedy for this difficulty. It is to simplify these subjects, and reduce them to their elements in such a way that younger minds can grasp them. This is easily done in several branches of natural history. Children can learn many subjects of natural science just as well at ten or twelve as when much older. A considerable gain in time may thus be made. Let children have the elementary facts in as many sciences as possible. The perceptive powers are then as vigorous as they will ever be; the imagination and memory are well developed. But the power of generalization and induction is still weak. Give the child the facts; teach him to observe the objects and processes of nature all about him; teach him to be interested in such things. Later on, when he is perhaps sixteen or eighteen years of age, he can comprehend the principles and laws which underlie the facts which he has learned. Everybody has observed the interest with which children investigate a new toy or if properly presented, any other novel object. There is no reason why we should not utilize this impulse and give to children, from a very early age, something useful to learn as well as interesting to study. Here, I think, is an opportunity to do something to bring into our courses of study at an early age, much that is left out until the time is too short.

Remarks of Regent Martin I. Townsend.

Mr. Chancellor:—I want to vindicate one school as having had as far back as 1831 and 1835, the facilities that enabled us to study science very successfully under Dr. Reynolds, in Williams College. I remember pursuing the study of geology to some little extent with the professor, and when he came to the point of teaching us that mineral substances had tendencies to crystalize in definite forms, the college had no specimens to enable the doctor to exhibit to us the appearance of those crystals. He was equal to the emergency, however, for he had a large supply of potatoes, and by cutting them into various figures he showed us the crystalline forms which mineral substances would take, thus using the vegetable world to illustrate the world of mineralogy. I can testify that the potatoes served a very good purpose.

Remarks of Professor Cady Staley.

Mr. Chancellor and Gentlemen:— As the Chancellor has called upon me, I must obey, and say a word with regard to the teaching of science, and my particular branch of science — civil engineering, in Union College. I cannot give the exact date when the scientific course was established in Union College, but I think it was about fifty years ago. At first it was only a three years' course. Afterward it was extended to four years. In 1845, Professor Gillespie was called to the college to establish a school of civil engineering. His method of teaching has been followed since then. We use text-books and lectures for giving instruction, and at the same time, have practical illustrations of what we teach. When we take up the adjustment and use of an instrument, each student is required to use the instrument, and so is not only given its theory, but is taught to use it in the field. That accords with Dr. Steele's method.

The science department of Union College has grown from the time of its establishment given by the doctor in his paper, until it is to-day one of the prominent features of the college. The apparatus has accumulated until now only part of it can be used in the general classes. Practical work with instruments and apparatus, is a marked feature in the training of our students. This has necessitated large collections of apparatus. Part of the apparatus is used in class to illustrate general principles; the rest is for the use of those who desire to pursue special lines of investigation. I agree with the gentleman who suggested that the study of science commence earlier, so that in college we shall not be obliged to begin with the rudiments.

V.

THE RELATIONS OF THE UNIVERSITY TO THE COL-LEGES AND TO THE HIGHER EDUCATION OF THE STATE.

By Professor W. D. WILSON, D. D., LL.D., L. H. D.

I have been requested to prepare a paper on " The Relations of the University to the Colleges of the State and to the Higher Education." The subject is eminently appropriate to the occasion of this our centennial anniversary, and my only regret is that the subject has not been assigned to some one who can do it more ample justice.

After a brief reference to the origin of the University and its history, with a view to exhibiting its legal status and the work it was expected and designed to do by those who created it, I shall devote whatever time I may have to some considerations of what, as it seems to me, it *may* do, and — if I may be permitted to use the expression — what it *ought* to do, to accomplish to the fullest extent its mission and to justify the grounds for its existence.

The first act of the Legislature creating *"The University of the State of New York"* was passed May 1, 1784, and amended November 26 of the same year. This act of May 1 was, however, but an effort to revise a previous institution and to put it in working order. It begins by reciting the fact, that, " *Whereas*, by Letters Patent under the Great Seal of the Colony of New York, bearing date (October 31, 1754), 'a certain Body Politic and Corporate was created (by the King, George II) by the name of the *Governors of the College of the Province of New York*,' etc., etc. *Whereas*, there are many Vacancies in the said Corporation occasioned by death or absence of a great number of the Governors of said College whereby the succession is so greatly broken in upon as to require the interposition of the Legislature, and, *Whereas*, the remaining Governors of the said College, desirous to render the same extensively useful, have prayed that the said College may be created into a University, and that such other alterations may be made in the

Charter or Letters of incorporation above recited, as may render them more conformable to the liberal principles of the Constitution of this State," etc.

The "College" here referred to was not what is now "Columbia College," for that was then known as "Kings College," and its name was changed to Columbia College by this very act (§ x). The "College" here changed in name into a university — and in nothing else that I can see — was vested with power to "make ordinances and by-laws for the government of the several colleges" — Columbia College among them — "which may or shall compose the said University, and the several presidents, professors, tutors, fellows, pupils and servants thereof." (§ iv.)

The Board of Regents of the University, thus constituted, consisted of the Governor and Lieutenant-Governor of the State, the President of the Senate, the Speaker of the Assembly, the Attorney-General, the Secretary of State and the Mayors of the cities of New York and Albany, twenty-four other persons by name, and, then, in addition thereto, one member chosen from each of the religious denominations, that might choose to make a choice of one, and, in certain cases of the founders, presidents, fellows, professors and tutors of the various colleges. (§§ vii, ix.)

But the Board thus constituted was found to be ineffectual and clumsy, so that in 1786 or 1787, the Regents appointed a committee to consider the defects of the old organization; and a new scheme was reported to the Legislature, which was, to a large extent, the product of the genius and patriotism of Alexander Hamilton, one of the proudest names in our nation's history. The plan thus recommended was adopted and enacted into a law April 13, 1787. This statute took the precedence of all previous statutes on the subject, and expressly enacted their repeal.

At the time of the passage of this act of 1787 there was but one college in the State, namely, Columbia College, in the city of New York. The act constituted the Board of Regents in its present form consisting of the Governor, Lieutenant-Governor, and nineteen other members, and enacted moreover the three following among other points, which are pertinent to our present purpose:

1. It provides that the Regents may confer "all such degrees, above or beyond those of bachelor or master, as are known to and usually granted by any university or college in Europe." (§ iv.)

2. It provides that the Regents may incorporate colleges in any part of the State, under certain restrictions (§ vii), and also that

they may erect any existing academy into a college on condition its funds and the quality of its instruction should be sufficient to justify the elevation. (§ xii.)

3. It provides that if "the trustees of any of the said colleges shall leave the office of president of the college, or if the trustees of any academy shall leave the office of principal vacant for the space of one year, it shall, in such cases, be lawful for the Regents, unless reasonable cause shall be assigned for such delay to their satisfaction to fill such vacancies." (§ iii.)

And although it was provided (§ xx) that "no president or professor shall be ineligible for or by reason of any religious tenet or tenets that he may or shall profess, or be compelled by law or otherwise to take any test-oath whatever;" yet it was provided (§ iii) that the Regents are "authorized and required to visit and inspect all the colleges, academies and schools which are or may be established in the State and examine into the system of education and discipline therein."

It will be observed that the act speaks not only of colleges and academies, but also of "all the *schools* that are or may be established in the State."

A system of public or common schools, supported by a tax upon the people, and controlled by officers elected by them, was first introduced and established in this country, so far as I have been able to ascertain, in Massachusetts, by an act passed in 1647. It appears, however, that schools had been established on the same plan, in some of the cities and townships of Connecticut as early as 1642, the law providing that "the town shall pay for the schooling of the poor and pay for all deficiencies." The first act in New York providing for the support of common schools, was passed April 9, 1795, at the suggestion of Governor George Clinton.

We have then three grades of schools — the colleges, the academies, and the common schools. In 1812 this latter system had reached such proportions that, by an act of that year (June 19, 1812), the office of "*Superintendent of Common Schools*" was created and these schools placed under the supervision of its incumbent. The title of the office has been changed, so that he is now called the Superintendent of Public Instruction. He is also member *ex-officio* of the Board of Regents.

The extension of the system of academies by the increase in their number, so as to meet all the wants of an education of a higher grade than the common schools could give, was limited alike by the necessity of an endowment as a condition prerequisite to the incorporation of an academy and the necessity also of depending for the support of the current expenses of the academies upon the receipts from the pupils in the form of tuition or rate-bills.

This state of things led to the formation of union schools in many of our thriving villages. In these schools a grade of instruction similar to that in the academies was provided for, while the schools were furnished with buildings and supported by a tax on the people, and controlled, like the other public or common schools, by officers elected by the people themselves. In this way the grade of academic instruction was brought within the reach of many for whom it would have been otherwise unattainable.

Meanwhile there had been growing up and accumulating from an early day, what is known as the *Literature Fund*. By the addition of what is known as the United States Deposit Fund, the income of this fund was raised by the act of April 17, 1838, to the sum of $40,000, to be distributed annually among the academies. The desire to get a portion of this $40,000, per year, toward the support of the union schools, as well as a sense of the importance of the Regents' supervision, led to the establishment of academic departments in the union schools. To this effect an act was passed June 18, 1853 (chap. 433, §§ 11, 6, and 16), providing that "the board of education of any union free school district shall have power to establish in the same an academical department whenever in their judgment it is wanted by the demand for the higher instruction that is given in the academies."

The limit between the instruction given in academies and to be provided for in the common schools has been fixed at English grammar, arithmetic, geography. In 1865, the Regents established, without any special act of the Legislature calling for it, what is known as the Regents' examination. The certificate issued to those who successfully pass the examinations in these three subjects constitute the entrance examinations to the academies and the academic departments of the union schools. And as the literature fund was distributed to them as to the academies, they, with their academic departments, have come to take the place of the academies to a very large extent in the educational system throughout the State.

Another act of the Legislature, passed June 6, 1877 (chap. 425), provided for another very important step in the progress of the work of the Regents. The act provides for and makes *imperative* a system of examinations in the academies and union schools under the supervision of the Board. It also *authorizes*, but does not make imperative, a system of examinations for higher degrees — among the graduates of our colleges, and in accordance with the words and in conformity to the spirit of the act of 1787, already quoted.

Under this statute the Regents have instituted and put into operation a system of examinations, and provided three grades — or qualities of diplomas — the "*college entrance*," the "*academic*," and what is known as "*the Regents' intermediate;*" that is, a diploma or certificate intermediate between the primary certificate on the one hand which constitutes the title to admission as an academic student, and " the college entrance " or full " academic " diploma on the other.

The last named, the " academic diploma," was intended for those students who have completed a full course in the academy and do not intend to enter any one of the colleges in the State. " The college entrance " was intended for those who intend to enter college, with the preparations in Latin and Greek required for admission. And it was hoped that such a diploma would soon come to be accepted in all our colleges, in place of an entrance examination conducted by the colleges themselves. The "intermediate" diploma was made to include all the English branches required for admission to our colleges, and it was expected that it would be accepted instead of the required entrance examinations, in so far as the English studies are concerned, even if in some cases there should be hesitation about accepting the college entrance diploma for the Latin and the Greek.

These academic examinations have been in use now for about six years. I believe the system is universally approved, so far, at least, as its general and essential features are concerned. I think that all will admit that they have afforded quite a stimulus to study and done much toward raising the standard of scholarship and scholarly attainments in all our public schools.

But the scheme for the higher or post-graduate examinations has not yet been put into use. A committee — a joint committee of the Convocation and of the Regents — was appointed in 1878 to devise a plan for these examinations. The committee met October 21, 1879, and reported a plan in detail which, in the following January, was submitted to the Regents. The plan thus submitted was, as I understand, generally acceptable. The statute of 1877, however, appropriated only $5,000 for both systems of examinations. The academic examinations having been made imperative they were of course first to be put into operation ; and it was found that the sum appropriated was not sufficient, after paying the necessary expenses of the academic examinations, to carry out or even to attempt to carry into effect the higher. And there the matter rests for the present.

The original plan reported in January, 1880, was subsequently modified by a smaller committee and accepted as the basis of operations. The changes consisted chiefly in the omission of some matters of detail so as to make the plan more flexible.

The plan as thus modified was substantially as follows:

§ 1. That the Regents establish the following academic degrees to be conferred by them in accordance with the provisions of the sixth section of the statute of June 6, 1877, namely:

(*a*) The degree of Master of Arts.
(*b*) The degree of Doctor of Philosophy.

§ 2. That there be a board of university examiners which shall consist of at least nine members, with more to be added from time to time as occasion may require.

§ 3. There shall be an officer to be called president of the board of examiners, to be appointed by the Regents, who may, or may not, be one of the examiners.

§ 4. That the examiners, or so many of them as shall be summoned thereto by order of the Regents, shall meet annually in Albany, on the Tuesday next preceding the week in which the annual Convocation of the University is held; and at such other times and places as they may be summoned to meet by order of the Board of Regents.

§ 5. Any six of these examiners with the president of the Board shall be a quorum for the purpose of examining, determining and reporting upon the qualifications of any applicant for the degrees above named, Master of Arts or Doctor of Philosophy.

§ 6. The applicant must in all cases give to the Secretary of the Board of Regents, at the time of his application to become a candidate for any degree, a statement of his age, the time and place of his graduation, his pursuits after graduation, with satisfactory references in regard to his character, and a list of the subjects in which he proposes to be examined.

§ 7. The examiners shall, in all cases, take into account the character, standing and general reputation of the applicant; and they may take notice of and give credit for any scientific work or literary production that the candidate may submit to their consideration.

Then follows a list of some sixteen or twenty departments in which examinations might be held, with the expectation that one or more examiners would be appointed at an early day for each of the departments and indeed for such other departments as it might be found advisable to add to the list as the result of experience or the increasing demands for the examinations might call for.

As to the expediency of providing for degrees for those who have not graduated at any of our colleges there was difference of opinion, and some doubt, in the minds of the committee.

It was found, on looking over the reports of our academies and high schools, that quite a large portion of those who are doing most excellent work in them as teachers have taken no Baccalaureate degree anywhere; they are persons, who, as well from their numbers as from their position and influence, may well claim our favorable consideration.

I see no reason why the Regents may not be allowed to provide examinations for the Baccalaureate degree to be taken in some cases by such persons before the higher degree, and as a preparation for it. The statute of 1877, as already intimated, removes all restrictions and authorizes the giving and conferring "such degrees or diplomas * * * * * as the said Regents may deem expedient." (§ 6.)

The following is a schedule of the general departments as given in the amended report already referred to, namely:

1. Latin Language and Literature.
2. Greek Language and Literature.
3. South European Languages and Literatures.
4. North European Languages and Literatures.
5. Anglo-Saxon and English Literature.
6. Comparative Philology and the Science of Language.
   (To constitute the first group.)
7. Mathematics, Pure and Applied, including Astronomy.
8. Physics, or Natural Philosophy.
9. Chemistry and Mineralogy.
10. Botany and Vegetable Physiology.
11. Zoölogy, including Physiology and Comparative Anatomy.
12. Geology and Palæontology.
    (To constitute the second group.)
13. Moral and Intellectual Philosophy, including Logic and the History of Philosophy.
14. Ancient History and Antiquities.
15. Modern History and Political Science.
16. Roman and International Law.
17. American History and Literature.
    (To constitute a third group.)

The plan thus presented, it will be observed, provided for only examinations and the conferring of the appropriate degrees. For this plan I claim no merit and must disclaim all pretense to originality in regard to it. It is indeed true that I was on the committee and took a somewhat active part in drawing up the report and arranging the details of the plan. But I must now, as I did then, in justice to an honored name, as well as to myself, say that the plan did not originate with me. It was often suggested to me by the late Chancellor, the Hon. John V. L. Pruyn, LL. D. The plan was near his heart and much in his thoughts; and it was often discussed with me, as I happen to know that it was also discussed with others whom he chose to take into his confidence and his counsels in this matter.

As I said, the plan was one for examinations and the conferring of degrees only. It made no provision for higher and post-graduate instruction. And I venture now to suggest, for the consideration of the Regents and this Convocation, another feature or element which, as I think, will add very much to its value. What I propose is, that we make these examiners, TEACHERS as well; and thus provide for the work of carrying on the higher education in our State.

When the University was created in 1784, and when it was remodeled in 1787, the three great departments or faculties of professional education—law, divinity and medicine — were well understood to be comprehended in the proper scope of university work; and schools in these departments have been established within our State, in numbers and variety sufficient to meet the wants of all classes of people. But the other great co-ordinate branch of university work has changed greatly since that time. I refer to what is now regarded as the college work proper, or the undergradaute course, leading to the degree of Bachelor of Arts. Then Latin and Greek were regarded as the only languages which it was worth the while to provide for. In natural philosophy the amount required was easily accomplished, and could be crowded into a very small space. Even mathematics had not attained its present proportions. Chemistry was hardly thought of; and the various branches of natural history received no attention. Geology was unknown. And although much — very much — less was required for admission then than now, it seems to have been thought that even with this little to begin with, what could not be acquired in the four years of undergraduate life was hardly worth teaching.

But now how changed! We have crowded out many things — squeezed many others into much smaller spaces — and yet in the four years required for the Baccalaureate degree, one can hardly get more than the merest outline and vague idea of what there is that may be known. The young man leaves college only just well prepared, and often in his own estimation scarcely so much as well prepared, to begin study in any one of the many inviting fields that open before him. If he has a genuine love of study and is so fortunate (which, however, is seldom the case) as to have ready means to go abroad, he is provided for. But if he cannot do that, his only resource is to seek a position and go into some school as a teacher Here besides his work as teacher — and its value to him as a means for his own education and culture can hardly be overestimated — he will find *some* time for study and the pursuit of truth in his chosen department.

Now, what I propose exactly meets the wants of such cases.

To bring the matter distinctly before the mind, let me recur to some actual examples.

We have, and have had at Cornell University several cases in point. One man, a graduate of Rutgers College, wished to pursue the higher mathematics. We received him as a candidate for a second degree. He remained at his school many miles away. But he came to Ithaca occasionally, conferred with our professors of mathematics, and when he could not come he wrote stating his problems or his inquiry and received an answer by letter. In time he completed his appointed course, took his diploma just as though he had been with us all the while.

We have another man now, a graduate of Williams College, a most successful and highly honored principal of an academy and union school, who comes into town once a week, on Saturdays, and spends the day with our professors of Latin and Greek, and in this way he is preparing for, and will doubtless soon take, the degree of Doctor of Philosophy.

Now what I propose is, that we make our examiners teachers also. Where a suitable person makes application to be received as a candidate for a degree, let him name his subjects of study, and name also, if he has any preference, the examiner and teacher in the department to whom he would wish to be referred or assigned, and then let him commence his studies under that guidance and with that help. Let him visit his teacher as often as he can. Let him write to him as often as a mail goes out, if need be, or whenever he finds occasion to do so. The University should not be expected to pay these teacher-examiners for such work. Leave that as a matter to be arranged between the teacher and the pupil. I believe that our professors at Cornell ask nothing. In fact, they assure me that they find this work a pleasure rather than a task, and they look upon it as the most agreeable, the most satisfactory, and the most inspiring work they find to do.

In looking over the reports of the colleges in the State I find but very few resident graduates at any of them. Most of them have none. Only Cornell, I think, has more than four or five. We have had, for a few years past, from fifteen to twenty actually with us and at work. This year we have twenty-one. Many of the colleges have no provision and can offer no inducement for them. With the exception of Columbia and Union I do not now remember any one of our colleges that can make residence an object worth the time and expense which it would involve.

But with the University it is otherwise. Whoever is in the State may be considered as *in residence*. All the professors of all the colleges are, in a sense, *our* professors. We can enlist them in this work. By a careful selection we can have a better faculty than any *one* of them can have, if we will take only the best. Select not one only, but two or more, if need so require, of your best mathematicians, linguists, chemists, natural philosophers, metaphysicians, political economists from all the colleges and in all parts of the State. Give them an opportunity to do some of this higher work, to say nothing about the chance to earn an honest penny or two by doing it. You will make them better scholars — *docendo discimus* — more enthusiastic and inspiring teachers, even in their ordinary work. And, above all, you will give to the ambitious, aspiring young scholars of our State an opportunity, which they now have not, to pursue and acquire that which they love and desire more than money; and, in many cases, more than life itself.

The men and women for whom you will provide are not *undergraduates*, still less mere school-boys and girls, to need control and personal supervision. They have learned to study *by themselves*, and have become, to some extent, self-reliant; they need only the occasional visit and personal conference with their teacher.

I have spoken of the usage at Cornell and of its success, but, before the time of Cornell, I had had experience as a teacher of theology in this way for some fifteen or twenty years, and it was about the most successful and satisfactory teaching I ever did.

There is one consideration more in favor of the plan now proposed. These instructor-examiners will be acquainted with their pupils and their attainments before coming to Albany for the examinations which are to be held here, and thus be in a better condition to judge of their qualifications for the degree they seek than they could be by any mere examination, conducted either orally or in writing or in both ways. And, perhaps, it might happen that the examiner could, in many cases, report to the board of examiners, or their quorum, assembled at Albany, and thus save the trouble and expense of personal attendance for the mere purpose of the examinations.

I will not stop to consider objections to this plan. I can see none. I do not believe that there are any that are worth considering.

I turn, then, in conclusion, to the more prosaic and humdrum aspect of the case — the attendance at Albany of the few, seven or eight, who will be needed here during the week before the meeting of Convocation. It will not only take time, but it will cost money. The time will be freely given. I am sure we can get enough of the very best men in our State who will at first and for the sake of inaugurating the experiment, come and attend to these duties for a while for merely their expenses. Mr. Chancellor and gentlemen of the Board of Regents, I believe that there are men who will come for this labor of love and *pay their own expenses*, if need be, until the experiment can be fairly tried and the people of the State shall have become so well satisfied of the value of the work that they will willingly appropriate enough money to pay reasonably well for the services thus rendered to what so intimately pertains to and promotes the highest welfare of a people.

I have spoken of the professors in our colleges. But I see no necessity of limiting your choice of examiners to them. There are many others in our State, honored names, whom I would be glad to see enrolled on our list if they are in sympathy with our work.

We have had in view thus far, only one of the four great branches of university work. I think that all four of them are clearly included within the scope of your powers, and responsibilities, as defined and implied in the acts of 1784 that created your corporation and defined its powers. But by special legislation since that time, the Regents have been especially directed to appoint a board of examiners to examine into the qualifications for, and confer the degree of Doctor of Medicine in certain cases (1872, chap. 746, § 1). I see no reason why they should not exercise the same powers with regard to one other great department — the law. They do confer the degree of Doctor of Laws, as an honorary degree. Why not appoint examiners and confer the degree for merit as well as for honor? I cannot doubt that there are many young men who would be glad to try such a test of their qualifications. Nor can I doubt that the measure would do something to elevate the standard of legal attainments. With regard to divinity the case is somewhat different and more delicate. It is doubtful whether it would be expedient to attempt any thing in that line just now.

I come back, therefore, to the one great branch of the work, with reference to which I have already said so much and for which this paper was chiefly undertaken and prepared, the department of arts, literature and philosophy — including, as it is now understood to do, all of education and of learning that is outside of the three great professional schools — law, medicine and divinity. This has been from the first the one department in reference to which and for the promotion of which "the University" and the Board of Regents were created. And, as I think I have shown, it is the one branch which in one most important respect has been the most neglected, and which is now most demanding attention. It is the highest field, and that in which its influence for good would be most widely felt.

I would begin then at once and select a president of the board of examiners, if you have in mind a man that is at all well fitted for the place. I would also select and appoint examiners as fast as names occur; and yet with such slowness and deliberation as to make no mistakes in the selection. I would publish the names of the president and the examiners with every report of this Convocation and of the Board of Regents, and invite the young men, and the young women, too, of the State who are qualified to become candidates for one of the degrees of Master of Arts or Doctor of Philosophy, to send in their names — indicating the departments of study which they intend to pursue — and also indicating or not, as they may choose to do — the examiners with whom they would prefer to consult in the pursuit of their studies, or from whom they can most conveniently and most agreeably to themselves receive instruction. Do this, Mr. Chancellor and gentlemen of the Board of Regents, and I have no doubt you will soon have a list of post-graduate students of which you and all of us may justly feel very proud.

I will add one consideration more in conclusion.

Much has been said of late years of the wide-spread abuse of *honorary* degrees; and doubtless something has been done to arrest the evil. One cause of this prostitution of a commendable prerogative has been, undoubtedly, the fact that there was nowhere any provision for such examinations as we propose to hold, and the conferring of the degrees as the result of such examinations. I know of nobody who is at all *worthy* of the degrees who would not much rather take the examinations and have their worthiness of the degrees fairly and fully tested and the degree itself granted, or if need be, *withheld*, according as the applicant shall be found, as the result of a pretty thorough examination, fairly entitled to it or not, than to receive any kind or amount of degrees as a mere matter of favor and of honor. Put in use such a plan as is here proposed and, as I believe, all those that are really deserving of such testimonials and certificates of proficiency and attainment, will seek them in this way and by this means, and then, as a most desired result, the unworthy will not seek them, nor will colleges be willing to grant them in the manner now so much complained of as an abuse of a power that was conferred on the colleges for a higher and a nobler purpose.

I have spoken of publishing in all your reports the names of your examiners; and so I would, but I believe the matter will need no special advertising. If I understand the case, there are a plenty of the best men in the State who are ready to engage in the work of instruction and examination. Nor can I doubt that the number of young men and young women who would be glad to avail themselves of the opportunity for improvement and distinction thus afforded them will be so great as to surprise and delight us all. And the inspiration to study and improved scholarship and attainments thus given to those, even if they should be comparatively but few in number, who are at the head of our academies and high schools, would be felt for good throughout the whole State, and down through all the grades of our system to the humblest hamlet and the most unpretending cross-roads in our land.

REMARKS OF PRINCIPAL JOSEPH E. KING, D. D.

Mr. CHAIRMAN : — I have two or three things in my mind that I propose to ventilate. It may have a wholesome effect with reference to the relation of the University to colleges. I am not myself a college-man of New York. An alumnus of a New England college, for thirty-seven years, with one exception — when I ran over to Europe — I have been present every year at the anniversary of my *alma mater*. I have official relations with that college. Last night there was an allusion to the subject we have come up to, tentatively, the relation of the University to the colleges. We have seen progress made. The colleges have grown nearer to each other. We have seen something printed of the work done by the colleges in the reports; some of the college-men come up to our Convocation, notably this year, attracted by the centennial. The question is, what is the relation between the University and the colleges? We had the ideal conception presented to us last evening in the centennial oration of Regent Curtis. It was very charming. Still there is another side to it, I think. I do not know but that there are compensating features in this independence, as well as in the sovereignty, which are of too great value to be given up. I fail to see any sufficient equivalent which the Regents as at present constituted can confer, unless their power is very largely increased. They should also have a larger purse. Now what compensation can the Board of Regents offer to the colleges for giving up their sovereignty to the University of the State of New York? I fail to see. You cannot expect a common business man, with a shred of the thrift which the average man has, to invest his money where he has no voice—where he cannot speak. How can you then expect that trained intelligence, which was so beautifully illustrated as well as recommended last night, to give something for nothing, or for a mere added prestige if you please. Now this question of examinations: I can well understand how, in these relations which are growing up, something of progress may, in the process of time, be evolved with reference to examinations. Notwithstanding the wholesome and natural jealousy of colleges there may, under the lead of the Regents, come to be a uniformity, a symmetry, and an aggregate power in the examinations for college degrees, most desirable and most valuable. We do not know. The whole matter of examinations may be deferred. What if some inspiration should happen to the Board, or to the Legislature, a hint of which I once heard, when I was on the committee concerning ways and means to make the Convocation profitable and interesting, by which the colleges should have a voice — a hint coming from Dr. Murray, I think, when he had just arrived — something about "a senate of the Colleges!" Now you think of the analogy of the nation when under the confederation just prior to the adoption of the Federal Constitution. Let the nineteen colleges of our State represent the thirteen old States. An ideal constitution originates, say in the brain of Dr. Murray or the Chancellor, and it is proposed that the colleges shall give up important rights, retaining what they do not give up, in consideration of which they shall have certain grand things. In the formation of our Union, little Rhode Island was the last to come in. I wonder she ever did. If she had not been bulldozed she would not. I beg pardon for a term not classical, but peculiarly effective. What can the ideal University offer to the colleges — what to our Rhode Islands? Why, the prestige of a great name, which shall make your degrees equal to the degrees of the oldest and greatest college! May it not happen that the little college will say as Webster did, when pleading for Dartmouth, "Sir, it is a little college, but there are those who love it." She has within her circle men of rare mind, of high merit, whom she thinks entitled to the degree of Doctor of Divinity—men of whom the Regents possibly have not heard. She knows their merit and she desires to decorate her men. How does she know that her recommendation will pass? The Regents are grand men; there is no greater name or grander man than the Regent whose picture we here look upon. Men serving without pay; the choice, the pick of the very foremost men in letters and in wisdom; and yet they are so busy that even in this annual gathering they have so much to do they cannot give us their society! they cannot afford to hear some of the best papers here. They do come up annually, but perhaps not so many as a majority, even to their own centennial and to hear the golden-mouthed orator of America. And these are the men who are to sit upon and determine the merit of candidates for the degrees we want from our little college. I do not wonder men hesitate. I should want a consideration if I gave up that power. Let us face some of these hard facts. Some think if the colleges were not selfish they would walk right in and see if they could get under the wing of these grand men. But they are not represented there. The genius of the constitution of the Board of Regents did not provide for any organic, vital relation of these colleges to the University. They are ignored. What is the relation of the Regents to academies? That of a parental autocracy. The academies are not represented here but by courtesy. We come here, are entertained and we go home inspired, encouraged. We have no power. The Regents, by courtesy, put us on a committee. We can demand nothing from them. These are the important points. This parental relation may be the best thing in the world. The bounty of the State comes to us through the Regents. We of the academies do not complain. If we had more power some of us might get puffed up. Why should the Regents expect the colleges to say: "Come take us under your protection." There is, I believe, common sense in these ideas. While I will rise as early as any man to champion the Regents, I still feel reasonably jealous for the colleges. I know how we, who are college trustees, work over the nominations for degrees that come to us from our faculty. We know our constituents. We do not have to adjourn. We attend the whole day and the whole night, two days and two nights. And the question of degrees is a very serious matter. We demand to know the whole thing and take time for it. Suppose the Regents had occasion to retire and pass upon these questions, how would it be? Somebody would say: "Do you think that all right, Mr. Secretary?" 'Yes, all right," and so, even if he were a very Nestor of a Regent but a very busy man, he could give but little attention to this grand matter. Of course the new constitution might provide that the Regents should be paid. I think they ought to be. They might then have sessions as courts hold sessions, and give their time. It may come one of these day that we should give up our sovereignty in the matter of both examinations and degrees. I do not see sufficient reason for it as yet. Rhode Island by coming in was made equal in the Senate to the highest States. It may be that the Legislature will offer such inducements that the colleges will be glad to come and range themselves under your wing and have a voice in your Board, and not be obliged to come with hat under your arm and say, "if you please." We might then have some of these grand new departures. It is now all in the air. You must give solid grounds for it. Give compensation and you will then get it.

Dr. WILSON: — It may be well, before this discussion proceeds any farther, to say that there is no proposition, no suggestion, no wish or inclination whatever to interfere with the entire independence of the colleges. We do not propose, in what has been suggested, to take from them any right, but merely to provide for such examinations as they do not hold, and to give such degrees as are appropriate to the examinations that are held.

REMARKS OF PROFESSOR C. W. BENNETT, D. D.

Mr. CHANCELLOR: — I suppose it is the desire of all that the paper just read should be historically correct. Probably Dr. Wilson desires, that above all things. He does not seem to recognize the fact that we have a University at Syracuse, and he seems to ignore a paper of last year in which this subject was brought before this Convocation. Two years ago you appointed me to prepare a paper on degrees in colleges and universities. We have had the system here outlined, in operation at Syracuse, for the past eight years. Alumni from more than twenty different colleges are pursuing our post-graduate courses. They are scattered all over the land, and are doing the very work which the paper suggests may be possible. It is only that we may be historically correct in our reports that I make this statement. By the suggestion and direction of Chancellor Haven, who was then at the head of our institution, and who is well known to this body and to the educational world at large, our system was developed. We have students doing this work all over the world, in China, in Japan, in India, in Canada and in many States of the Union. They keep in very close relation to ourselves by correspondence, and by visiting us as often as possible. The examinations are conducted at Syracuse in case the candidate resides within the United States, and by a board of examiners if he resides in a foreign country. This work has been going on now for eight years at Syracuse, and we desire that it shall be recognized as part of the history of this grade of work in this State.

REMARKS OF PRINCIPAL ALONZO FLACK, PH. D.

Mr. CHANCELLOR: — One of the professors at the institution of which I have charge, asked to be relieved this vacation from all work, in order that he might give his time to German literature and the German language, which he learned in Germany, for a degree that the Syracuse University proposes to confer upon him. I think that he does not know a professor in the Syracuse University. He simply knows the plan that Dr. Bennett has referred to, and which was brought out by Dr. Haven. This young man, who wishes to be professor in a college, expects to study eight hours a day for six days in the week to fit himself to receive one of these diplomas. It seems to me it is more appropriate for a graduate of a Pennsylvania college, a professor of an academy under this Board of Regents, to be examined by a board of examiners nominated by the Board of Regents, and that the degree conferred by the Board of Regents in this examination would have greater weight than if it came from so honorable and distinguished a University as that of Syracuse. Therefore, it seems to me there cannot be any thing more practical than this paper and the idea suggested in it.

The diplomas of the State which we are now receiving, the English academic diploma and the Latin diploma the Regents have provided for, are infinitely more valuable than if they came from an academy. I have a wonderfully high opinion of the virtue of a diploma from Claverack, but I clinch my fist and raise my voice when I say to my students that a diploma from the Regents is infinitely higher than one from Claverack, I say it is of just as much more value as the great State of New York is more valuable than the little town of Claverack, and I press this upon my pupils. I most earnestly indorse the paper of Dr. Wilson, and hope the examinations recommended in it will be established.

The CHANCELLOR — LADIES AND GENTLEMEN OF THE CONVOCATION : — In reference to the discussion of this paper, I want to say one or two words. I thank Dr. King for his remarks. There are certain things which may be taken for granted as to the Regents. In the first place they are most of them graduates of colleges; most of them when appointed Regents were trustees of colleges, but as by law they cannot be trustees of colleges and Regents of the University at the same time, they have been compelled to resign the former office. Whether for that reason or from some other cause I do not know, they are men of not very thin cuticles. They are quite ready to accept decided expressions of opinion from men like Dr. King. I am glad to hear from them. As I said in the beginning, this is the place for the free lance. The doctor complains of the little power we give — why we give to you the power of expression and we cannot further endow you. You come here with a wealth of knowledge, that your studies and long experience have given you, and you confer it on us. We are absorbing knowledge from you. We wish this and we wish your criticisms, if they are needed, not because we can reply, but because we can do better. What is our work? If we have any work to do it is to assist you in educating men and women. Now in regard to the Regents receiving pay for their services, I trust that time will never come while I live, and so far as I am concerned, I hope it will not come while my memory lives. I hope there will be one body of men who are so honored by the work they do, that in doing it they will receive their full compensation for the services they render. Pardon me, gentlemen, I was very glad to hear the doctor. I hope to hear more of the same sort. We do the best we can by you. We are grateful to you. And as I look around to-day and see here men who have grown gray in the work of education, and whose services command our gratitude and admiration, and when I see men like Dr. Wilson, Dr. Clarke and Dr. King, who have been the constant and always acceptable participators in these gatherings from their very beginning, then indeed I realize the dignity and value of this Convocation. And when I look back over the papers and discussions published in successive years, comprising the thoughts of some of the ablest educators of this country, I am ready to aver that no more valuable service has been rendered to education by this Board than the establishment of this Convocation.

VI.

THE RELATIONS OF THE PUBLIC-SCHOOL SYSTEM TO HIGHER EDUCATION IN THE STATE.

By Hon. W. B. RUGGLES, Superintendent of Public Instruction.

The necessarily brief remarks which, by the courtesy of the Executive Committee of the Convocation, I have the honor to make, will be confined to outlining a few thoughts having some bearing upon the relations of the public-school system in this State to higher education.

The last thirty or forty years have developed, in our State educational systems, two very marked tendencies; one, in our higher or collegiate institutions, toward a broader culture and more practical adjustment of instruction to the actual needs of society; the other, in our common or free-school system, toward a wider scope and greater thoroughness in studies and a higher reach of instruction, the result being an increasing approachment of the two systems to each other, and closer and more dependent relations between them. The colleges are undergoing a gradual process of popularization. The free schools are gradually rising to a higher plane of influence. And thus the gap between the two seems steadily closing up.

Previous to the year 1849, the legal school age for pupils in the common schools was the period between the ages of five and sixteen years. That year, however, this period was extended five years, by a statute making the legal school age the period between the ages of five and twenty-one years, and the same statute declared the common schools free to all persons resident in the several school districts within such limitation as to age.

This inducement of free tuition, with the extension of its benefits to the more mature class of pupils, ranging in age from sixteen to twenty-one years, naturally increased largely the attendance in the common schools, and, at the same time, created a necessity and demand for a corresponding expansion of the range of studies.

With the schools full of pupils, of ages all along from five to twenty-one years, instruction could no longer be restricted to the few simple elementary studies, if the system was to fulfill its beneficent object. The extension of the privilege of pupilage would have been to little purpose if the vaunted free-school system was to "keep the word of promise to the ear and break it to the hope," by forcing pupils to lose the practical benefit of the last and best part of the school-age period, and to leave the schools only because they failed to furnish the wider instruction which they needed, and for which their maturer years and larger capabilities fitted them.

Fortunately, the history of the common-school system of our State, from its origin to the present time, shows a movement steadily forward, seldom halting, never going backward.

And so we find, four years later (in 1853), the enactment of a general law, authorizing the reorganization of common-school districts into union free-school districts, with increased powers and facilities for establishing a high order of graded schools with courses of academic instruction adapted to these expanding educational needs.

It was almost a matter of course that these schools should at once take root and begin to thrive. They have been steadily increasing in number and in usefulness, until now there are four hundred of them in the State, including sixty-five organized under special acts.

Their growth has not been without serious opposition, principally on the score of the increased taxation involved in their maintenance, but this argument has been so often discussed and satisfactorily answered that it calls for no especial examination at this time. Another feature, however, of the large development of this class of schools deserves notice. It is sometimes observed that the extensive establishment of union free schools involves a process which is gradually tending to weaken the weak districts and to strengthen the strong ones. The fact, I think, must be admitted, and it may, in time, come to be a subject of serious consideration. What may be the proper remedy, if, indeed, any effectual remedy is possible, seems to me a question easier to ask than to answer. A superior class of schools must be considered a natural and necessary concomitant of centres of population, industry and wealth, and an inferior class of schools is as naturally to be expected in sparsely-settled and impoverished districts. And that the better schools of the former should draw away pupils, and parents with them sometimes, from the surrounding localities, unfortunately in the latter predicament, can only be attributed to the operation of the inevitable law of supply and demand.

The Regents' examinations, preliminary and otherwise, established for such of the higher departments of these union free schools as are under the immediate visitation of the Regents of the University, indicate but partially the extent and variety of the studies pursued and the thoroughness of the instruction given in most of these schools.

To-day they are carrying their pupils quite up to the line where the college course begins, and many of them are amply competent to take them well along into the college course.

Should the preliminary entrance examinations be considerably advanced by our colleges, as has been earnestly and forcibly urged by eminent educators, to enable them to eliminate from the curriculum and relegate to the high schools and academies a larger portion than at present of their classical course, thus making room for an increase of that class of studies which can be more readily turned to account and made practically available by the average graduate on leaving college and suddenly finding himself in the whirl of the activities, the rivalries, the competitions of the "struggle for existence" in the business world, I doubt not the high schools and academies would be found well prepared to meet the new and additional draft upon their resources.

To meet the demands arising from the constantly increasing tendency toward specialization in knowledge, we see springing up on all sides schools thoroughly equipped for supplying special instruction in particular lines of professional and industrial pursuits. Law, medical, scientific, polytechnic, commercial, trade, industrial, art, normal and other special training schools are getting a very strong foothold in the country. With courses of instruction usually considerably shorter than those of the colleges, and turning out young men ready to grapple successfully with practical affairs, who carry away in their pockets certificates of proficiency, diplomas, or whatever their graduation papers may happen to be called, which have a very appreciable value in the eyes of business men and are apt to be successful passports to quick employment, these institutions are presenting attractive inducements to young men, and, I may add, young women, to continue longer in the high schools and academies, and to go from thence (skipping the college altogether) directly into these finishing schools, and from thence into their life-work, professional or otherwise.

To meet this certainly increasing tendency it would seem to be a wise precaution for the colleges to face the situation and to set about the adoption of such adequate modifications in their courses of instruction as would be most likely to bring them into closer sympathy with, and more general adaptation to, the intelligent and enlightened activities of modern enterprise.

On this point it is not my purpose to depart from a very general line of remarks, except in a single particular, in which it occurs to me that our colleges and universities, by incorporating into their courses of study an additional branch of instruction, might be enabled to bring a far-reaching and lasting benefit to the cause of popular education, while incidentally, and probably directly, benefiting themselves. I refer to instruction in the science and art of teaching.

For half a century the one thing which has, at all times, seemed most desirable, as best calculated to promote the efficiency of our common-school system, has been some practical and adequate means of enhancing the qualification of teachers in the public schools. Measures adopted at various times, to this end, have been, and still are, working improvement in this direction. But the head-way has been slow, for the undertaking has been a very large and very arduous one, not to be accomplished by sudden and radical, but by considerate, judicious and gradual processes.

There was a good deal of sound significance in the remark, attributed to Bulwer, that "we shall never educate the children till we have educated the parents;" and the same line of thought may suggest that "we shall never educate the teachers till we have educated the public at large who employ and pay them." But the public have been, for a good while, getting educated up toward the point of appreciation of the fact that in this, as in other professions, special study, instruction, training, are the best guarantees of the best results. And this is shown in the constantly increasing demand for teachers who have had the benefit of such special training. Such teachers are having a very decided advantage in the competition for employment, and especially in the matter of compensation.

The teachers employed in the free schools of our State now number over thirty-one thousand. About four thousand go out of the business, leaving their places to be filled by other teachers, every year.

I am not able to state, with accuracy, the proportion of our college graduates who find their first business in life in the schoolroom. But I am satisfied that it is much larger than is usually supposed. Three years ago Professor North, of Hamilton College, put the number of graduates of that institution who engage as teachers, temporarily or otherwise, after graduation, at fully one-half. This is probably an exceptionally large proportion. Ten years ago a committee of the Board of Regents having instituted a pretty thorough and systematic inquiry, reported that about one and three-fourths per cent of the teachers employed in the public schools were college graduates. From the best sources of information now at hand, I think the number does not at present exceed two per cent. One and perhaps the principal, reason of this low percentage is to be found in the fact that graduates just from college usually lack this special training which is becoming more and more a matter of inquiry among the best paying trustees and boards of education. Ten years ago normal school graduates constituted a little over two per cent of the teachers employed in the public schools. They now number about four and one-half per cent. Counting graduates and those who have taken a partial course, but who have not graduated, the normal schools now furnish a fraction over eight per cent. Such of the remainder of these thirty-one thousand teachers as have had the benefit of any considerable period of special training come from the teachers' classes in the academies and academic departments of the union free schools.

These, from the short time allowed, necessarily obtain a less thorough and narrower range of instruction. The teachers' institutes, while reaching larger numbers and operating directly upon the great mass of teachers actually employed in the schools, are yet cramped and limited in their influence from the shortness of their annual or semi-annual sessions in the several counties. Aside from the practical information imparted, the institutes are doing much to incite and keep alive among the teachers interest and zeal in their work, to impress them with a sense of the dignity, responsibility and requirements of their vocation, and to awaken in their minds a desire to avail themselves of whatever opportunities may be within their reach to further advance their fitness for successful teaching.

A chair in each of our colleges, classed by the Regents as those whose object is to train for a Baccalaureate degree, including those for the exclusive education of females, established for the special training of students intending to teach in the public schools, would enable them to turn out teachers more thoroughly informed and equipped for the work than those coming from any other sources, except, perhaps, from the normal schools, and would tend to considerably increase the supply of the better class of teachers, especially in the graded schools.

The propriety of including the female colleges, and indeed of giving them first rank in the consideration of this idea, may be apparent when we remember that of the thirty-one thousand teachers in the public schools over twenty-four thousand of them are women.

The instruction proposed should, of course, be free, and should terminate, upon satisfactory final examination, in a diploma conferring an appropriate degree, and a permanent license to teach in any of the public schools of the State, revocable only for cause shown and after opportunity to be heard. Thus the higher institutions of learning and the common schools of the State would naturally gravitate into still closer and more practically useful relations, and would approximate nearer to a completely rounded and homogeneous system, embracing in its scope the entire range of primary and higher education.

The measure would not be a pioneer enterprise, inasmuch as, to say nothing of its introduction in European universities, it has already been tested in a number of progressive and prosperous colleges and universities in this country with marked success.

In conclusion, I have only to add that should this Board think favorably of action in the direction indicated, the Department of Public Instruction stands ready to join hands heartily with the Regents in the endeavor to promote its success.

Remarks of Principal Sias.

Mr. Chancellor: — I believe, sir, that our teachers in all the schools need, first of all, aptness to teach; secondly, breadth of culture; and thirdly, special, thorough preparation for their work. The breadth of culture certainly comes from college life, its studies and its experiences. And if connected with the colleges we might have such advantages as cannot otherwise come, and which would give a training in the methods of teaching, I would be glad to see it; for the great deficiency of our teachers is in the knowing how to teach. But I would surely have them learn, above all things, in taking this course, how to forget; for a great deal must be forgotten or laid aside when they come into the practical work of the school-room. Culture is needed in methods of teaching. And yet our method, as covered even in our normal schools, does not thoroughly equip for the lower grades of teaching. Not that the normal schools have failed in their work, for they have done it nobly and successfully, but it is a failure on the part of scholars not having aptness to teach. They could not apply what they had received in their normal school or college course of instruction. Therefore there lies at the foundation of all that can be gained, an aptness to teach. You cannot make a classical scholar of one whose trend is naturally toward some mechanical trade. You cannot make a first-class mechanic of one whose trend is naturally toward literature. You can, however, make his hours pleasant aside from the labor hours of the day. Not so with the teacher. He must be able by his breadth of thought to grasp every subject, and by his methods of instruction to adapt himself to the poorest and dullest intellect as well as the more advanced. First of all comes aptness, therefore let such as prove by some experience either in the district school or in the instruction of classes in academies that they are endowed with that wondrous sub-stratum of a teacher's life, be granted the privileges of this higher culture and training. Then they will come out and show to the world that they are teachers indeed. We must have breadth of culture. One great fault with the ordinary teachers of our district schools and academies is narrowness of thought. They are confined down to one routine. They can work in that and in no other. Now, there are no two minds working alike, and to meet this variety the teachers should have culture, and that culture, if properly molded in college or normal school work, will enable them to adapt themselves to surrounding circumstances as teachers, even as it does polished persons of a higher grade in society to adapt themselves to the circumstances in which they may happen to be placed. Give us, therefore, first, aptness to teach; second, breadth of culture; third, thorough preparation either in college or normal schools in the methods of teaching.

REMARKS OF PRESIDENT DODGE.

Mr. CHAIRMAN:—Perhaps I might be allowed to say a word on this paper, and I want to make, at the outset of my remarks, one of a general character. If I were asked what was the great defect in the relation of the academies and higher schools to the colleges, I should say, perhaps, a want of downright and thorough sympathy between the two, a want of mutual appreciation of the work and sphere of labor in which each is engaged. Now I have for myself, personally and individually, a profound interest in the work of academic instruction, and I will only state one reason for it. From my observation in life and from my experience as well, I believe the pupils that are under the charge of teachers in the academies are pupils who receive from them their great decisive impulse in life. I think that at that period most young men that count more than one in character and promise, receive their life impulse and their life direction. Certainly, when I was a boy between twelve and fourteen, I had as definite a plan for myself, and had more ambition to carry out that plan than I have ever had since ; and the impulse which I got in that period I think I have not wholly lost. And if there were no other reason than that, I could not fail to have and on suitable occasions to express a profound sympathy and profound interest in the men who teach in our higher schools, our graded schools, and in our academies, but so frequently in our district schools. At that time of life the soul is ready to take on an impression. Any teacher that comes to a young soul and voices the aspirations of that soul, has gained that pupil not alone for himself, but has gained that pupil to himself and to the community in which he is to live. The pupil becomes himself. He is, in theological terminology, born again. I do not mean in the churchly, but in the genuine and real sense. Now, sir, I want to make a remark or two of a more special character. I believe that the college and the academy or the public school are constantly reacting, one on the other. I do not think that the action is by any means always direct. I think, indeed, it is largely, very largely, indirect. The truth is, both these and the professional schools are affected by the intellectual and moral atmosphere, which both have in part created. And this indirect influence I hold is much more important than the direct. And, gentlemen, whether in college or academy, you and I know very well that the unconscious influence is the most subtle influence, and so the dominant influence in doing good to the pupil. What we are, often tells not what we meant to be. I do not mean to say that the work we perform is not of great value. It is of great value. But that which moulds it together, that which gives it unity, common direction, which makes it potent and lasting, comes unbidden, unspoken from the fountains of manhood in the teacher himself. Now I attach great value to this unconscious influence. It comes not at one's bidding. God takes the initiative. It is not of one's making, it makes itself. Now my point of contention is just here : when the question is raised whether or not to have in college a special class for teachers, my answer is this: that you will find that the aptitude is a great factor in life. I would take a teacher that was born right and had a fit education in spite of the absence of any professional training in a teachers' class. For if the man has no well of sympathy in him, you cannot dig a place for it and make a reservoir to answer the purposes of a living fountain. Such a man will work his way out of the den of scholasticism, and work his way into the light of life, and he will be a power and a success. Now I can understand very well in earlier training the necessity of this, because the two go together very largely in making him master of the subject and master of the pupil; master of what he teaches and then of those whom he teaches. They are not to be separated. When you wish to teach any thing, study until you can put it in language which others will apprehend as well as yourself. No man masters a thought until he can state it and illustrate it in forms to attract and hold his pupils. And then you come to the question of address and etiquette. That is largely a question of general culture. The cultured man learns to join his life on to the life of his pupils. If he is a genuine man he finds or makes avenues and channels of approach. I would feel different, as I hope my remarks would suggest, if I were connected with an academy or high school. Why? Because many pupils would come to me with imperfect preparations and would stay with me for only a limited period, and so would not be able to gain a self-education in the art of teaching.

But when you come to college you are to remember they have added four years to the culture they had when they started. They have grown; they have gained self-mastery, self-possession and patience, which is the prime condition of success. Thus, they do not need, to the same extent, this work to be done in colleges as in academies. Besides we have not a chance to do it. But, as Dr. Anderson knows very well — a name honored and loved by all who know him — how we are pressed on all sides in the curriculum. Now this can have no claim upon us unless you can show, not simply that it is desirable or a good thing, which I admit it is, but that there is no better thing among the very many things pressing on us for a place in our course of study. There are plenty of good things we would like to do if we could do them, but the course of history has limited us to four years and we are, for the present, shut up to that limitation.

- REMARKS OF PROFESSOR EUGENE BOUTON.

Mr. CHAIRMAN: — I hardly know whether to regret or to rejoice that I do not agree with the last speaker in regard to the importance of the thorough training of teachers for our schools. I am not able to say that I have had as much experience in school-work as many of those here present, but I have had enough to convince me that the most vital defect in our school system is the poor instruction that is general, not simply in our district schools, but in our academies and in our colleges. We probably all agree that the teacher, as well as other persons, is subject to the law of nature which requires that he should be born before he achieves much success. No doubt a person with natural gifts, "who is born right," will make a better teacher than one who is lacking in these gifts and who is born wrong, even though he has received all the training that the schools and the colleges can give. For my part, I would prefer to take the work of a person naturally bright and earnest, without a college course, than that of a person of the opposite nature with such a course. I would expect to see him succeed better in the work of his life, but it does not follow that such a person would not be benefited by a college course. It seems to me that our whole system of education presumes that improvement is possible, and that to natural gifts must be added thorough training before one can be expected to accomplish the best work. I think I have seen enough of the teaching in this State in our district schools, in our academies, and in colleges elsewhere, if not in this State, to satisfy me thoroughly that about one-third of the effort that pupils make and that teachers make is absolutely wasted, if not worse than wasted, by a lack of knowledge respecting *how to teach*. I think that experiments enough have been tried to demonstrate to us that the most profitable work we can engage in for the purpose of elevating the standard of our schools is the better instruction of our teachers. The universities of England have taken steps in this direction, and their work is accomplishing good results, not only in their own country, but in ours. Those who are interested in educational work read the lectures that have been delivered there, and feel themselves thereby better prepared for teaching. Some of the colleges in our own country are providing similar instruction. Our numerous normal schools are based on the belief that such instruction is profitable. I hope this matter may be amply discussed, because I believe the State is throwing away its treasures in maintaining schools which are not provided with competent teachers. The State should especially look toward the better instruction of teachers, and should require more ability, experience and professional knowledge on their part. Such a measure as the Superintendent has proposed ought to receive the hearty support of every friend of children. Their time is being wasted by incompetent teachers, and it certainly is possible, and already the practice of many progressive colleges, to give successful instruction in this subject.

REMARKS OF PRINCIPAL J. W. COLE OF TROY.

Mr. CHAIRMAN:—I want to lend my testimony in favor of professional training for teachers. I was disappointed somewhat in the remarks of the first speaker on this paper. With all due deference to his experience it seems to me that, with his experience, he could say something to a young man who has just received his diploma from the college, which would be of service to him if he were going to teach. I believe with him that successful teachers are born so. So are doctors, physicians, surgeons, lawyers, musicians; but because a few with very rare natural talent have arrived at eminent success, with little professional preparation, and under unfavorable circumstances, it seems to me that the organization of so many schools in each one of those professions recognizes the fact that professional training is necessary, notwithstanding the existence of native talent, and I do not see why a chair might not be profitably provided in a college in this particular science of pedagogics. My experience is this — with all due deference to the culture and eminent success of gentlemen who occupy chairs in college: That while at school some of my professors did all the reciting, and all the students had to do to get good marks was to say yes. · I have a nephew who, within two years, has completed a course at one of the largest and most successful colleges in this country. He finished at about eighteen years of age and expects to obtain a degree of A. M. this fall, by a special examination. He tells me that at that college there are two eminent professors whose methods of instruction furnish a help in that direction, which the young gentlemen appreciate. I only mention that as a fact, to show that some eminent college examples might be pernicious; and it seems to me that some special culture is desirable, and, if in the right direction, it would help a young man who has just passed through his college course to step into the profession and have greater success. He would have a pride in the college that furnished it to him. I have met men who could give professional advice which would be profitable to me, which could be instantly assimilated without compelling a long, anxious groping around and finding it out myself.

Excuse me for taking up your time, but it seems to me that professional training is quite as profitable in the teacher's profession as in the physician's, the lawyer's, or in any other.

REMARKS OF SUPERINTENDENT A. J. ROBB.

Mr. CHAIRMAN: — I rise to say that by the paper just read my heart has been greatly cheered. When the gentleman stated that two per cent of the teachers of the State were college graduates, and only four per cent were normal graduates, and, a little further on, that of the thirty-one thousand teachers of the State, twenty-four thousand were ladies, it seemed to me that the proportion of our college graduates must very greatly exceed that of the male graduates of our normal schools.

There are at least four ladies to one gentleman among our teachers, and I think more than four to one among the normal graduates; we get, therefore, at least eight per cent of the male teachers of the State from the colleges, while we cannot get more than two per cent from the normal schools. This, it seems to me, speaks very well indeed for the colleges.

Judging from my experience with teachers and schools, I think the greatest want of our graded schools and academies at the present time is a class of teachers possessed of more general culture — of more extended knowledge.

This we cannot get from a two years' course devoted chiefly to the elementary branches, with a part of one year devoted to special training. The special training is greatly needed, and I think if the suggestions of the paper could be carried into effect and a chair of pedagogics established in each of the colleges of the State, the demand might be fully met.

I agree with the gentleman who spoke immediately after the reading of the paper, "so far as giving an impulse to the scholar is concerned, it is after all the *man* that is required." The best type of manhood is always accompanied with extensive knowledge and genuine culture.

REMARKS OF PRESIDENT DODGE.

Mr. CHAIRMAN: — It did not seem possible I could have been misapprehended; still we live in an age of surprises. I had supposed that four years in our colleges furnished some preparation. They give four years' training. They are four solid years of work, and must help them to be teachers. But change the point of view. The question is not so much about the mastering of subjects, as it is how, having mastered them, they shall deal with them in the best way in order to secure the desired end. I certainly am in favor of such a study. Personally and privately, I have done a good deal of what might be called oral teaching of young men. My pupils naturally call on me and talk to me about it. If we had not so much to do and were free to give public lectures in the art of teaching I might be in favor of it. There is one thing to be remembered, the art of teaching is a fine art and and comes of genius and patience. A gentleman once said to me, "Dr. Dodge, my boy is giving his whole time to his studies." I said to him, "Do you not make a mistake in not allowing him to go into society at all; won't you make a mistake in regard to his manners?" He answered, " He has an aunt, a very cultivated lady; I am going to send him to her for six weeks in order to have his manners all right." I answered, "You can never set them right in that way. Your boy cannot take on such education as that." And again the criticism that I sometimes am obliged to make when I go into the common schools is this: the instruction is just a little too mechanical, just a little bit too much cut and dried; all the minds are trained in one way, and there is but little chance for a free growth.

REMARKS OF PRINCIPAL A. MATTICE.

Mr. CHANCELLOR: — I rise to put together two or three of the things we have heard.

You remember the famous saying of the lamented Garfield to the effect, that a seat on a log with Mark Hopkins by his side was all the University he wanted, and surely Garfield was not a failure as a teacher, although he had not had the advantages of a training school. I would not be understood as saying one word against training schools for teachers; on the contrary, I am strongly in favor of them. And yet it seems to me that the experience of four years in college with the daily *example* of several professors who know how to teach, and of, say one or two who do not know how to teach, must lead any observing young man to form the highest ideal of the profession, since he has an example to follow and an example to shun.

Allow me to refer to my experience and observation during the past year. A college graduate of nineteen taught for me, and better work I have never seen done. How was it that one so young and with no special training for teaching could do so much and so well? No doubt he was "born right" and then in addition had learned in college how to do it, and perhaps how not to do it, and then set about doing it with all his might.

With the curriculum of studies in our colleges already overcrowded there seems to be no room for the chair of didactics, unless, as has been suggested, the course be extended to five years.

In the mean time I submit, sir, that, with the breadth of influence spoken of here, and the examples of both classes of teachers, we virtually have that chair now.

REMARKS OF PROFESSOR EUGENE BOUTON.

Mr. CHAIRMAN: — If the teaching that is done by a majority of inexperienced college graduates is based on examples set before them during their college course, it seems clear that chairs of pedagogics might be serviceable to some college professors. I graduated from a college which is generally ranked second to none in this country, and whose graduates succeed at least as well as those from other institutions. Our professors were eminent for their learning. But I must confess that in my judgment some of them failed in the very matter of imparting instruction. By their great attainments, they could not help inspiring their pupils. But the effect would have been much the same if they had not attempted direct instruction. It is a fact that a large proportion of the graduates of our colleges are not good teachers until years of experience have taught them the mistakes which they might have known from the experience of others. I am constrained to think that in most of our colleges the examples of poor teaching are so much more abundant than those of good teaching that the average graduate has had very little chance to learn correct methods, however familiar he may be with examples of poor teaching. That is the trouble. We have tried the experiment of showing students how not to teach. We need somebody to tell them *how to teach.*

The crowded state of the curriculum is largely the result of ignorance of the best combination of subjects and the best methods of imparting instruction. The reason why we have so much to do is that we know so little how to work. To ignore all attempts to improve our teaching, on the ground that it is exclusively a divine gift, is just as sensible as it would be to ignore improvement in any thing else. It is just as wise as it would be for a rustic to argue that he has so much mowing to do that he cannot spend time in learning how to use a mowing machine; or for a woman to insist that she cannot spend the time needed for purchasing and learning to use a sewing machine on the ground that she has already more sewing to do than she can find time for. If the time usually spent in the study of psychology, without any practical application, were spent upon it with a view to make it useful in finding out the best means of cultivating the mind, the study would be vastly more serviceable. The fact is that our colleges are making the same blunder as many of our primary and intermediate schools. They are cramming their students with knowledge, instead of teaching them how to make knowledge available in life. They have become so afraid of the "practical" in material things, that they have almost ignored it in higher things. The claim that the laws of mind considered in relation to the theory of education are any more mysterious than when considered for no purpose whatever, is a very gratuitous assumption. That it is impossible to learn any thing from the experience of mankind in the particular matter of teaching, while that experience is eagerly sought and is exceedingly useful in every thing else, is absurd. That institutions which assume to stand highest in educational matters should attempt to shroud their processes with mystery, and should claim some special divine and miraculous gift of imparting knowledge, is serio-comic.

REMARKS OF PRINCIPAL ELISHA CURTISS.

Mr. CHAIRMAN:—I was very much pleased with the paper, especially for this reason: never before has the Superintendent of Public Instruction met with and given us the ideas that his department holds in reference to plans that may promote the cause of education. He has designated lines of policy to be pursued to promote the cause of education, and for the consummation of that policy the Board of Regents and the Department of Public Instruction can work in unison. He has challenged the Regents to a course of action, and promised the efforts and sympathy of his department in furtherance thereof. Let us hope that there will be unity of purpose in every effort to secure better teachers for the schools. In regard to this breadth of culture, every teacher has confidence in his own ability to teach. Examinations have proved that he has standard qualifications. He can teach best what he knows best. No amount of special training will prepare one for a calling for which he has not a liking and natural aptitude. But most teachers have some special preparation, and they should see that pupils intending to teach are well instructed in the theory and practice of teaching. More than two hundred of the academies of this State are presided over by college or normal school graduates, and in the faculties of many academies there are both college and normal school graduates. Principals of normal schools here will tell you that principals of academies write them frequently for graduates of their schools to teach in some of the departments of the academies. Therefore, members of teachers' classes will have competent instruction, and soon nearly all the teachers in the common schools of the State will have special preparation.

Remarks of President Cowles.

Mr. Chancellor:— I have been waiting to hear these points presented more fully by college men. Presiding over a college for women it is, perhaps, more modest for me to be silent. There are two or three points involved here that I regard as of vital importance to the whole educational system. I have had some twenty-eight years' experience at the head of a college — the oldest of the fully chartered colleges for women. Our great difficulty has been the poorly prepared material that comes to us from the lower institutions. Now we could easily lighten our curriculum, and we could very easily open a place for a chair of didactics, if we could have all our freshman class made up of well-prepared students; if there were not conditions to be removed; if we had not all this extra burden thrown in upon us in our college course, we could do vastly better work. I think the presidents of colleges for either sex will agree on this point. Another very important point in this discussion is, what is the true end and aim of teaching? I have found that it takes one or two years of college life to really learn how to study. Those who enter college are all at sea in the way of using their own forces. They have been at work at class-room recitations. They have witnessed, with a great deal of pleasure and a great deal of profit too, the explanations of the teacher and have studied very busily to make a good recitation and get a good mark.

If a man wishes to engraft a scion into a stock, he is very careful to get the living bark of the scion joined to the living bark of the stock, or else it will not grow. He loses all his labor. We want the living forces of the teacher to touch the living forces of the pupil; then you will have a living education. It is a very common thing for teachers to make every thing depend upon mere recitation as the beginning, middle and end of teaching, instead of putting them in permanent possession of what they are trying to learn. Multitudes will recite well and forget the greater part of what was recited before the next day. I knew a clergyman once that committed his sermons to memory. He would commit one-half on Saturday night, leaving the other half to the morning just before the tolling of the bell. He could say it well in the pulpit, but forgot it on Monday. There was a special effort for a certain thing and then a collapse of the memory. That is the way when students study chiefly for recitation. We want a great reformation there. We want this culture of the mental powers to be made vital — something that will enter into the very constitution of the pupil, something that will grow in with all the vital forces. If this could be secured from our lower institutions our college work would be delightful. We could put our better forces, our better experiences, our higher types of training into practice, and then we should have teaching that would mean something. I was greatly pleased with the position of Dr. Dodge. I believe he is right. We want to introduce living forces from the living mind into the living mind.

Some twenty years ago the plan of uniting normal didactics with college instruction was thought of by Hon. Victor M. Rice, then Superintendent of Public Instruction. When the present normal school system was organized, a bill was introduced in the Legislature with reference to our college at Elmira, in which the way was prepared to have a normal department under the care and pay of the State — a college and normal department for women; but when we came to examine carefully how it was to be managed, we saw it to be wholly inexpedient; there would be a corporate board of trustees, and there would be the State Superintendent and the Regents — a triple-headed management with constant difficulties in the practical administration, and we abandoned it. We did not want it. If we can have a chair of didactics, supported and guided by the Regents, yet under immediate control of the college itself, I believe it would be a very good thing. Yet that chair should be occupied by a man of extraordinary ability, fully the peer of the other members of the faculty, one of broad culture who will command the respect of the entire college, faculty, students and all. There are doubtless some difficulties that will need to be carefully considered, but I am confident some plan of this sort will be a success and will prove a new departure in a really higher education. I hope we shall hear from Dr. Anderson and other men of college experience.

REMARKS OF PRESIDENT ANDERSON.

Mr. CHAIRMAN: — This has been the result of my experience, that no man can adequately instruct a pupil how to teach others, except in a department in which he himself is an experienced instructor. I question whether any general professor of pedagogics could train a pupil in the best methods of giving instruction in Greek, unless he himself was an experienced teacher of Greek. My own impression is that the men who are successful teachers in a department should take their pupils privately, in voluntary classes, and give them instruction in the method of teaching the department for which they are individually responsible. If a man himself is a thoroughly good Greek scholar and has been a successful teacher, he would be better fitted to give cautions suggestions and methods for elementary instruction than any professor of pedagogics without such experience. I confess to some suspicion about the capacity of one man in a chair of pedagogics to take and go through the whole range of our courses of college work, and give them information in the processes of giving instruction in all the departments. I would put the work of training teachers under the control of individual departments.

Remarks of Professor W. D. Wilson.

Mr. Chairman: — I rise not only because of my interest in the subject, but because at the outset of this discussion I was requested to say something, and the request has been made that all college men should say something. For thirty-five years I have been a professor in a college, and I think you will find that nearly all of us who have had that sort of experience are very much agreed with the gentleman behind me, President Dodge, and the gentleman before me, President Anderson, with respect to this matter. I would say for the successful teacher, as stated by President Dodge, change the order somewhat. The first thing, in my estimation, is that he shall be full of his subject. I never knew a man to succeed in teaching who was not thoroughly full — brimful, overflowing — with what he was to teach, and I have scarcely ever known a man who was full of it that did not make himself a successful teacher. He secures the interest of his pupils, and can communicate his knowledge to them and inspire them with the enthusiasm of his own soul. Undoubtedly here as everywhere, something may be done in the way of teaching the teacher, but the fact that has been suggested here, and to my mind I think it a controlling one, that one must have had an opportunity to learn — I recur to the action which the gentleman, Principal Mattice, alluded to some time ago. Ten years ago I made precisely that statement, and have made it again and again, namely, that a man who has been through college is not only supposed to have acquired the knowledge, but he has had the experience also all along. If he has looked forward to be a teacher, he has studied the methods of his teachers, perhaps that of a very successful teacher either in the lecture-room or laboratory. And the man who was not a successful teacher was not likely to be very much respected, I am inclined to think. If now the pupil was born with the natural gifts, referred to by Dr. Dodge, he could not go through college without getting that education in the art of teaching any more than a man born with a taste for color or a gift for painting, could go through an art gallery without learning methods from the various painters. He would get much more from such a study than he could get by sitting down in any room and receiving instruction from any teacher, even with illustrations on the blackboard. I think that this method of observing their teachers is the one great thing for those who are to be teachers; I think it is the very best opportunity for those who are to prepare themselves for teaching. As long as they continue to be pupils, they are studying men who, in some sense, the successful ones at least, are masters in the art of teaching. No one successful man has the same method as another. If he has it in him and is full of the subject he will make a teacher, and a good one, too, in the end. Doubtless he will make mistakes — it is only very mediocre men that make no mistakes — but if he is capable of making a teacher at all, a live and life-inspiring teacher, he will succeed, and without this it is hardly worth while for him to try to be a teacher. Doubtless much can be done for him by way of "teaching him how to teach," but without the habit of observation and analysis and the exercise of it during his college or academic course, I fear that but very little can be done for him by any system of pedagogics or training in the art of instruction.

VII.

CONFERENCE OF THE PRESIDENTS OF THE COLLEGES OF THE STATE OF NEW YORK.

REMARKS OF PRESIDENT ANDERSON OF THE UNIVERSITY OF ROCHESTER, CHAIRMAN.

GENTLEMEN OF THE CONVOCATION :— The subject before us is so broad that I hardly know how to introduce it for your consideration. I will, however, call your attention to a few points connected with the American college, not with the design of discussing them in detail, but to put them before the gentlemen here present, as subjects for consideration. First, I remark that the college system among us is an American growth. It is not an English college, it is not a French lyceum, it is not a German gymnasium, nor a German university, nor a French university. Though its germ came from the old world it is substantially an American product, reflecting American life, institutions and character, matured by our thought, experience and sacrifice. This college system has been reasonably well adjusted to our wants. My own impression is that we shall do our best service to education by improving and invigorating that system which we already have. The object of our colleges is to prepare men for the study of professions, or for business; to give them that range of knowledge and discipline of intellect necessary for all the duties of the man and the citizen. It is to give them capacity to study a profession intelligently, with such a philosophical outlook that he may be able to understand and apply the scientific laws which underlie it. The same is true in its relation to business pursuits. The number of educated men who go into business is increasing every year, and is destined to increase still more in the future. Our business relations are becoming so complicated, so interwoven with all the political, economical and moral interests of society, that a man who expects to succeed in mercantile life in the highest and best sense requires a liberal education just as much as does the lawyer, the doctor, or the clergyman.

Secondly, this training of youth, this special preparation of a man for the study of a profession, or the taking up of a particular line of business, must be accomplished by systematic study, not of all learning, for that would be impossible, but by the systematic study of *specimen portions of the great departments of organized knowledge.* Such a course of study will give a young student a conception of the methods in which these great lines of organized thought and investigation have been developed by the great thinkers of the past and the present time. We do not propose to make men mathematicians in college in the large sense of the term, but we propose to give them an idea of the laws and processes of mathematical inquiry. We do not propose to make men linguists like Grimm or William Von Humboldt, but we propose to give them such an idea of the growth and laws of language that they shall understand something of what is meant by linguistic science.

Thirdly, these specimen portions of organized knowledge which are to be made the basis of a systematic and broadly liberal education must be selected. This selection ought to be made by the professional teacher. Here I wish to say that I consider the business of the teacher a profession, and I hope the time will come when it shall be recognized as such, as universally as that of the lawyer, doctor or clergyman. It is not so now. I call a physician to the bedside of a member of my family who is ill. He makes a prescription, and I obey that prescription, or subject myself to an almost criminal responsibility. I go to a lawyer with a contract, which involves some doubtful question of construction, and he tells me what to do. I obey him, unless I undertake to be my own lawyer and have a fool for a client. But it has been my experience, and I have no doubt it has been the experience of many of you here, we find very few who do not assume to understand the laws which underlie the selection of the course of study best fitted to develop a young man's faculties better than the professional teacher. I think the teacher who has spent a life-time in studying the processes and results of disciplinary training, is entitled to respectful attention when he recommends certain portions of organized knowledge as best for the development of the mind and preparation for the business of life. The opinions of individual teachers are increased in weight when they harmonize with those of the great community to which they belong. There is a substantial agreement among the great body of experienced teachers in reference to the selection of those studies which shall be made the basis of liberal education. I say a substantial agreement. We should not be men if we did not disagree in some particulars. They believe in giving students their choice among studies to a certain limited extent, in the latter part of the college course, but in general, experienced teachers do not believe in permitting young men to select indefinitely from the various departments of knowledge, according to their own idiosyncrasies and tastes. Young men often make their election, when their range is free, without regard to the laws of scientific method, or the relations of the studies to each other, following a zigzag course like that of a brook through a mountain valley. Their intellectual tastes lead them to follow the line of least resistance. Most students select, naturally, the courses easiest for them, studies in which they can take the highest rank with the least effort. Human nature is human nature the world over. Neither they, nor their parents, have in general the knowledge and experience fitting them to make a wise selection. The professional teacher should make that selection. If they are not better prepared to make it than men who have not given their lives to the work of instruction, they are unworthy of a place in their profession.

Fourthly, the question comes up regarding the range to which this selection should be confined. Human knowledge is organized through symbols, whether language proper, or the lines and formulas of algebra and geometry. We should require knowledge enough of different tongues to enable the pupil to get an idea of the laws and processes of growth common to all language to give him a basis for understanding the principles of comparative philology — a science which is now one of the broadest that can come before the mind of a learner, for it bears immediately on every thing connected with the mental and moral development of man. He should have knowledge enough of expression in different forms of language to understand and apply its laws in studying the development of the human mind. Again he must study expression and language in order to master the vocabularies of the sciences of thought and the sciences of matter, for expression or language is the instrument and condition of all generic thinking. There can be no science without a study of the language in which the scientific truths and generalizations are incarnated. There can be no chemistry, no mathematics, no physics, no philosophy, no natural history, unless their generalizations are embodied in distinct, definite and coherent scientific terms. "Science is a language well constructed," as Condorcet aptly said. Right here we find a necessity for studying the classical tongues, for the whole range of science is embodied in a nomenclature which has been drawn from the Greek and Latin languages. This nomenclature does not need to be translated. When it comes before the well-educated, scientific man of any country, he can understand it at once. The generalizations of all departments of the physical and intellectual sciences are studied in a terminology, common to the whole civilized world. There has grown up a vast vocabulary which puts the scientific man, unfamiliar with the Greek and Latin, at an immense disadvantage. I have read passages from treatises on natural history, which contained more difficult Greek words than any passages of equal length in Plato or Xenophon.

These tongues should be learned also, because they are the deposit of all the processes of the growth of human thought in definiteness, breadth and clearness, among those people from whom our earliest culture has been derived. We may ascertain much of a nation's culture apart from literature as such, by the mere study of words in a dictionary. As the scientific culture grows and the thought becomes clarified, it is cast into terms, and by studying them we learn the history of man's thinking and the growth of his experience, and the development of his mind. We are thus able to compare the ancients and moderns with each other. This statement finds its illustration in politics, in religion, in morals, in civil law, and every branch of inquiry. We study this deposit of human thinking, which is fossilized in language, so that we may bring the new to bear upon the old; discriminate the universal from the particular, and the accidental from the fundamental; and thus solidify our thinking upon those fundamental principles which underlie the dearest interests of human society, as well as our own personal wellbeing. We must study the languages of the old world in order to learn history. To learn history we must trace the thought of nations in the words which they used to embody it. Take the word "idea" for instance. I defy any man to teach the history of psychology without tracing that word in its modifications from Plato to Locke. Around this word gather the analyses of human thinking attempted by the great philosophers of all time.

"Words are things," said the great Mirabeau. The history of legal terms and legal maxims gives us illustrations of this thought also. The scientific elements of our law are mainly of Roman origin. If we would learn their history we must trace the growth of these elements embodied in phrases, maxims, and decisions from the patriarchal or tribal period, until they developed into universal, ethical principles, which have been collected into codes that represent our highest notions of justice between man and man. For these investigations so valuable to the scientific lawyer, some elementary knowledge of the ancient languages is indispensable.

Without this also the history and laws of our own language cannot be adequately learned. The very words we utter day by day in our intercourse with each other have the same forms, laws and roots as those tongues used by the people of ancient Greece and Italy. The thorough student of English must have a knowledge of languages other than his own. Let any of you somewhat advanced in life recall what passed current for philology in the introduction to older editions of Webster's Dictionary, with its curious etymologies and vague speculations. Many of us can remember when that introduction passed current for philological learning even in New Haven. Now it has disappeared and is outgrown. Now a man must know something of comparative philology founded on a study of ancient languages in order to understand the etymologies and grammar of the English tongue.

A liberal education also requires some knowledge of the laws of mathematics, especially in their application to astronomy and physics. Shall a man be called educated who is without any knowledge of the methods in which the great mathematicians and physicists of the world have done their thinking, who has no idea what the verification of a scientific theory means? An educated man must have some knowledge of the laws of chemistry. He may not be a chemist in the proper sense of that term, but he should have some idea of what is meant by these wonderful attractions and repulsions which are the basis of those constant advances in knowledge from which we hope so much for the future. The organs and parts in the body of man and animals must be studied, in so far that he may be able to understand what the science of natural history means, and the methods by which the great masters of that branch of science have achieved and verified their results. These departments of the sciences of matter are to be studied in comparison with each other and with the sciences of mind. These two great departments stand over against each other and have a magnificent harmony in their relations as they illustrate each and all the Almighty's plan in the universe. These laws of thought and laws of things are systematic, coherent and interdependent, and no part can be adequately known without knowing something of the other. Hence, this systematic study of representative portions of organized knowledge, is necessary to give the student an idea of the totality of knowledge, and a grasp of the plan of

21

the universe; also to prepare him for study of the details of any one branch of scientific thought, or of a specific profession. Hence, I believe in the preparatory education; the old-fashioned college course, with such modifications and developments in details as the advance of human knowledge and scientific construction may justify and demand.

Very few persons realize how greatly the college course has been modified within the past forty years by those who are regarded as hide-bound conservatives. Its breadth has been enlarged until we are in danger of becoming superficial.

It has been said that the college studies are forgotten, especially Greek. Very well, we do forget Greek. Years ago I taught Greek, but I should pass a very poor examination now in Greek. But the marks of Greek thought, its terms of science, politics, literature and philosophy, are stamped upon the very form and substance of my intellect. I studied and taught mathematics many years ago, but very much of what I then learned has passed away from my memory. I read the differential and integral calculus, and I remember once applying it to the theory of the rainbow, tracing a ray of light in its reflection and refraction, by a drop of water, and deducing from them the phenomena of the primary and secondary bow, and I remember my feelings at the result of that experiment and the quantitative reasoning founded upon it. I shall never forget the emotions that thrilled my mind. I was intellectually translated; I was elevated to a new plane of intellectual existence. I could not differentiate or integrate a quantity to-day, without again becoming a learner; but I never teach a class in psychology and scientific method without feeling the influence on my thought of those discussions in the sciences of mathematics and physics which I went through, under the guidance of a venerated teacher, forty years ago. I have forgotten a great deal of my Greek and Latin and mathematics, and even my common arithmetic. I should not be worth five dollars a week as an accountant in our Chancellor's bank; but it by no means follows that these studies did me no good. The best lawyer in this country will not pronounce an opinion off-hand, but he takes time for consulting decisions and examining special treatises before he gives his conclusion. He cannot carry about the whole body of common law in his memory. It is the "lawyer's mind," it is the mark that has been left upon his intellect by years of legal study, that he always bears about with him and can never lose. That is what we mean by intellectual discipline. We cannot acquire it by reading books merely. We must get it by careful study of the works of the great thinkers of the world, by going again and again through their processes of thought.

Habit is a facility in doing a thing acquired from doing it frequently. A man who goes carefully and frequently through the processes and methods by which cultivated languages and matured sciences have been developed and constructed generates within himself scientific, constructive, and literary habits of mind. He comes, in a measure, to think over the thoughts and live over the intellectual life of the great masters of thought and expression. These intellectual tendencies and habits become part and parcel of such a man's existence, and he carries them to the farm, to the work-shop and the counting-house, to the pulpit, to the bedside of the patient, to the bar and the teacher's chair. This is what we mean by education, and I believe if the community were to hear the discussion by intelligent educators of their methods and the results of their experience, they would be less inclined to condemn teachers' methods and become more ready to respect their conclusions. There are men I am aware, able men, brilliant men, who believe that students should be educated only in harmony with their natural idiosyncracies and tastes. They insist that every young person has a special adaptation to some line of study, and that the elements of his education should be determined by this.

This idea was the basis of Fourier's system of association. In his Phalansteries it was assumed that different persons would be naturally attracted to different kinds of labor; and hence that when a person engaged in that special employment, labor would cease to involve self-denial and become amusement. This was held to be "living according to nature." The Brook Farm community adopted this view. Its inmates sought to find the work which was attractive; but it came to pass that few were attracted to the hard and vulgar work of farm-hands. Very few of the cultivated young ladies who went to Brook Farm were found to be "attracted" to washing blankets or scrubbing floors. It soiled their dresses and spoiled the delicate beauty of their hands. Just so with young gentlemen. They are not naturally attracted to work which is hard for them to do. Now, discipline of mind and will, as I understand it, is to enable a man to do any thing which becomes his duty.

When I was a boy I never wished to chop wood, I never wished to take care of a cow, but I was obliged to do it. My mother said "go" and I went; I am now thankful for the discipline. I did not like Greek nor mathematics; when I entered college I was not attracted to either of them. I thought that if I could only get rid of the mathematics and Greek, my college work would be delightful. But I could not change the curriculum. Under the spur of necessity I put myself doggedly to this distasteful work. I found out after a time that by hard work I was able to master these. I could get along with comparative ease. I came to be attracted to both of these departments, and I owe to this drudgery by which I overcame my distaste for them, very much of whatever capacity I have had for the subsequent hard work of my life. In actual life the true man does not follow his tastes, but the dictates of duty, and duty often requires to us do what is most antagonistic to our natural tastes or tendencies. Self-denial lies at the root of all worthy achievement in every department of labor. It is the power of self-control — the power to do disagreeable work — which makes a man. He who goes through life shunning all unpleasant duties, indulging his idiosyncracies, following the line of least action, will be a man without vigor, without power to lead men and to stand by his country in the hour of its peril. It was not for pleasure that some of the gentlemen here shouldered muskets and went to the war of secession, it was not that they liked it, but they did it. It was terrible drudgery — those long forced marches, the shock of the battle was a terrible strain upon the will — but their duty bound them to the sacrifice, and they came back men who will be honored for all time. Education should be a training in intellectual and moral self-denial. It should aim to correct a young man's moral and intellectual deficiencies. If the logical capacity is weak he should be rigidly trained in logical processes till a just proportion is established among his powers. If his taste is defective he should be made familiar with literature and the arts of design. We should not neglect the strong points of his mind, but we should take special care to strengthen and develop those which are weak or defective. While there may be courses of training differing from each other, it seems reasonable that all courses should be systematic and that the selection of studies should not, except within very narrow limits, be left to the caprices or fancies of uneducated young persons. An education to be in any sense liberal must be systematic, representative of organized knowledge, and adjusted to all the faculties of the mind.

REMARKS OF PRESIDENT A. D. WHITE OF CORNELL UNIVERSITY.

Mr. CHAIRMAN :— In common with all here I feel grateful for the admirable presentation you have made of the ideas which should guide, and the system which should unite the colleges and academies of this State. You have said much, sir, in which we can all agree; but there are some limitations which, in my judgment, ought to be placed upon one or two of your statements, and these I desire very respectfully to suggest.

And first, you speak, if you will allow me to say so, very nobly in regard to teaching as a profession. Teaching *is* a profession. There is no other, in my judgment, more honorable. Yet I feel obliged to dissent somewhat from your idea, as I understand it, that because a teacher is to be regarded as a professional man, therefore his opinion should be necessarily final in regard to what should constitute a course of study. I think, sir, that your analogy between the profession of teaching and other professions would carry you farther than you would yourself wish to go. It is doubtless true, as you have said, that when we put ourselves into the hands of a lawyer we expect to follow his advice, and that when we put ourselves under the care of a physician we expect to follow his advice; and so in regard to other professions; but it does not follow that, because the member of a profession in a given instance may be expected to give good advice, the members of that profession as a whole, and they alone, are to fix the limits and the character of the work to which that profession shall be devoted, and determine absolutely and finally as to every reform. If it did follow, sir, where would the profession of the law be now? We should be following in this State the old chancery practice of England. If the lawyers alone had been heard, without any interference from healthful public opinion outside of their profession, we should have cases dragging on interminably now, as they formerly did, to the misery and discomfiture of suitors, and in substantial denial of justice. Again, take your own illustration as regards the medical profession. If it alone had determined finally just what it should be without regard to interference from healthful influences outside, and especially from the masters of various sciences which touch it at many points, we should all be back under the old regime of calomel, jalap, and frequent bleeding, much, I fear, to the detriment of your own health and of the admirable work in which you are engaged.

In the profession of theology, also, if the world had listened to the overwhelming majority of its professors and teachers, neither you nor any of us would be occupying the places we now hold. Just so with regard to the profession of instruction which you have so ably depicted. If we had listened merely to the men occupying professors' chairs where would education be now? Hardly a word of Greek would be taught in our universities; hardly a word of the modern sciences. You and all of us would be devoting ourselves to the scholastic philosophy. The substitution of classical for scholastic studies was due mainly to men outside of the teachers' profession — such men as Erasmus and Ulrich von Hutten, the former one of the two greatest literary men who ever lived. To him it is mainly due that the universities of the world have come out from the study of the scholastic philosophy, and made the teaching of ancient literatures, and especially of Greek, what it now is — one of the most beautiful instrumentalities in the culture of the human mind. My contention, then, on this point is that the profession of teaching, like other professions, must be adjusted to the advancing needs of the world, and that this will never be done wholly by men who sit in the chairs of professors or presidents of universities and colleges. A very important agency in such adjustments must always come from the general literary and scientific tendencies of each age, voiced by thoughtful men, both inside and outside the teacher's profession. Thus alone can the spirit of routine, inevitable in our profession as in others, be overcome.

Dr. ANDERSON* — I must still insist that reform in every profession must come from that profession; especially is this the case in the profession of medicine.

President WHITE — I cannot think that the example of the medical profession, now insisted upon by my learned friend, is selected with his usual acumen; indeed, I can think of hardly any more unfortunate illustration of his view, or any more apt illustration of my own. Take, then, the profession of medicine, as you, sir, would have us do. What is at this moment the greatest progress making in it? Certainly there can be no doubt that it is the development of the new theory of the origin of disease. Call it the germ theory, or the theory of the *microbe*, as you please; on it, evidently, the theory and practice of medicine are to turn; in accordance with it, medical methods will undoubtedly be vastly modified in the future.

---

* The above remark of Dr. Anderson and the answer by President White were made at the close of the latter's speech; but it is thought better to insert both here, since they thus come into more proper connection with the subject discussed.

Now, how and by whom was this change wrought? We all know that the main agents in it have been Pasteur in Paris, and Koch in Berlin. Neither of them, certainly, would be classed as belonging to the medical profession; even if either or both of them had in his early years some medical instruction, no one would call either of them a member of the medical profession. Koch, in his recent investigations on the cholera, while pointing out some absurd methods of medical treatment in the past, and indicating some better methods in the future, took pains to declare that medicine and medical practice were not in his department, that he was not a medical man. The methods of both Pasteur and Koch, as I have myself seen in their laboratories, are not those of the medical profession.

I must then thank my friend, the chairman, for suggesting an illustration which strengthens my own view of the question at issue, namely, that progress in every profession is made, not only in obedience to the ideas of those within the profession, but of those working upon it from the outside, and that the teacher's profession comes under this general rule.

And now, sir, I come to your second point, from which I must most distinctly, though respectfully, dissent; I refer to your argument regarding elective studies. And first of all, it is clear that in this matter either you, or all the leading universities of the land, are at fault. To say nothing of so many other of the principal institutions of learning in this country, which have been giving increased scope to elective studies, within a month past Yale College, the last great bulwark of the old system, has announced its conversion to the new system, giving a greater range of choice among studies.

Dr. ANDERSON — I conceded the propriety of elective studies, but the argument I used was against total election.

President WHITE — I am surprised and delighted to see that my honored friend has got so far; but the correction is not necessary. Our honored chairman would seem to be arguing against what Carlyle would call "an extinct Satan"; for there are no universities in this country where total election, as he has depicted it, is allowed. The analogy you have drawn, sir, from the history of Brook Farm was certainly very amusing, and your statement of the absurdity of allowing students to "go meandering about" among studies, choosing the easiest, seemed cogent; but I may safely challenge you or any other person to produce a single example of any university or college in this country, of any standing at all, which permits the system you have depicted. The only cases, so far as I can learn, in any such institutions where students are allowed to make up a course entirely of their own selection are the exceptional cases where men come of advanced age with large preliminary preparation, knowing perfectly well what they want with reference to some profession already fully decided upon. The Brook Farm illustration, I venture to say, does not correspond to any fact in education within the knowledge of either of us.

Dr. ANDERSON — It was an illustration. I am not accustomed to going on all fours.

President WHITE — I do not quite get the force of the chairman's remark; perhaps I shall reach it as we go on. The elective system as it is pursued in various universities is generally carried out in one of two ways. It either gives the student a choice between various courses of study, allowing him to select, with the advice of his parents and teachers, that which is most in accordance with his aims and tastes: or, secondly, it allows him in a certain specified course to add to a certain nucleus of studies absolutely required a certain number chosen with reference to his aims and tastes. In either case there is a basis of hard work absolutely required. In both cases, too, it will be remarked that the student after consulting with his teacher and family, after thinking upon his own aims in life and his own purposes — and that is a very healthful thing for any young man to do — selects one, two, or three studies additional to those positively required. Such is the main system of election in the United States, and when fairly examined by you, gentlemen, I believe it will be found one of the greatest advances in the history of education. Will it be said that a young man at the age of seventeen or eighteen years cannot select two or three studies supplementary to a fixed course? I answer that you leave to a young man of that age, at present, subjects of far greater importance and difficulty. The great majority of young men in this country have to decide at about the age of seventeen on that which determines the whole after-course of their lives — what profession they shall take, where they shall study for it, the men with whom they shall associate in business, and scores of other questions equally important. If they can decide these weighty matters at seventeen or eighteen years of age, they can certainly decide after advising with professors and fellow students whether they shall make up their supplementary course with more or less Greek, or Latin, or mathematics, or moral philosophy, or science, or history, or literature.

But, Mr. Chairman, all this has led me entirely off from the idea

I had intended to take up at this meeting. Nothing was further from my mind on entering this hall than a thought upon teaching as a profession or upon the elective system. I would gladly indeed, were not other subjects more pressing at present, go on to a more adequate discussion of this latter subject. But I will only say regarding it, that while differing from you, sir, on these two points I have named, I would gladly sit at your feet as a learner in regard to the main range of subjects which you have so ably presented.

And now as briefly as possible, I will put forth a suggestion which was in my mind before your remarks diverted me from my original purpose. This suggestion was based upon the very eloquent and noble address which we heard last night from our distinguished fellow citizen, Regent George William Curtis—an address worthy of the occasion by its eloquence, its valuable historical references, its philosophical grouping of facts, but most important of all, so far as we are now concerned, by its admirable suggestions as to the future work of the Board of Regents.

And first of all, regarding Regent Curtis's advocacy of a closer union between the colleges and universities of this State: Here, in my opinion, is the most important subject that the Regents have to deal with in entering this second century of their existence. How shall this body of colleges and universities work more vigorously together? I believe fully that every one of them is doing good work in its own way. I believe that they form a group of educational institutions of which any country might be proud. And yet I believe as strongly that they are shorn of half their power by the fact that they are not really working together; that each college or university knows little of the methods and means in the others. How shall this be remedied? Two ways occur to me. The first may be classed as heroic treatment, and I merely mention it now as a matter to be thought of, not to advocate it at present, or even to declare it at present practicable. This first plan is to make the University of New York what Alexander Hamilton intended it — a university — in its parts a teaching body, but as a whole an examining and a degree-conferring body. I can, of course, speak only for the institution from which I come, but so far as that is concerned, I would pledge myself, if the heads of other colleges would do the like, as far as my influence goes, to relinquish wholly to the Board of Regents the power of holding general examinations for degrees and of conferring them. The reasons why this was not formerly done are not far to seek. Most important among them is the fact that these colleges and universities were formerly far removed from one another and from any common centre. Now they are brought close together by the railway and telegraph, and the reasons that obtained in former days for falling short of the system which Alexander Hamilton and his compeers evidently had in mind as regards examinations and degrees no longer exist. Whenever such a system is adopted, the Regents of the State of New York as an examining body, will doubtless employ examining experts in the various sciences and literatures. These experts would probably hold examinations either by papers forwarded to each institution, or by meeting candidates at various accessible centres in the State. When those candidates worthy of degrees, had thus been tested, the degrees would be solemnly conferred by the Chancellor of the Board of Regents. A degree thus obtained and conferred would, in my opinion, be worth more than that of any other institution on this continent.

You have observed, sir, that our system of colleges is "an American system," and, if I have understood you rightly, would present this as an argument why little or no development or advance can be made in it. In this, too, I must respectfully insist that while you are partly right, you are largely wrong. Our college system is indeed an "American system," just as our judicial system is an American system; but there is not a session of the court held in another part of this building, or, indeed, any important court in our country where principles, and even cases, are not cited from Westminster Hall. The fact is that the roots of our legal system run far into the jurisprudence of the old world. So in regard to our systems of medicine and theology. It may feed our national vanity to call them "American," but when we come to study them we soon find that we are drawing largely both from the past and present of the same departments in other countries. Just so with education. If there is any thing good in an English or in a German university, or in any other foreign institution of learning, let us seek to adapt it to our needs. Let us not fall back on the declaration that what we have is "an American system," and therefore capable of no betterment. This would simply be Chinese Mandarinism. There are many reasons why it is well worth our while, at least, to think of the possibility of such a reorganization of our system of advanced education in this State, but I will refer to just one, and that is, the need of better examinations. The weak spot in our present system is, that the students in all our institutions are examined by the identical persons who teach them. An experience of my own revealed to me a better way. It was my fortune, a few years since, to attend the best exercise in classics that I ever heard in my life. I had heard classical exercises in German and English universities, but I never heard any thing which could be compared to the "Normal School," at Paris. You are aware that this school is not a normal school in our sense. Its students are the picked scholars of the University of France. The exercise to which I refer lasted two hours. It made the classical author live again. The discussions which took place between the professor and the various students, on points which arose in the reading of Cicero's letters, were the most instructive I have ever seen. I will not go into details, but come at once to the point. At the close of the exercise, the professor said to the class: "On all these points which we have discussed, you must be very careful, for those examining gentlemen, who are to meet you over there at the Sorbonne, are a very particular body and they demand very careful study of this whole range of subjects." It was clear that this fact, that the examining and the instructing bodies were not the same, formed a most powerful incentive to bring the students up to the required work. I agree entirely with my friend, Dr. King, that the colleges ought to be, to a reasonable extent, jealous of their rights and not let any valuable right they possess be taken away from them without an equivalent. But, in this case, I think that thoughtful study of the whole subject will show us that we shall gain far more than we shall lose, by confining each institution individually to the work of instruction, and allowing the work of examination and conferring degrees to be done by all the institutions together acting through the Chancellor of the Board of Regents.

And here I leave the first means of bringing about a better union of our colleges and universities — not claiming it to be immediately practicable, merely leaving it as a germ which I trust may develop into something good hereafter — and take up my second and last proposal, which is far more important, and which, it is my belief, is entirely and immediately practical. This is, that provision be made for a series of examinations for scholarships and fellowships, conducted under the auspices of the Regents of the State of New York, by examiners whom they shall choose—these scholarships and fellowships to be sufficiently endowed. First, as to the scholarships: I would have the brightest and best young men from the academies and high schools in all parts of the State, compete for them at examinations in various subjects, and I would have a certain number of scholarships worth three or four hundred dollars a year, for four years, conferred upon ten or fifteen or twenty of those who pass the best examination. Each of the successful young men should be allowed to choose the college or university at which he will continue his studies. Next, as to the fellowships. I would have the Regents establish examinations carefully carried out, in the more important studies which are pursued in our colleges and universities. These should be open to candidates from the graduating classes of the various colleges and universities, and I would have fifteen or twenty of those so endowed as to yield an income to the successful competitors of six or seven hundred dollars a year for, say two years, thus enabling these choicest young men to perfect themselves in their chosen studies for the good and the honor of the State. You, Mr. Chairman, in your long and honorable experience, must have known, among the excellent men you have trained, many whom you have longed to see in possession of means sufficient to enable them to perfect themselves in the studies in which they excel, and you have been saddened to see these men, who might have added vastly to the honor and strength of the State and nation in their chosen departments, obliged to sink down into the ordinary ranks of some profession for which they were not especially fitted, never to be heard of more. Such cases, sir, I venture to say, have come within the experience of every one of us who has been long engaged in advanced education. I maintain that the best political economy shows the necessity of something of this kind. The most precious treasure which any nation has, is its young men of talent and genius. If we suffer the talents of such men to lie undeveloped we cast away our most precious possession. Build this Capitol twice as great and gaudy as it is, increase the tonnage of your ships and the mileage of your railways a thousand fold, multiply your wealth to billions, and if this be your only object and all talent be restricted to money getting we are simply destined to the fate of Tyre and Carthage. On the other hand, let some catastrophe sweep away all our accumulated wealth; imagine a cataclysm, if you please, sweeping the nation of all existing buildings and shippings and railways and accumulated capital, but if you have fitly developed the treasure of talent and genius among your young men you shall have all your wealth back again and more.

It may be claimed that such scholarships and fellowships would inure to the benefit of the richer class. No idea could be more mistaken. It is generally among the children of the poorer classes that the greatest treasures of vigor, self reliance, talent and genius are found. That no doubt is your experience, sir; it is mine; it is the experience, I venture to say, of the whole body of teachers here present.

And finally, as to the advantages of such a system of scholarships and fellowships: In the first place, it would be a most powerful stimulus to all the students of the State. The scholarships would stimulate earnest study in the academies and high schools; the fellowships would do the same thing for the colleges and universities. Next, it would tend to bring out any excellences in the system of instruction at each individual academy, high school, college or university. Each would thus have the benefit arising from the experience of all. One institution would show itself especially strong, perhaps, in classics, another in mathematics, another in the moral sciences, another in the natural sciences, another in applied science, and each of these thus revealing strength would serve to stimulate the excellencies and improve the methods of all the others. I can think of nothing so fruitful for good in the whole educational system of the State as a plan like this. Next, it would tend to elevate and strengthen the teacher's profession, and especially to invigorate the teachers and professors themselves. A successful teacher or professor in any department would become rapidly known throughout the State; would secure promotion and advancement; would rapidly obtain the reward to which he is entitled. His reputation would not be circumscribed by the little village in which he teaches, but would extend throughout the State — even throughout the nation. Again, it would greatly strengthen the Board of Regents and the State University, including all the colleges and universities combined in it. It would raise all in the estimation of the citizens of the State. Its influence would be felt in the humblest cabin of the State where there is a bright boy; and I am convinced that, as the Board of Regents goes into this second century of its existence, there is nothing it could do by which more good would be accomplished to the institutions under its charge, to itself—to the State—to every youth in all our institutions of learning of every grade, than by offering this incentive.

And now, as to the practicability of such a plan and the ways and means for its accomplishment: Such a plan would require a yearly use of some money. I believe that with the proper agitation of the question, the State can be made to see its duty in this matter. There is no way in which a small sum of money could be made to do so much good in education throughout this State as in this way. The appropriation necessary might possibly be made from existing funds without the slightest increase of taxation; but even if there were an increase of taxation for this purpose, it would be infinitesimal, so slight indeed that it would not cost a single being in the State a single slice of bread during the entire year. I trust that, so far as the State is concerned, some statesman will arise and carry out this plan, and thus prove himself a worthy successor of such men as Hamilton, Clinton and Seward. But if not done by the State it might be done by individuals. No more useful and no more lasting memorial could be created by one of our princely millionaires than the capital sum required for this purpose. Three or four hundred thousand dollars placed at the disposal of the Regents, the income to be used in the establishment of scholarships and fellowships and the payment of examiners, would be ample. I might adduce a great number of examples within my own observation, which prove to me that there are many wealthy men who would take such an endowment into consideration, if the matter were properly displayed to them.

And now, last of all, Mr. Chairman, though you and I may differ as to some of the minor questions raised here this morning, allow me to say that I shall ever respect and honor you none the less, and I hope that this feeling may be reciprocated. I believe that John Stuart Mill never said a truer word than when he declared that the greatest misfortune to a nation is to have all its citizens educated in exactly the same way. While then we differ as to minor plans and methods, we can certainly agree in the great work of strengthening the hands of the Board of Regents by making the University of the State of New York more and more a reality — more and more powerful for good in the future of the State and of the nation.

Dr. ANDERSON remarked: — I feel a little anxious for the honor of my profession. I recall the fact that the most of the modifications that have been made in law have been made by lawyers; those made in medicine have been made by doctors; all the modifications made in theology have been made by clergymen, and I know that the great part of the modifications made in education were made by teachers. I have been thirty-one years in the position I now occupy, and not a single year has passed without introducing something new. I want to say one word about the elective system. I spoke with reference to the fact that the tendency of the elective system, when carried to extremes, is calculated to supersede American training colleges by a system founded upon the German university, which is designed to be a professional school, and not one for elementary education — that work in Germany being provided for by the gymnasium.

REMARKS OF PRESIDENT DODGE OF MADISON UNIVERSITY.

Mr. CHAIRMAN : — There is one thing I like in this discussion, and that is freedom of thought, connected with high courtesy. I profoundly believe in both, though if I should be obliged to yield one, I should be obliged to yield the matter of courtesy. First and foremost I say, here and everywhere, we must have freedom of thought. I hold it even in a theological seminary, where it might be supposed to have a hard time. I say to my students, in my talks on the laws of intellectual growth, that the first and the fundamental law, without which no advance can be made, is freedom of thought. I listened to my honored friend, Dr. Anderson, with great satisfaction, and I listened with equal satisfaction to my honored friend, President White of Cornell. But I must express my dissent from his view that, in the future, the University of the State of New York will hold relations to the colleges of the State analogous to those which the University of Oxford or Cambridge holds to the colleges which make up the university; and I dissent because the University of the State of New York is not made up by the colleges of the State. It is an organization quite independent of them in very many respects. Now, the colleges at Cambridge and the colleges at Oxford are all state institutions. They belong to Great Britain. They are kept alive, regulated, largely by acts of Parliament. The university represents these colleges. They are geographically in the same locality. They have grown up together. They have their individualities, to be sure, but the points in which they are unlike are insignificant compared with the points in which they agree. Well now, sir, see how different it is here. The colleges are widely separated. Each college has its own individual type, its own individuality. Each college has its own distinctive body of constituents ; each one embodies a genius of its own, and has its own idea and its own sphere of labor. I have no doubt if President White and myself could talk together we should find we agree, perhaps, more than we seem to do. I can conceive of a University of the State of New York so organized that it would embrace and be made up by all the colleges of this State, and that it could do just what President White has suggested.

I have only two suggestions, and I will be brief, because I know there are gentlemen here who must have something to say. I must say first that it belongs to college men and to the presidents and faculties of colleges to be conservative. Conservative men in life do not have their names flamed and flared in public print. Perhaps they will in the future, but they do not now take prominent places upon the roll of history or of fame as the more radical and the more progressive men do. But without the conservative man in life, the bulwarks of society would go down, and society itself would fall. I say it belongs to them to be conservative. Why? Because they honor the traditions of the past, because all men as a rule who go through life as they do, have to be conservative. Their life is one of thought rather than of action, and their opinions are given under a sense of responsibility. It is hard for a man to be a genuine reformer and be in all respects a perfectly true man. I know only one such man. I hardly want to mention his name, but you know whom I refer to — the ideal man, in fact the sole man of the race.

Now, sir, all who have grave responsibilities are inclined to conservatism. The father must be conservative; the mother must be conservative, and I hold that the teacher ought to be conservative. The other *rôle* I sometimes think is the more attractive part to take in the great drama of life, but I honestly believe that individually and personally, it is my duty to take the part of the conservatives, and I do. But by that, I don't mean that I will not accept whatever is good and true in college reform. A man must surrender himself to the truth. To do otherwise, a man has to put his feet on the laws of history, on religion, on science, on all that is noble in life. I often thought I had learned more from reading books outside of the men who belong to my denomination; I often thought I got more from sources about which men have their misgivings, because we shall find this to be true, that there never has been a great thinker, give him whatever name you please, believer or infidel, but has made positive contributions to the sum of human knowledge.

Why, sir, out of the very shipwrecks of philosophic thought found all along the shore of time, you can gather the most valuable cargo, the very richest freight. For there have always been in those great systems something good and true. The soul must be free and open to the truth, by whatever name it is called, and by whomsoever it is supported. This is liberty without license, because it is liberty to receive and to follow the good and the true. So I am a liberal conservative.

There is a tendency, how large, how strong it is I do not know, but there certainly is a tendency to give up the study of the so-called dead languages, the Latin and the Greek. Now there is an illustration of precisely what I mean. I certainly did not believe in the study of Latin and Greek as it was taught when I was a student. I do not believe a case can be made out for the old method. You can drill a student to death; you can take all the life out of him — positively impair his creative powers. You know in college the great test of intellectual culture is the power to write and to speak.

A man's power to think and give utterance to his thought is, I hold, the one best criterion of the college discipline. Now I hold that the languages can be so taught as to help a man to do just that thing. Why, sir, what is language but the one sole monument in the building of which every member of the nation has a part. It is the creation of the nation or of the race. Now the Greeks and the Romans have created, each for themselves, a great and enduring monument. And then be it remembered that language ought always to be taught in the class in connection with its literature. It should be made, as my friend has said, vital in the teaching, and by lectures and by essays. The connection should never be separated between the language and the life and the literature, and between both and the life in which they depend. Language should ever be a means to a higher end. Now, when you look at the Greek speech, and the Greek literature, and see how much they have done, and remember also that the Greek thinkers were the first, as they were the foremost teachers of the human race, we must admit our indebtedness to them has been vast indeed.

Plato and Aristotle reigned through all the middle ages. We study to-day these two great lights; the one has given us our methods, and the other our philosophic inspiration. We inherit the culture of Greek art as well as the spirit of Greek philosophy. Take now the Roman side — the old Latin tongue and remember the great fact that all the common law of Continental Europe has its rise in the old Roman jurisprudence; that the municipal regulations in early European history were really creations of Roman administrators, and we have something there that is independent of the Greek language and the Greek literature and the Greek philosophy. Shall we then give up the study of the old Latin tongue? Besides, the study of the language itself has its own worth. The mere act of translation is an intellectual exercise. It gives culture of what I will call the synthetic impulse, a tendency which needs to be as largely cultivated as its opposite. You know the natural process of education is analysis. But now the synthetic processes are very important. It is the seeing things in their unities — seeing things in their living connections that is also of supreme importance. Analysis has its limits; thus, we say we analyze it in thought, never in fact; but in reality, this last is impossible. Can you separate, for instance, the volition from the intelligence? Can you conceive of human volition without intelligence? Can you conceive of genuine human intelligence without the concept of the will? The power of analysis is splendid, grand; but so also is the power of synthesis. A boy has a sentence to deal with. He will never translate by a simple, analytical process. There is one complex thought in the sentence and he has got to master that thought, and he determines, when he finds there the real thought, whether the translation is correct. He thinks it quite probable that the writer was a sensible man or sensible woman. The translation, the real translation, into his own tongue cultivates just this synthetical power. If you translate word for word you do not give us English, and I do not believe in that way of teaching. I do not believe in teaching Greek or Latin by any such process. The pupils must be taught to translate the Greek or Latin idioms into good English forms of speech or the culture and discipline of process is all lost. Now, that is what we do not find in regard to this, and I want just a word on another thought that my friend has brought out. I really wish the colleges of this State could be brought nearer. We tried to get the presidents together. I never saw President White there, but —

President WHITE — I was about to make the same remark in regard to you.

President DODGE — But after all, the meeting of the presidents seems a little bit like a secret conclave, and if there is any thing I hate it is a mystery. If presidents have private grievances, nobody wants to hear about them. Introspection is the most dismal of all mental operations, most unheavenly, and it ought to be unearthly, but it is not. If there are any grievances, it is better to speak of them openly. There is nothing like open confession in college or out of it · nothing so good as free ventilation.

REMARKS OF REV. BROTHER ANTHONY, PRESIDENT OF MANHATTAN COLLEGE.

Mr. CHAIRMAN, GENTLEMEN OF THE CONVOCATION : — After listening, as I have, to such men as the venerable President of the University of Rochester, Professor Wilson of Cornell, and others who have grown gray in the noble work of education, I feel some diffidence in rising to address you. I came here to listen and to learn rather than to talk. Let me say, however, that I have been gratified beyond expression with what I have listened to during the interesting sessions of this assembly of the foremost educators of the Empire State.

The gentlemen composing the Convocation are a unit on the importance of maintaining a high standard in the study of the classics. I agree fully with those who argue that too much time ought not to be consumed in the study thereof at the expense of other important studies, and I believe that with *live* men teaching the classics they may be mastered in considerably less time than is consumed in some colleges.

Another and a consoling fact, which must be patent to all who attend these Convocations of the University, is that beyond a doubt a strong, earnest desire exists among us to impart a Christian education to the youth of the land. As long as this is kept clearly in view, our nation's institutions are safe.

Dr. Anderson very truly said that amongst other things the object of our colleges is to train up youth for all the duties of *the man and citizen*. Yes, the mission of the American college is to perpetuate our government by the education of those who are called on to govern. History shows that in proportion as the higher education of a country has been thorough, just in that proportion has been the influence of that country. In consequence of the excellence of her universities, Scotland, with her comparatively small population, exerted a world-wide influence. England owes more to Oxford and Cambridge than to her navy and fortifications. To her universities Germany is indebted for her unification. * * * The mission of our country is broader and higher, because our people are the outcome of the best elements of modern European nations. Our mission is to prove the brotherhood of man on a broad and high plane, and by securing the individual the fullest liberty, make it his interest as well as his duty to exert his best energies to the development of the industries of his country and the perfection of a wonderfully wise government in all its departments. No government is stable that is not based on the principles of justice and liberty, and whose people do not cherish these as their greatest earthly boon. Governments are good in the degree that they bring out and elevate the nobler characteristics of the people by the encouragement of industries and the impartial administration of the powers intrusted to them.

Knowledge is power. The knowledge given in the college is based on the principles which underlie human society. The student, whether he likes it or not, must investigate things in their causes, and must, therefore, recognize that there can be no stability for human institutions if they are not in conformity with divine ideals. An educated man may not always be a good man, but if his training has been solid he will cherish the institutions that gave him the opportunities of being great, and will, if necessary, prove his gratitude at the peril of his life. * * * While each of us in his department is animated by the high motives which alone qualify him to educate, holds up before the youth that comes under his influence a high standard of virtue, and endeavors, day after day, and week after week, by appealing to their generous impulses and sincere convictions of duty, shows them that success is always the fruit of sterling integrity and unswerving fidelity to the principles that enable them to see in their fellow citizens a member of the same human family, and to look up to our Father in Heaven as the Alpha and Omega of all that is good, the results for our country cannot be other than great and lasting, and the influence on the family of the nations happy in the evidence furnished of union and harmony with diversity and liberty, each man respecting the rights of his fellow man, and all working for a common good. It is our privilege, gentlemen, to be the laborers in this noblest of fields, and if we are to gauge the future by the past, how magnificently grand is the vista that breaks on our view.

REMARKS OF GENERAL A. S. WEBB, PRESIDENT OF THE COLLEGE OF THE CITY OF NEW YORK.

It was not my intention, Mr. Chairman, either to detain or to interrupt you in these proceedings; but, called upon by name, I will promptly acknowledge that I have been placed between the upper and the lower millstone by the remarks of my respected friend, the presiding officer, and the comments and declarations of Dr. White.

In these days one has to choose between these two able and instructive presentations of our duties as college officers, and each must manfully declare himself to be on one side or the other.

For my own part, until I receive further enlightenment, I shall be forced to express myself very strongly against the elective system as presented to us at present. In fact, I have already decided, in the case of my own son, that I am opposed to it unless I can be assured that the course of study once declared to be most fitted for him is to be the one settled course from which he will not be permitted to depart during the first three years of his college life.

During the past fifteen years I have known of so many applications of parents for permission to select the studies for which their sons were supposed to have had some especial aptitude, and have seen so much that is good result from the youth's being required to master subjects for which he had no liking, that I am convinced that it is better to keep each young man at some settled course of study until he has mastered it. Many parents have rejoiced with me upon finding that their sons were successful in the acquisition of a knowledge of subjects for which they had had, at the outset, a positive dislike.

But Dr. White touched upon a subject which is of the highest importance, since it involves the question of the consolidation of the colleges under the University. Perhaps it would be feasible to do this, but it is a large proposition, and one we must approach only after a careful sifting of all the questions which will arise when we take into serious consideration such grave alterations in the care and government of our colleges. To accomplish such a result would require the exercise of the highest authority in the State. You will be called upon to consider the origin and source of growth of each college, and when you find as I did (when obliged to write upon the subject in an address made before the Phi Beta Kappa Society) that each college is guarded by trustees, and its faculty is required to carry out certain principles, and to teach certain doctrines, belonging to powerful and influential churches, you will realize the difficulties attending the attempt to bring all under one directing body. It would be like bringing oil and water together to try and combine the whole number under this University.

Remarks of President E. N. Potter of Hobart College.

President ELIPHALET NOTT POTTER, responding to the call of the Chairman, said: — Mr. CHANCELLOR AND MEMBERS OF THE CONVOCATION: — In the historical address which I delivered at your commencement, and which was published and circulated by the Regents, I referred at some length to the development of the university ideal, and to Alexander Hamilton (of whom my grandfather, President Nott, was the confidential friend and eulogist) as enunciating the idea of a State university. This venerable institution, as indicated in the centennial address last evening, represents that conception, and this corporation has consistently and successfully sought to develop it.

For the fulfillment of the great design it only remains that the educational institutions of the State shall co-operate with the Regents to the full extent of their powers. President White, concurring in this position, does not, I presume, propose that the chartered right of any of our colleges shall be sacrificed; for colleges like those of Oxford and Cambridge, or those of this State University, can retain all their chartered rights and property unimpaired, and yet unite for certain common ends, under a system or University charter similar to that which is being tested by this State Board of Regents. Representing one of the oldest colleges connected with the State University — Hobart College — I am happy to say that, in compliance with the suggestion of this corporation, it indicates its connection with this University and willingness to co-operate in the fulfillment of legitimate and practicable university purposes by printing on the cover and title page of its college catalogues the words, "University of the State of New York."

The State University can aid us, each and all, and we might with advantage relinquish somewhat in return to the State University. Would it not be a relief to every college president and corporation if we turned over the annually perplexing and "pestering" appeals for honorary degrees to be disposed of by the Regents? A competent committee of examiners, appointed or maintained by the State University, might not only decide upon and confer honorary degrees, but, in conformity with the suggestion made this morning, confer other degrees.

Should State enactments enable the Regents to exercise authority over all the primary instruction in this Commonwealth, or should those intrusted with authority over primary instruction co-operate with the colleges of this University, a much larger number of pupils could be prepared and admitted for higher education. And each collegiate institution might develop along the line of its own appliances and aptitudes. Admirably equipped for imparting classical training as it is, to Hobart College, for instance, might, with advantage, be assigned that department as a specialty ; while its younger neighbors, especially that institution so lavishly dowered by its founder, Ezra Cornell, and by public and private munificence, with collections and buildings, might stand unrivalled in the field of what is popularly known as higher scientific training.

In this connection, I may also refer to electives, to which attention was called at the opening of the morning's discussion. There seems to be no difference of opinion as to the principle involved, but solely as to its application. President Anderson rose promptly to repudiate the idea that he opposed electives altogether. President Anthony, whose institution is related fundamentally to an ancient source of church authority and classical learning, and who spoke so clearly of education as essential to the progress of the nation, admits the propriety of electives, under sufficient restrictions. My honored friend who told us of his own son, in relation to electives (and our best aspiration is that the son may be the father's peer), doubtless recognizes the fact that most of our sons must elect for themselves in the more momentous matters of life. It may be well to prepare them to do so judiciously by previous training, and to see that we are educating boys to be men in our colleges. Electives, regarded as American in character, are growing in favor ; and it is competent for our colleges, admitting the principle, to regulate their own practice, deciding as to a well-regulated elective course, whether they will have more or less of it. None, we may trust, will substitute for the time-honored college system a sort of literary restaurant, where each youthful applicant may call, in place of wholesome solids, for whatever sweets he likes, however injurious to his health or destructive of his force and future usefulness.

Surely this discussion indicates not discord, but unity of sentiment, such as we may hope will ultimately prevail in all departments of educational work among the representatives of our several institutions.

There is no need of unseemly or injurious rivalry among the colleges of this State, since we are yet but as drops in the ocean of a vast and growing population. The endowments, faculties and students of every one of our colleges might be doubled, and the prosperity of each but prove a benefit to every other college. When we accomplish ten-fold what we do now, we shall stand but on the verge of the great work which remains to be done in the higher and wiser education of our people. The college president or "beggar," admitted from the ante-rooms of merchant princes, after anxious waiting, remembering the millions that, of late years, have gone from this State to swell the plethoric coffers of institutions outside of it, sometimes feels that the liberal New Yorker might, not inconsistently, meet him with the exclamation: "Is the college you represent within my own State? If it is, I cannot conscientiously aid it!" Standing and laboring harmoniously together, we may rouse the people of the Commonwealth to a recognition of the merits, to the endowment, and to the more general patronage of colleges within their own State; and the Empire State, under the system of the State University, might then freely extend the blessings of adequate education to the whole body of its citizens.

The pillars which support the arches and upper walls of this resplendent Senate chamber in which, we assemble for our Convocation, are they not symbols of our colleges and of the college men? Polished monoliths, but well-knit and strong, they stand on the marble walls below them, as the educated man stands upon foundations of all the past. He is also the hope of all the future, as these pillars support not only their capitals, flowering into forms of beauty, but the arches and solid walls above, and then the towers and heaven-pointing pinnacles! For the educated man is not only the source from which the future art and culture spring, but the support of solid progress as well as of our hopes of Heaven itself.

If we regard those large, well-rounded monoliths, to which I have pointed, as emblematical of the particular colleges of the State, each adequate to its own work, complete in its chartered rights and religious principles; then, the arches above them, connecting each with its neighbor and uniting all in one under the roof and dome of this noble public building, suggest the union of the colleges of the State in the University, so that, without losing individuality, the colleges may all form part of one great educational organism. Because it is right, we may believe that, in future years, the waste, if not wrangling, resulting from the lack of intelligently adjusted co operation among the educational institutions of the State will be ended, either by wise voluntary concessions or by the authority of law. Instead of colleges each tempted to try both to own and to do every thing, instead of dissevered or warring members of a disjointed edu-

CONFERENCE OF THE PRESIDENTS OF THE COLLEGES. 185

cational body, each then could have a character and do a work so specifically its own, that no other institution in the State would need to compete with it or oppose it in its special sphere. Thus, without jar or waste, misunderstanding or discord, each contributing its perfected part, the State and nation would gain the undiminished utility and harmony of the whole under this extended university system.

The splendid portrait, by Eastman Johnson, of the late Chancellor Pruyn, which hangs before us, and the tributes which have been paid to his memory and to the life and services of Dr. Woolworth who, as Secretary of the Board, co-operated so efficiently in the progress of this University, and the memorials of others connected with it, recall the great Richter's declaration, that " however modest and free from self-seeking, those who labor for education are among the greatest benefactors of mankind."

Frank and free discussion here, combined with earnest, loving, Christian effort, in our separate spheres of duty, will enable us to help on the good work. When the second centenary comes, may the University of the State of New York have even a better showing to present than the honorable record which is celebrated in this centennial.

REMARKS OF WARDEN FAIRBAIRN OF ST. STEPHEN'S COLLEGE.

Mr. CHANCELLOR : — I did not expect to address you this morning, but I shall not disobey your call. I shall occupy your time only a moment or two. I suppose that the real object that we have in view is to show what the colleges of this State have done and are capable of doing. Many of the objects which we have in view in the administration of our colleges have been brought to your attention. I think that people generally are beginning to learn, from our discussions here, what is the particular purpose of the American college. They have come to see that it is not a university, but that it is intended to furnish a preliminary education, which shall enable one to enter on the study of a profession. They have thus come to look for a less extensive range of studies in our colleges than they did formerly. It has been the custom to speak of an American college as if it ranked with a German university. On the contrary, it appears to me that our colleges rank only a little above a German gymnasium, and that they are preparing young men to enter on this higher stage of education. Now it has frequently occurred to me in listening to the discussions in this Convocation, and especially this morning, that there is one class of students, and that class I think much the larger, for whom we do not feel it incumbent upon us to make any provision. A great deal has been said this morning about elective studies. If studies are to be elective, as President White, himself, has shown, it requires a very great deal of ability on the part of the student, even with the advice of distinguished persons, to make that choice. It is not something that is to be left, according to my notion, and in which we all will certainly agree, to the student himself. Then, also, we have had presented to us the subject of examinations. The removal of all examinations in collegiate studies from the college itself, and placing them in the hands of the Board of Regents have been advocated. This proposition is founded on a certain notion, that a degree granted under such circumstances will indicate a great deal more than if granted only by the college. I have no doubt of this. But here is the simple point that I wish to place before you, and which seems to me to be so often forgotten in our discussions in this Convocation, that we have to provide an education for men of mediocrity. Most of the students of every college are simply men of ordinary ability. They are not, as we have heard this morning, bright young men, coming up from the academies to our colleges. Those are the exceptions. The colleges have to provide for the education of men of slender ability as well as for those of superior capacity. The world is really not governed by men of genius — by the Beaconsfields and the Gladstones. They no doubt in their day exerted a great and superior influence. But the world is governed by men of much less ability, because there are not those geniuses. They do not exist in such abundance. Those bright scholars, of whom we have been speaking, who would win fellowships, and for whom examinations are to be made, form only a small proportion of each college. The large majority of young men in all our institutions are men of ordinary ability.

This is a question, it appears to me, that we should take into consideration to-day, on this Centennial Anniversary. Have we made provision for the education of men of mediocrity as well as for the men of superior natural capacity? Are we prepared to educate them to the extent of their ability, so that they can be sent out to take their share in the affairs of the world? A distinguished person of this State, listening to a conversation on the arrangement of a curriculum for a college, turned and said: "The persons you have in view are simply persons of genius. You seem to forget that you are to provide for the education of those who are men of only ordinary capacity, and yet it is those who will be called to fill the offices in the State and in the church." This gentleman was one of the most distinguished citizens of the State, and had been a professor in one of our colleges. He was certainly correct. The larger number of every profession — clergymen, lawyers, physicians — are not men of superior ability; they are men of mediocrity of talents. The most of those who are educated at our colleges cannot undergo such a training as will fit them for an examination for a fellowship. The men of superior parts are the exceptions. I appeal to the presidents of colleges now in this room, if such is not the case in each of the colleges which they represent. The men of mediocrity, then, it appears to me are worthy of our attention and consideration.

I remember a dozen years ago or more Dr. Anderson, who, I am sorry to see, is not still with us in this room, giving us an account of a conversation which he had with some of the deans of Oxford. He said to them, "you seem to let men through on very slender examinations." And they said that they did — that it was part of their purpose that the larger number at Oxford and Cambridge should get their degree on an examination which was certainly not a severe one. But, they said, they had two courses, the one an *honor course*, the other called a *pass course*. The honor men were trained scholars, of superior ability, who gained all fellowships. The passmen were those who had no real disposition for study, who were men of only ordinary capacity. But they also said this to him, and this is what the president of Rochester University said was their reason for giving to this latter class a degree on very moderate terms: he said that they told him that a residence of three years in the University would give a tone and character to these men, so that they would go out into the world better men, better prepared to do the duties of life, better prepared to take their place in that station of life for which they were designed by Providence. Now this is one work which our colleges are doing — and it is one of the most important of our works. But it is one which does not receive the attention which it should. We think almost only of the higher education — of bringing forward our distinguished scholars — those who will shine in examination, and who will give us a name before the State. But ought we not in our curriculum, and in all the arrangements of our colleges to remember that there is such a class of students as I have had especially in view? Ought we not to make provision for their wants and their instruction, because they fill offices in every department of society? We must not, then lose sight of that larger class — the ordinary men.

Remarks of President White, in Reply to Dr. Fairbairn.

Mr. Chancellor: — I will detain the Convocation for but a moment. I entirely agree with what Dr. Fairbairn has said, namely, that the great majority of young men in our colleges and universities are not men of genius, or even of the highest order of talent; the majority are certainly men of moderate ability.

It is none the less true that from these men frequently come those who do admirable service in the nation; I doubt not that this is the experience of us all. But the system of degrees to be conferred by the Regents, and the plan of fellowships and scholarships, which I have suggested, do not at all militate against this idea. We do not thus prevent the men of moderate talent from obtaining an education. They would obtain the same education which they obtain now, and all scholars who at all deserve it, could secure a degree from the Regents. But every scholar who could do work good enough to keep him in college at all could at any rate receive a certificate — call it a licentiate certificate, if you will — showing just what he had done, and this, in my opinion, would be just as honorable and just as valuable as the degree which he now receives.

But the degree itself should require somewhat more labor. I repeat that the taking of these degrees would not be confined to geniuses or even to men of the highest talent; there is a large class of men of moderate talent, strong enough to get the degree.

The whole purpose of my suggestion is, not to prevent any mediocre man from getting all that he can get now which has any real value, but to enable the better and stronger class to have a greater incentive to good work, and to give various institutions and the country at large a means for their better training and identification.

REMARKS OF REV. BROTHER JUSTIN, PRINCIPAL OF THE BROTHERS
OF THE CHRISTIAN SCHOOLS.

Mr. CHANCELLOR AND GENTLEMEN OF THE CONVOCATION : — The distinguished President of Cornell would seem to intimate in his very able address, that specialists have done more for the world than men of a wider range of education. The deserved eminence of the men he cites cannot be questioned. I am sure Mr. White does not contend for special as against general training. No man knows better than he, that the higher and wider the culture of the intellect, the greater its influence. History proves that the world has ever been governed by intellect; and experience in our own days proves that the Disraelis, the Bismarcks and the Gladstones have more to do with the world's government than less educated men.

General Webb, in saying the professor is not always the most honored man in society, did not mean that he did not deserve it; for there can be no doubt in the mind of any intelligent man, that the worthy professor is worthy of the highest honor, since he does the noblest of works, the bringing out and perfecting of the best qualities of youth.

In comparing our colleges with those of Europe, the venerable President of St. Stephen's, one of the most earnest and worthy educators of the country, has, I think, said that they are no better than the German gymnasiums. In this my friend will permit me to differ. I grant, if you make an education consist in the details of a Latin or Greek grammar, there might be some reason in the statement; but if you take all that goes to make the man an educated gentleman, then there can be no question that our colleges excel. Apply a test that no one can fail to appreciate. Put the young German, the young Englishman or the young Frenchman side by side with the young American in the battle of life, and you will soon perceive the superiority of the American. His acquirements are of a wider range, and his ability to apply them in the daily walks of life is much greater than that of his competitors. Apply another test, the highest in civil society, take our National Congress and compare it with the English Parliament, the German Reichstag or the French Senate, and the vast superiority of our Congress is evident to the most casual observer. It is true indeed that in these countries specialists of a superior order are found, but this is the growth of ages. There is a life position waiting such men.

They know it and they work for it. It is in order to create such a class of men that Professor White, who has witnessed during his long stay abroad its benefits, makes his proposition. He has seen the London University. He knows its workings. It is just such an institution as this Board of Regents should be — no college buildings — a board of competent examiners, well paid by government, are there to test the ability of whoever comes looking for a diploma; and if he deserves the honor he receives it. There can be no question that if this Board is clothed with the authority it so richly deserves — look at its record of a hundred years, spotless, not a stain on its banner — and if the necessary funds are placed at its disposal, that the results will be most cheering to every friend of liberal education. Why should New Yorkers be obliged to go to Yale or Harvard? Why not make provision here for the highest intellectual development? Why not encourage a noble emulation? Our population, wealth and enterprise are admitted to be second to none. Then why not have the highest intellectual culture? I know of no better way to bring this about than by giving practical effect to President White's views. It is not too much to say that it is within the province of this Convocation to pass a resolution for the appointment of a standing committee, whose duty it shall be to take such action as may be deemed necessary to give effect to the plan proposed, and to obtain such legislation for the enlargement of the powers of this eminently respectable Board as the situation demands. If you found scholarships and fellowships, you will have some of the brightest and best intellects of the State striving for the prize; and the four or five hundred dollars a year you expend for education of a youth of genius will be repaid a hundred fold by the superior ability you will develop, and which will become a part of our national culture. You will turn out specialists of a superior order; professors whose services in educating the coming generation will be a national blessing, and whose fame will add new luster to the excellency of our institutions. If all the colleges do not come in to the plan at once, there is no reason to be discouraged; only start the good work, and in a few years it will become a grand success. Announce that there is a standing committee of the Board of Regents which is ready to receive donations for the founding of scholarships and fellowships, as proposed by President White, and you will find no man with funds to invest in so noble a work, who wants higher security or a better guarantee for his investment than the integrity and ability of the gentlemen who do honor to the position they hold in this Board. In furtherance of this project, I suggest that President White, its originator, propose a resolution empowering the Chancellor to appoint a committee to give effect to his proposition.

VIII.

THE LIMITS OF NORMAL SCHOOL TRAINING.

By Professor JAMES M. MILNE of Cortland Normal School.

When your executive committee invited me to prepare a paper on the subject announced, my impulse was to decline the honor, that it might fall to the lot of one more competent, but reflection corrected my impulse and decided me to assume the task, even though but little could be expected, and hold your executive committee amenable for any failure.

In the brief paper to be presented, it would be impossible to traverse the various avenues leading from the question; hence we shall have to content ourselves with considering only the two divisions more frequently discussed in connection with this subject, viz.: Whether academic instruction has any place in normal school work, and if so, whether the higher courses therein are essential or desirable.

The first practical foundation of normal principles and practices was established in 1697, by August Hermann Francke, a professor in the University of Halle, Germany. It comprised a single class of twelve in connection with an orphan asylum in which he was interested. The aim of the professor was to train an efficient corps of teachers for the orphan school.

Satisfied with his success, he, seven years later, opened a teachers' seminary, purely for training and practice in teaching.

So marked was the excellence of teachers trained therein, that normal schools began to be founded over all Germany, and finally over all Europe, until to-day there are nearly one thousand normal schools in Europe.

The system was transplanted into Massachusetts with but few modifications, through the enthusiasm of Rev. Charles Brooks, in 1839, and was firmly established by the energy of Horace Mann.

The public sentiment on education in New York State may be best read in the recommendations of her illustrious executives, and their variations from year to year. The growth may be seen in the want felt by the earlier, and in the means of relief suggested by the later, executives.

The messages of Governors Jay and Morgan show clearly that they saw the necessity for a systematic education for teachers.

Even as early as 1818, Gov. DeWitt Clinton recommended the system of training teachers founded by Joseph Lancaster, an English Quaker, and his subsequent recommendations on that subject show how firm were his convictions. Various methods were suggested to supply the demand; notably, that of Governor Marcy, suggesting the establishment of county normal schools, and that of Governor Seward advocating the engrafting the normal school system on the academies of the State.

Public opinion, educated by these discussions, in 1844 established the first normal school at Albany as an experiment, and the subsequent establishment of the other normal schools throughout the State testify to its success.

We have thus hurriedly outlined the history of these schools in this State to make evident that many of the measures of relief — the so-called original plans bruited about from time to time by would-be reformers have, in fact, been already hammered out on the anvil of debate by the intellectual giants of the Empire State.

All the normal schools of this State were founded on the same principle, embodying the German Normal system and the Lancasterian system as well; and our normal schools are more nearly identical with the German normal schools of to-day than with those existing at the time our schools were established. They comprise also some of the elements and practice of the pupil-teacher system so prevalent in England. They embody, then, some of the excellences of the German and English system with perhaps some of their defects.

As the normal schools of the State have not yet enough of a history to establish a system, the corresponding action of other States and countries must be applied as the historical test and measure of experience. Their establishment in this State was not a new and untried course of uncertain issue.

Germany, as we have stated heretofore, established her first normal school as an annex to an orphan school, and all the earlier normal schools founded were adjuncts of preparatory schools; but by a careful study of the general educational regulations of different German States we find that although the immediate supervision and direction of all schools are under the same control, there has been a growing necessity to introduce scholastic work into their normal schools to obtain the necessary technical knowledge of subject-matter to teach, and general strength of mind sufficient to grasp the principles of the science of pedagogy.

Hence there has been an increasing necessity, not only to raise the standard of admission, but also to extend the study of subject-matter throughout the course.

The educational statistics of Europe clearly indicate the universal tendency to raise the scholastic standard for admission into the normal schools, to extend the time and to teach academic matter throughout.

In those we have examined, we find that academic studies are *universally* taught throughout the course. You will please note that the idea somewhat prevalent now-a-days, that normal schools should be schools of method and practice only, was the basis of their establishment in Europe; and all have been compelled to abandon that notion, and add the teaching of subject-matter.

Prussia. by the last general regulation, has a three years' course in her normal schools. Baden, in fact all the German States, have a three years' course and a final examination one or two years after graduation. Denmark has a three years' course and likewise Switzerland. Netherlands experimented for a number of years with different courses, but finally, in 1880, by a decree of the Minister of the Interior, adopted a four years' course. Finland has not only extended its normal course, but has also required that all applicants be at least eighteen years of age before entering. Some of these countries have provided a special preparatory school in connection with the normal schools, for the sole purpose of perparing students for entrance into the normal schools.

Canada a few years since was compelled to extend the course in the normal schools and review the non-professional studies in order to get maturity of mind.

The Michigan normal school is trying the experiment of teaching only professional studies, but at the same time there is in connection with it a large and crowded academic and preparatory department. The city normal schools of Boston and Washington are succeeding admirably, although they are only schools of pedagogics and practice, yet they are simply a normal department of their city system proper, which, taken together, differ in no respect from the system of normal schools in this State.

Moreover, city normal schools and State normal schools have an entirely different province. The former prepares teachers for their city schools which are graded and classified, the latter prepares teachers for the schools of the whole State and country with their multifarious conditions and wants.

In the forty-seventh annual report of the Massachusetts Board of Education we find the following statement of one of the normal principals concerning the result from imperfect preparation: "If we had no other proof of the need of a higher standard for the public schools of the State, we should be well convinced of it, from the results that come to notice as the successive classes present themselves for admission; and the saddest feature of the case is, that no subsequent training can ever make up for the lack of a good foundation laid in the earliest years of school life."

In this State a few years since several of our normal schools tried the experiment of a five or ten weeks' normal class in connection with the normal school, for the benefit of those who could not complete a full normal course, but the results were alike unsatisfactory to the teachers and the taught, and in some cases lack of candidates compelled the abandonment of the experiment.

Unless we greatly err the normal schools of this State welcome all candidates to advanced standing and are only too anxious to receive them, and that the number entering advanced standing is steadily increasing is gratifying.

Not alone from the practical experience of other countries is the conclusion reached that the teaching of subject-matter is at present a necessity in normal schools, but from the deductions of reason we may also arrive at the same conclusions.

From the idea that a person can teach only what he knows, the corollary does not necessarily follow that teaching is only the communication of so much knowledge.

There is, perhaps, no mistake more fatal as to the proper education of youth than the practical error of imagining that because a man possesses knowledge, therefore he will be able to communicate it. That there are degrees of success among teachers and that these must depend in no small degree on their formation in early life, derogates in no measure from the importance of natural gifts and aptitudes. As the late Dr. Armstrong wisely said in his report to the Superintendent of Public Instruction in 1876: "That many persons who have never been trained in any systematic manner have attained a high degree of excellence in the art of teaching, is freely and gladly admitted."

Having a natural aptitude for teaching they spontaneously do every thing just right.

Without being aware of following any system or having any method they never fail to produce the best results and attain the highest success. These persons have genius. They are our law. We bow to them and recognize fully that our humble business is to study what they do, what costs them no study; to analyze those processes which their genius enables them to conduct without labor; to methodize those ways which to them are spontaneous, hoping to make it possible for others less highly endowed to profit by their genius, hoping to be able by this means to make common those arts which otherwise must be exclusive.

Lord Bacon voiced the advanced thought of his age when he said the art of well delivering the knowledge we possess is among the secrets of life to be discovered by the future generations. Dr. Watts was wont to say that there are some very learned men who know much themselves but who have not the talent of communicating their knowledge.

Both these giants recognized the same defects that Professor Francke observed in his teachers in the orphan school.

This want all the normal schools seek to relieve, and maintain that beyond subject-matter to be taught must be an aptness to teach which embodies a knowledge of methods and processes.

Methods have for their aim to produce unity, but not sameness in teaching. Methods of teaching are but ways of applying principles.

Principles are necessary and laws of application. Facts are necessary and the natural relation of facts.

The teacher thoroughly equipped must possess both. But the success of method teaching depends on the facts acquired and the processes employed in the acquisition. Rightly prepared for the work methods can be mastered by the teacher in embryo, otherwise he will be completely mastered by the methods, and while the former state is desirable, the latter is indeed suicidal.

Among the hindrances in this State at present preventing normal schools from devoting themselves more exclusively to the teaching of methods and practice may be noted: —

First. The lack of homogeneity that must exist in the classes; and every practical teacher will admit that the best results of definite work cannot prevail under such conditions. A harmonious development would be impossible when the laws of their unfolding had been so varied and their strength of mind so diversified.

We would note *secondly* as a hindrance, that in the teaching of subject-matter there is at present a radical difference both in aims and ends between our preparatory schools and normal schools.

It is the aim of academies and high schools either to be good preparatory schools for college or to give the pupils thorough instruction that they may be fitted for the practical duties of life.

It is the aim of normal schools in teaching subject-matter to trace it to principles which will be the basis of fitting these teachers in embryo to teach others. The former teaches subject-matter for its own sake and for the sake of the general discipline; the latter teaches the same for its own sake and for the sake of special training; that is, the power to teach others.

The former has for its especial aim facts, results; the latter, strength.

The former considers knowledge as an end; the latter uses knowledge as a means.

The work of the former looks to knowledge acquired; the latter to the power to acquire it.

The pupils of the former are directed toward knowlege as a possession; the pupils of the latter are more engaged with the processes.

The pupils of the former will give readier results; the pupils of the latter will more surely apprehend embodied principles; hence we must conclude that the work of our academies and high schools, excellent though it is, must of necessity drift in a different direction and produce elements of strength in fields where normal schools may not reach by reason of that oneness of purpose which is marked out by statutory enactment.

With the history of the experience of other countries in trying to divorce scholastic training from normal school work, with the general nature of the training of our preparatory schools in the State, with the lack of unified methods and results, we can but conclude that the normal schools of the State have a scholastic work to do, as well as the pedagogical work — their especial function. In the query whether the higher courses have any place in these schools is embodied the discussion of whether the high schools have any place in our State system of education. As that question was discussed fully at your last meeting, we shall waive its discussion here and assume the right in the normal schools, only in the school system as it now exists in the State.

We may be permitted, however, to note in passing, one or two bases that must be assumed in the discussion of State aid to higher education:

First. That all our school systems are the outgrowth of higher education, as both our preparatory schools and common schools are the progeny of our universities.

Second. That opportunities for higher education tend to strengthen the republican spirit and prevent class distinctions.

Third. That the people and their rulers must be educated together, and equally as much, else a government of the people, for the people, and by the people cannot exist. These and other kindred thoughts will ever rise in our minds, and although the constitutional basis of this question was ably discussed a few years since by the Hon. Charles E. Fitch, the scholarly editor of the Rochester *Democrat*, in a paper both clear and convincing from its standpoint, yet when we consider the social and ethical questions allied to it, our mind wavers between the desire and the inability to believe all the conclusions reached.

The normal schools, when established, had a special work *assigned* and a general work *expected:* the especial work, to educate and train teachers for the public schools of the State; the general expectation, that they would be centres of educational thought and foci of all educational influences relating to the public schools. Hence their work has not only a present but a future outlook. They must observe the coming as well as apprehend the immediate demand.

Richter, on Education, says: "To elevate above the spirit of the age must be regarded as the end of education, and this must stand clearly developed before us, ere we mark out the appointed road. The child is not to be educated for the present, for this is done without our aid, unceasingly and powerfully, but for the remote future, and often in opposition to the immediate future."

If such be the archetype we entertain of education for the child, we must entertain as high an ideal for the education for the teacher. Consider the drift of education. The university course of fifty years ago was but little more than the preparatory course required in some of our colleges to-day, yet the number attending college is increasing proportionately with our population. Twenty-five years ago the district school was the problem for educational men; to-day the graded city school is the greater factor.

The tendency in education, like the tendency in industry, is to drift to centres. There are not as many of school age residing in the districts of the State to-day as there were twenty years ago, while those of school age residing in cities have nearly doubled.

Note the following statistics, taken from the reports of the Superintendent of Public Instruction: There were, in 1864, residing in the districts of the State, of school age, eight hundred and sixty thousand three hundred and fifty-three, while in the cities there were four hundred and forty-seven thousand four hundred and sixty-nine. In 1869, in the districts, there were eight hundred and fifty-five thousand seven hundred and sixteen; in the cities, six hundred and seven thousand five hundred and eighty-three. In 1874, in the districts, eight hundred and fifty-seven thousand and thirty-six; in the cities, seven hundred and thirty-nine thousand eight hundred and ten. In 1879, in the districts, eight hundred and thirty-five thousand seven hundred and ninety-eight; in the cities, seven hundred and ninety-two thousand seven hundred and forty-nine. In 1883 (the latest statistics) there were, in the districts, eight hundred and six thousand eight hundred and seventy-six; in the cities, eight hundred and seventy-eight thousand two hundred and twenty-four.

Thus we see there are more children of school age residing in cities than in the country districts, although but nineteen years since there were nearly twice as many in the districts as in the city limits, and we must also bear in mind that those classed as district schools have changed their character and embody as well both union and country graded schools.

The influence of these graded schools is readily seen, for while there has been a decrease of the children of school age in the districts during the last ten years, there has been a gradual increase of children attending district schools out of their own district. In 1873 the number attending district school from other districts than their own, eighteen thousand one hundred and thirty; 1880, twenty thousand seven hundred and six; 1883, twenty-four thousand six hundred and nineteen. So that while the number of children residing in the district schools had decreased nearly sixty thousand in ten years, those attending other district schools than their own had, in the same time, increased about six thousand five hundred, showing that schools classed as district schools are not so homogeneous as formerly. We also find that the numbers attending private schools in the country are decreasing, while the number attending private schools in the city are increasing.

In the light of these facts we can fairly assume that if the normal schools of fifteen or twenty years ago had recognized the temporal and not the permanent demand, much of their best usefulness to the State would have been lost.

Moreover, we firmly believe, that the number of permanent teachers from these normal schools has been lessened by yielding too much to the demand for temporal rather than permanent relief. Again, unless teachers are prepared to supply that coming demand they will abandon the profession, for they will soon realize that they have not the power to rise, and will not be content to remain stationary. Observation of graduates of these schools, especially of the young men who were graduated from the highest course, shows that, after teaching a few years with marked success in the schools of the State, they leave these schools for a time and enter the university, to better prepare themselves for their life work, while those young men from the lower courses, crippled from the beginning, rarely pursue an advanced course in the university, and after a few years abandon the work of teaching for some business in which they have a better chance for the highest success.

If the demands of the future are to be as advanced and varied as the trend of popular opinion would indicate, the State will in time receive a better return from the students of the higher courses in the normal schools than is possible from the students of the lower courses. But fearful of trespassing beyond the limits of your patience we must stop in this brief outline. We have kept constantly in mind that there is a reverse side to every picture. We have aimed to present fairly, although doubtless imperfectly, some popular tenets which both experience and reason would seem to indicate as fallacies. We firmly believe that, if subjects are discussed in a fraternal spirit, with an honest determination to sacrifice all personal considerations for the sake of the common cause of education, some good must result. Even differences may become likenesses, for although we may be honestly looking at the picture, we may be making the mistake of looking on the reverse side.

Truth finally will prevail, but in urging her on we ought not to hazard the success that may have been reached by any false steps. Our visions ought not to be limited by the little days upon which the eternal sun describes from the morning to the evening of our lives, but look beyond, to that influence which thoughts surcharged with the spirit of humanity will wield on all the coming ages.

Remarks of Dr. A. B. Watkins.

Mr. Chairman: — I feel that this paper ought not to pass without an earnest commendation on the part of some of those present here, hence I rise to commend it. I know it to be true that the normal schools are doing excellent work in certain directions, as I have seen that work in visiting teachers' classes which were under the instruction of graduates of normal schools. Those classes under normal school graduates who have had some experience in teaching, have been the classes which have done the best work. I was pleased to hear the subject treated historically, and to learn in regard to this subject what has been done in other countries as well as in this. I believe there is a widespread feeling among academy men that the normal schools should not trench upon the domain of teaching the branches, but should be kept closely to teaching pedagogy. There is a strong conviction that this can be done, in spite of what the paper has told us, for we are told that in the schools of Boston and Washington, pupils receive instruction in the branches themselves sufficiently good to make their work effective when they become members of training classes.

If this be true there, and it is true also in this city and in Rochester, where classes are organized by the superintendents of schools, if this be true in the cities, making due allowance for the fact that the normal schools may not get that uniformity of scholarship or grade of talent that the city schools furnish, the question arises whether pupils cannot be prepared in the best academies for the normal schools and prepared successfully. The objection is made that the aims of preparing pupils for the normal schools and for purely academic work are different. It is said that the one directs its preparation to a knowledge of principles, bases it upon principles, that the other aims to impart a knowledge of facts, to make instruction practical. I think most of the best teachers in the State would contend that they in their teaching strive to lead their pupils to a knowledge of principles as well as of facts. I throw out these suggestions to open what I am sure will be a profitable discussion.

Remarks of Dr. Noah T. Clarke.

Mr. Chancellor: — I remember when the State normal school of this city had had a little experience, and when the late Secretary Woolworth was at the head of it, of having an interview with him in reference to shortening the course of study. Both he and

Secretary of State Randall were anxious to make the work of the normal school purely professional, and to bring the work down to a course of not more than six months, and possibly of three months. The experiment was thereupon tried and the result was that they had to go back to a two, three or four years' course, as the students who entered were not found to be prepared for professional study.

These students, many of them coming upon the recommendation of school superintendents or school boards, or upon examination, were found deficient in the subject-matter of an education and needed much academic work before they could profitably enter a training or professional school, which I think shows that the elementary work of that day did not generally prepare scholars for the professional training proposed by the Albany Normal School, which I think has adhered to its proper work more closely than any other of our normal schools.

But the academies have done a good work in this department for many years. They have educated men and women in the subject-matter necessary to make them good teachers in the common schools, and they have added to that the professional training to an extent but little, if any, short of that furnished by our normal schools. I was pleased with the paper and very much interested in the author's view of the proper work of the normal school. So far as that work is concerned there should be no conflict with the academies, and the field is large enough for both. But if the normal schools are mainly free academies preparing scholars for college or for business, outside of their work of preparing teachers, then there naturally arises a feeling that the academies are brought into an unfavorable competition with these schools with their free tuition and backed up by the strong aid of the State, in which competition the academies must inevitably suffer. But I think we must all agree that if the normal schools are to succeed they must do not only professional but educational work, and therefore there should be no jealousies between them and the academies. The normal schools I look upon as an outgrowth of the academies which had laid broad and deep foundations of the great work of educating teachers for the common schools, and I hope these schools will never forget "the rock whence they were hewn, and the hole of the pit whence they were digged."

Remarks of Principal C. T. R. Smith.

Mr. Chancellor: — I, too, was very much interested in Professor Milne's historical researches. There is one question I should like to ask in regard to the historical aspect of this question. It is this: Has the experiment ever been tried in this State or any other country, in the normal schools, of requiring pupils to enter normal schools upon examination? They should search thoroughly their qualifications for admission, and admit them to the normal schools only upon such examination.

Remarks of Professor J. M. Milne.

I think I can answer that very readily. As I said of the German normal schools, pupils are eligible to entrance only after graduation from the preparatory school, otherwise they would not admit them; hence I think the authorities assume that they are prepared when they enter. Also in Canada, some of you will remember that a few years ago a person was eligible for admission to the normal schools there only from a graduation which might entitle him to a second grade certificate. They had to abandon their plan because they could not get sufficient maturity of mind to comprehend the purpose and plan of them in the given time, which was one year.

Remarks of Principal E. A. Sheldon.

Mr. Chancellor: — I feel deeply interested in this particular discussion. It seems to me, sir, we have had some experience of this kind in our own State — an effort made to establish normal schools upon the basis of academical work. In 1861, we organized at Oswego a training school for the training of primary teachers. It was essentially a city school for the training of the teachers for the public schools of the city of Oswego. The work was strictly professional, consisting of discussion of the principles of education, their application in teaching, and actual teaching work under criticism. Pupils were admitted to this work on an examination, covering our high school course. The result of this experiment, which ran through three years, was the abandonment of this plan. The theory was that the training school ought merely to do the professional work, and that the high school should do this preparatory work.

So far as the city of Oswego is concerned, the graduates from the high school were prepared to enter directly upon the professional work, but pupils from outside experienced the trouble alluded to in the paper. Pupils came to us, supposing they were prepared to meet all demands; they had been over the subjects required, but as the standards of excellence were different in different schools, they were often found wanting. Consequently we were obliged to begin academical work. I think it is not expecting too much to suppose that the academical schools may do this work, but there are some practical difficulties just at this time in regard to it. These difficulties have been indicated to a great extent already. We have no uniform plan in our educational work in this State. We have, under the Board of Regents, something that seems to be working into a uniform plan, but the Board of Regents have charge of a portion only of the preparatory schools of the State.

If all the schools that are supported in part or wholly by the State funds were under a board of education who could direct the courses of study quite definitely, not only in regard to the studies and the thoroughness with which they are pursued, but as to the methods that should be employed in the work, it seems to me this problem would be practically solved. Examinations could then be had that would indicate the thoroughness of the scholarship and the method pursued in the preparation of teachers for our professional schools. If we will begin here and so unify our educational work in the State that we may have unity of plan, unity of method, and thorough testing of scholarship at the end, then relate the normal schools to these preparatory schools, and we have accomplished the work. This does not seem to me a Utopian idea. It is thoroughly practical. It is what we ought to aim at, and I believe the time is coming when we may realize it.

REMARKS OF SUPERINTENDENT A. J. ROBB.

Mr. CHANCELLOR: — The gentleman who has just taken his seat, referring to the city of Oswego, tells us that they find the students from the high schools and academies of that city and vicinity well-prepared in subject-matter to enter upon professional work, and that after three years of experiment they abandoned the special work. Now I would like to ask one question in regard to the result of that experiment. Did the city of Oswego, after having tried the experiment for three years, abandon this professional work on the part of the students of their high school, because it was believed to be unnecessary work, and that their pupils, coming directly from the high schools and academies, were fully qualified to teach in the public schools of that city; or was it because they concluded that with the addition of one year's professional training these pupils were still unqualified to teach in the public schools and that the city of Oswego must depend upon the normal school for its teachers. I think the cities throughout the State may find this a very important question. It is a question which is being discussed in more than one city that has at present neither normal school nor normal department of high school.

If the pupils coming from high schools and academies were found to be fully qualified to fill the position of teachers in the primary and intermediate departments, it seems to me that other cities need not go to the expense of maintaining a normal department. I would like more light on this subject. There is another question connected with that of the paper. The high schools of the cities and the normal schools of the State are being continually brought into comparison with each other and the complaint made that our academies and high schools do not furnish sufficient subject-matter for the pupils that go to the normal schools to get professional training.

If statistics were at hand I would like very much to know how large a proportion of those entering the normal schools come from academies and high schools, and how large a proportion from the little country schools on the hill-sides, where they had received no regular training; where they had one teacher in summer and another in the winter. A large number is made up of a class who have never been inside a high school or academy or who, perhaps, may have attended such school for a term or two. I would also like to know how large a proportion of those who enter the normal schools with this low grade of preparation is composed of those who have been unable to sustain themselves in their classes in the high schools and, therefore, have left them to enter the normal schools. Are there any statistics on these points?

REMARKS OF PRINCIPAL E. A. SHELDON.

Mr. CHANCELLOR: — I omitted to say that this training school, which was at first a city training school, grew into a State normal school. Doubtless as a city training school, it might have succeeded by taking graduates from the high school. The training schools of Boston, New York City, Philadelphia, Cincinnati, Chicago, Indianapolis and other leading cities of the country are now training their teachers on this basis of academical work alone. The same would have been true in Oswego had it not grown into a normal school and received pupils from outside. The gentleman has alluded to a point which, I believe, is very just; indeed, so far as my own experience goes, those pupils who are most poorly prepared are not pupils who come from our best academies and high schools. They are, as he says, from the "hill-sides." They have not the advantages which come from our best schools. It is for this reason that they come to the normal school. They want education and they want to get it in the cheapest way possible. If we could have some plan by which these academies and high schools could be related to the normal school, so that the latter could take pupils who had graduated from the former on the recommendation of the faculties, I believe the result would be different from what we have already experienced.

REMARKS OF PRINCIPAL ELISHA CURTISS.

Mr. CHANCELLOR: — I am very glad to hear this criticism. I believe, myself, you will find quite as diversified a practice among normal schools as among academies. I do not believe they have the same method in view. I suppose they are different in different localities. They are not uniform in system. But I very much doubt there is that diversity of opinion in relation to subject-matter being taught. I very much doubt if the purpose and plan of instruction is the same in every normal school or in every academy. Who can take it and make a good theory out of it? There are those who know the schools who differ from me. There are those who have been prepared in academies who have just as good aims for teaching as those in the normal schools. The subject-matter presented in academies has different ends and aims in view. Those desiring to become teachers have to make application to the commissioners and stand high in the professional studies, and they become, I doubt not, fully as well prepared and competent to teach as those prepared elsewhere, if they have the genius and tact and earnestness to become good teachers. Simply because a person comes well prepared to the normal school does not signify that all are well prepared. I have no doubt that many do come, as the doctor suggested, from the "hill-sides," and have no knowledge with reference to subject-matter.

REMARKS OF PRINCIPAL JAMES A. CASSETY OF ALBANY.

Mr. CHANCELLOR: — Some three years ago, when I had the honor to be connected with a normal school, at a meeting of the principals, which was held here in the city of Albany, it was proposed that we should accept the Regents' examination as a basis for putting the pupils in the training class. We all agreed I think — if I am wrong, Dr. Sheldon will correct me, I think he was present — we all agreed that in the first-rate high schools, in the first-rate academies, the pupils were properly trained and ready to enter the professional work of the normal schools. But we also found out that we could not accept them without examination and put them into the training class. The statute did not permit it. It requires that all shall be examined. It has been the practice, so far as I know, ever since the normal schools have been established, to accept, on examination, properly prepared persons coming from high schools and academies and put them directly into the training class. I do not quite see the point of this discussion. I do not think anybody has made the point that high schools and academies do not properly prepare young men to enter normal schools. In many of the high schools and academies it is due to the difference of their aims and ends that many are not prepared properly to enter the class, but, if found properly prepared, they are always put into the training class. Am I not right, Dr. Sheldon? So far as mere knowledge is concerned, I would not wish to say they do not fit better. I believe we prepare boys in knowledge, better here in the Albany Academy, than in the normal schools, but we do not fit them to enter training classes, we fit them to enter college. In the normal school they ask, why do you proceed in this way? We try to create a different attitude of mind in our instruction in the normal school from what we do in the high schools and academies. I have been in a normal school about twelve years, and in academies about thirteen years, and I claim to have a certain amount of opinion upon the subject, at any rate. When we are teaching a boy or a girl simple knowledge, we are creating one kind of attitude of mind toward that knowledge in his or her mind; when we are preparing him to teach that knowledge, we give him a totally different attitude of mind. All of you — all teachers — know very well that a man who stands up as teacher before a class looks at his own knowledge and his own mind very differently from what he did when he stood upon the other side and faced the other way as a pupil. The only reason for putting academic work into the normal school, as I look at it and understand it, is that the pupils should look at their knowledge from the proper stand point, not why is this so, but why are we proceeding in this order — why do we present it so. I do not think there is any conflict between the two kinds of schools. When I was in a normal school we certainly accepted boys and girls from academies and high schools very thankfully. It saved us the labor of preparing those boys and girls from the hillsides; but those boys and girls thoroughly unprepared, I suppose, form very largely the class of pupils for which the normal schools were made. They were established to help boys and girls who have not the means to prepare themselves for teaching, and yet have all the enthusiasm and earnestness and patience that is desirable.

REMARKS OF PRINCIPAL D. C. FARR.

I am not one of those persons who believe that there is any antagonism between the normal schools and academies. No one would deprecate more strongly any such thing than I. At the same time I am at a loss to understand if the eight normal schools of this State are teaching the same subject-matter that the academic departments of union schools are teaching, why this great State of New York should not extend to both the same advantages in point of compensation. The latter do the same work as the normal schools. If she provides money to pay for this instruction and furnishes free text-books also, why in all fairness is she not called upon to do the same thing for all the academic departments of union schools which do that work?

REMARKS OF DR. N. W. BENEDICT.

Mr. CHANCELLOR:— Part of what I had to say has been said by the gentleman who has just taken his seat. I was very much pleased with the paper because it gave me so much information which I had not before obtained myself. The point just alluded to, I was about rising to ask in reference to that. Are the normal schools fitting students to enter college — some of them or all of them? Do they so fit them when they go through, if it is their choice? In the next place, what has been the result in such cases in the State? What have been the facts? Here, for instance, is an academy that gives academic instruction to some who can go no further, and it gives instruction to those who expect to go to college, and by the side of it is a splendid normal school. Each school has given the same kind of instruction, and those pupils, after being prepared in the normal school, will perhaps go to college, some may go to teaching. What has been the result in respect to those academies, I would like to know, if the normal schools are doing college preparatory work, and students going to academies must pay a tuition fee and pay for their own books, and by going into the normal school they avoid the expense, with perhaps better advantages than in the academies? That is all I would add to what has been said.

REMARKS OF PRINCIPAL E. A. SHELDON.

Mr. CHANCELLOR AND GENTLEMEN: — I do not understand that the work of the normal school is to fit for college. The idea is to prepare teachers to teach in the public schools of the State. We start out with that proposition and we ask students to come to us for this purpose. As many as come prepared to enter upon professional work, to study principles of education and their application in teaching, are admitted at once to this work. If there are those who come to us not thus fitted, what shall be done with them? Shall we turn them away, or give them the necessary preparation? It is doubtless true, as has been suggested, that both these things should be done to a certain extent; that professional work should stand at the head of the work of normal schools, and then, so far as is necessary in preparation, that this academic work shall also be done.

It is true that some pupils go from the normal schools to college, largely, however, after they have entered upon teaching work, and they enter college with the view of subsequently taking up the work of their profession. The college, in other words, supplements the work of normal schools, and prepares teachers for a larger range of instruction.

REMARKS OF PROFESSOR J. M. MILNE.

I think the gentleman, perhaps, fairly makes the criticism. I would add for his information, however, that I have been connected with three normal schools in this State — Brockport, Geneseo and Cortland. With all due diligence, I must confess, have I sought to find any difference in their methods; thus far I have been unsuccessful. As to this college work that has been referred to, we do prepare pupils for college in this way. There comes to my mind now four young men who are graduates from Cortland, who have taught in the union schools of this State. They are boys from the hill-sides, and by teaching they have earned money to go to college, and they will go forth this fall to better prepare themselves for the grand work of life-teaching. We had to prepare them for college in that way. Mr. Chairman, the pride of these normal schools is, that their boys and girls are from the hill-sides that they have nerve, sinew and muscle. They are not there to squander money;

they are there under the beneficent influence of the State, which nourishes the pride to reach the highest place in the profession of teaching. I can recall nearly one hundred normal school teachers, not one of whom ever went to college directly from the normal schools, and who have taught continually since graduation. So we see there are a great many ideas afloat and bruited about, and are becoming embodied in the minds of the people, which are not true. We had in Cortland a few days ago, three who were graduated and who never received an iota of instruction in the normal school. All we ask is, send us properly prepared teachers and we will be very glad to receive them. All the normal schools will gladly lay down their charge and delegate to the academies, academic instruction. We all want to do the same thing, only our ways differ. Again do I want to emphasize here in the University Convocation, that the boys and girls of the hill-sides are the pride of the normal schools, and the back-bone of the Empire State.

IX.
SOME SUGGESTIONS ON THE STUDY OF MODERN GERMAN POETS.

By Vice-President KIRCHER of Niagara University.

The increased attention bestowed upon the study of modern German classics in our higher schools cannot but be a source of gratification to a German, and as such you easily recognize me from my accent. The scholar cannot be indifferent to the fact that by the study of those classics the cause of literature may be greatly advanced.

However, the object of this paper is not to dwell on this point. I would respectfully beg to draw your attention to the question whether, and under what conditions, young students may, without detriment to sound ethical principles, be encouraged in the study of modern German classics, as the representatives of which Goethe and Schiller may be safely assigned.

I readily grant all the advantages claimed as resulting from this study in a literary sense, but I cannot close my eyes to the grave perils attending it when young pupils, unguided by the skill and vigilance of a conscientious educator, are allowed free access to all the works of the modern German poets.

In giving my reasons for this conviction, I must beg to dwell at some length on principles of ethics and æsthetics, allowing those familiar with our great German master-poets to critically apply these principles to their works, because I cannot, in the attempt at illustrating these principles, enlarge this paper to an extent both unreasonable and fatiguing to my kind audience.

I would remark also that these principles may equally apply to many of the classics of other tongues than the German; but I do not propose to pass any opinion on these latter, this being foreign to my subject.

The artist — and the poet has to be, of course, eminently an artist — must have before his mind the true ideal of art, when engaged in the composition of his works.

What is that ideal?

Let me submit to you my conviction, that the true ideal of all art should be the purely spiritual, the supernatural, the divine.

Christianity, by communicating to man the most profound revelations concerning his origin and destiny, concerning the world and its Creator, and by holding up before him the Divine human ideality of the God-man, shed a brilliant light over, and imparted a sublime transfiguration to the artist's conceptions. Christianity, and it only, shows forth the highest moral, intellectual, and æsthetical ideas which constitute the empire of the True, the Good, and the Beautiful. The mind of the Christian artist is not altogether directed toward and circumscribed by the sensible and the things of this world; in his works the spiritual and the things of the other world take the foreground; his view is expanded to the Infinite. The Christian artist does not fatigue us with his strivings after sensual enjoyments and earthly glory; he idealizes the renunciation of the world, pleasure in poverty, patience in persecution, the striving after spiritual fruition and the possession of God. His art is not merely beautiful in form, but it spiritualizes the sensible, raises it above the mere natural to a higher sphere, and makes it the reflex of Supreme Beauty itself. (Compare Wedewer, D. Literatur u. d. christl. Jugend erziehung, Frankf. Brosch. 1868, 4 Jahrgang, No. 5.)

From this I infer that if an artist be an alien to true Christianity, he will be estranged from the true ideal in art. Christianity, and true Christianity only, can inspire the true ideal. The denial of Christianity, or indifference to it, or the holding of tenets more or less opposed to it, will necessarily be more or less fatal to art.

Many, indeed, want religion and art to be divorced. They are willing to let religion go her own way, but they require also that we should not ask their supreme goddess — art — to bow before Christ and Christianity.

To them I reply that there can be no art, no beauty, outside of or opposed to religion. And for this reason, that which is moral is beautiful, because it is an essential development of man's nature. The immoral, on the contrary, is ugly, because it is an unnatural phase of being. But Christianity alone proposes true morality, and places before us the highest ideal of morality and beauty in the person of its Divine Founder. Let the unbiased artist judge from this whether religion and morality can be indifferent factors in art.

How is it, then, it may be asked, that we sometimes find lofty ideals in the works of our modern infidel and materialistic artists, as well as in the creations of those who, being more or less removed from true Christianity, have their ideas warped in their lofty flight or may have them even placed on a basis positively hostile to all Christian art? It is true, their ideals are not the highest possible, because they partially disregard, partially ignore, all that which has the highest real value; but still they have some lofty ideals.

The reason is, that though they are estranged from Christian faith and Christian life — though they may discard God, ignore the Redeemer, and slight all or a part of Revelation — yet they cannot altogether divorce themselves from the all-pervading, civilizing spirit of Christianity, in spite of themselves or their tenets. Had they never been imbued with any true Christian ideas, they could have no such high ideals at all as they sometimes hold up aloft before us. But unfortunately they look for the highest and noblest to which the human spirit may aspire in the manifestations of human life; they promise to themselves from human efforts or even passions all that which only the Christian religion can give to man. (Compare Wiseman, Essays, 6, p. 95; Kraus, Kunst bei den alten Christen, Frankf. Brosch, 1868, 4 Jahrg., No. 9, p. 5.)

I repeat, then, that the artist's ideal must be the purely spiritual, the ever good, true, and fair, the Creator, the Redeemer, the Holy Spirit, God.

Why? If the ideal were not God, it would be necessarily man; if it were not the Creator, it would be the creature; if it were not the purely spiritual, it would be the material.

Very well, it will be said, art is nothing else than the imitation of nature; and nature, therefore, in its grand simplicity, is the true ideal of art. To set up a higher ideal than nature would be to act against reason, against exact science, against all the great achievements of antiquity, against the dominant spirit of our time. And as nature consists of matter, it follows that materialism in art, or realism, is not only perfectly justified, but is the only proper tendency of modern art, as well as modern culture in general.

I reply that, though these assertions may sound plausible, and flatter human nature, they can bring no conviction to the Christian philosopher. They are only indications of what spirit those are who make them. They want us to conform to the depraved spirit of this age, which demands of an artist nobly-decked frivolities, and insists on his degrading art to become an apotheosis of low sensuality. Their idea of the beautiful is the flesh; of the true, fancy; of the good, matter. Certainly, truth must be the principal aim of art. We attempt nothing higher. But our realistic opponents, though they clamor so much about it, will never attain it; because what they call truth is simply falsehood, brought forth by an anti-Christian philosophy, by Materialism. Is our ideal a phantom, as they say? No; the very reverse is true. For things corporeal constantly change; they are but appearances, and not realities; whereas a genuine artist's true ideal, which is but the reflex of the Ever Good, True, and Fair, is the correct image of an unchangeable reality.

They desire only to copy nature? Ah, it is a pity that there is so much money squandered on musical instruments, so much time lost in learning how to play them; so much hardship gone through to cultivate the human voice! Try to imitate the trilling of a nightingale, or the warble of a lark, or the whistling of a sparrow — and you will be perfect artists! A phonograph would be a better musician than any human being! Photography reproduces nature with mathematical precision. Hence any piece of photography would be the most perfect work of painting, as soon as a person would succeed in photographing colors. The greatest painters would be bunglers by the side of this imitating machine.

A manufacturer of wax figures, who forms his puppets correctly according to nature, would be a master of sculpture. The highest achievement architecture could aspire to would be to imitate a cavern. And poetry would have to cease altogether; at most, it could only carefully copy nature; carefully, so that no idea would be mixed up with the copy.

What, indeed, would be the use of art at all, if its object were only the imitation of nature? Cannot every one hear and see nature? Why should the artist toil any longer, since he is forbidden to ennoble nature by an ideal conception? Since he is not allowed, by unity and harmony, to remove the disturbances and discords found in creation?

For nature is not always beautiful, not always pleasing and charming. Does not creation at present bear the stamp of misery and suffering? Do we not see discord everywhere in nature? Discord among the elements; discord among animals, of which one seems to live only to devour the other; discord in human society, where injustice, misery and corruption shock us at every step; discord even in the breast of man? As Goethe says in Faust, every thing seems to be worth existing only in order to perish.

Do not destruction and desolation stalk over the earth? Does not pain reign supreme here below? Marks of the curse are lying before the feet of the attentive beholder at every step. Men with their eyes open, men who think and feel, cannot become glad in this valley of tears. Delight and pleasure are but drops of irony in an ocean of bitterness. Those are foolish, indeed, who are talking forever about terrestrial joys and grandeur. Those who dream of happiness here below are infatuated and deceived, and at last they awake to a wretched reality. We are an enigma to ourselves. The corporeal is often repulsive by its appearance and its sickly forms; our spirit groans as if it were in chains; our soul weeps in its banishment; our *Ego* tends to bright heights of unchangeable rest. (Compare Bolanden Raphael.)

Is there any terrestrial beauty? To the superficial observer there may be, though even the apparently beautiful hides itself before most eyes. But the attentive observer cannot help seeing a hereditary disease in all things, the germ of death in the very bloom of life.

These difficulties crowd the mind of the young, sensitive student as he reads the works of a poet whose highest ideal is nature. At first he will be astonished to perceive such a want of harmony in nature; then he will ask himself who caused this abnormal condition, and in the end he will doubt, or even deny, an all-ruling Providence. With the true ideal in art he throws overboard his faith in Revelation. He will tell himself that a kind Heavenly Father or an all-wise Governor and Preserver of His creatures exists only in the Bible and the imagination of the ignorant, but nowhere in reality.

In proof of this, let me quote for you what Goethe says in his "Sorrows of Young Werther":

"That the life of a man is but a dream is the opinion of many, and this feeling pursues me everywhere. When I consider the narrow limits within which our active and inquiring faculties are confined — when I see how all our energies are wasted in providing for mere necessities, which again have no further end than to prolong a wretched existence, and then that all our satisfaction upon certain subjects of investigation ends in nothing better than a passive resignation, whilst we amuse ourselves with painting our prison walls with bright figures and brilliant landscapes — when I consider all this, Wilhelm, I am silent. I examine my own being and find there a world, but a world rather of imagination and dim desires than of distinctness and living power. Then every thing swims before my senses; I smile and dream my way back into existence."

And further on Goethe compares all the grown people to children, not "knowing whence they come or whither they go," like them little influenced "by fixed motives, but guided — by biscuits, sugar-plums and chastisements."

Thus, according to this master-poet, man is ignorant of his destiny, ignorant of the cause that brought about desolation in nature, ignorant of Providence, guided merely by brute instinct.

But not so with the believing Christian artist. He knows the reason for this abnormal state of things. He knows that every thing in nature is impaired in consequence of original sin; that therefore creation at present expresses the idea of the Creator but imperfectly.

Our first parents had in Paradise the true ideal constantly before them. Then all creatures bore the aspect of the Creator.

This constant presence of the ideal was forfeited in consequence of the fall But an indescribable longing after something no more to be found on earth in its perfection — an indestructible desire after something which never presents itself to the senses while on earth — a bent toward the heavenly — remain. We feel impelled to embrace the Ever Fair, which can never be effaced by the gnawing tooth of time or soiled by the filth of earth.

Thus the Christian artist, by the very defects he now so very easily discerns in the natural order, is forced to look for his ideal to nature in its primitive, virgin beauty, before it was marred by sin, or to represent ideal beauty in material forms. He feels impelled to ascend on the wings of faith to an ideal which, exalted above the sensible, is the highest reality. The sensible is to him no reality. He knows it to be a mere fluctuating shadow; he is convinced that the ideal is the reflection of the Ever Good, True and Fair.

An artist imbued with such sentiments may safely admire and study nature and try to idealize her in his creations.

For I am not opposed to the study of nature, or to the attempt of depicting her, if this be done in the proper spirit. For entire nature, even as she is now, marred by sin, is still a sublime representation of the power of the Creator. She is a grand pictorial made by the hand of God Himself, in which, by visible figures, He represents what Revelation teaches in words. The artist who looks at nature with an eye of faith will gradually understand the pictures which that grand art gallery contains; or, rather, the entire visible world will be to him an immense temple and every object in it a stirring sermon. He will understand and appreciate the words of Job: "Ask the beasts, and they shall teach thee; and the birds of the air, and they shall tell thee. Speak to the earth, and it shall answer thee, and the fishes of the sea shall tell."

In fact every thing created symbolizes or copies the Divine idea of the Creator, just as the work of our hands portrays the idea we had in making it. Plato calls the sensible "mimesis" or the "mimetic." It mimics, copies, or represents the Divine idea, or the ideal. This ideal, being found the same in every object of creation, cannot be particular, but must be universal; it being supersensual, it must be intellectual. Hence, God is the only ideal conceivable, to Whom we soar upon the wings of intelligence and love. God is essentially the true and the good, but the true and the good are not identical with the beautiful, which must be considered subordinate to the great ideal in every true work of art.. For the beautiful is not an absolute idea. There is no beauty in itself. It is only the splendor of God, not God Himself. "There is no beautiful, except to an existence endowed with imagination and sensibility, and, therefore, the beautiful is relative." (Brownson's Review, April, 1833.)

Hence, we properly should define the beautiful, "whatever is according to God," in conformity with God, representing some impress of His perfections, exhibiting some vestige of God's wisdom and goodness. "Whatever is beautiful," Jungmann says, "is like unto God, insomuch as it is beautiful;" and whatever is not beautiful is unlike God, insomuch as it is not beautiful. Consequently, substances purely spiritual, their activities, perfections and properties, will, as to beauty, irrespective of the order of grace, rank uppermost of created things, being images of God in a far higher degree than things corporeal, which, for that same reason, partake of a far less share of beauty. Thus Scripture says of the human soul, that she is an image of the Divine nature. (Compare Cæcilien-kalendar, 1880, p. 47.)

To the eyes of a Christian artist every creature is but a symbolical figure, expressive of moral and religious truths. These truths, disclosed to himself in his sublime contemplations, he wishes, by means of art, to open to attentive beholders. Thus art has often been a more successful evangelist than the most eloquent preacher.

Goethe, Schiller, and their less able imitators did not entertain such lofty ideals, except in a few of their works. Under the guidance of these great geniuses German poetry descended from its lofty Parnassus and went the way of the Prodigal, the way of misery. Are not the glorification of the Modern Babel, with its sinful love, and the deification of vice and suicide the frequent themes of their works? And when they leave such excesses, to glorify noble human achievement, do they not place man above God, the created above the Creator?

This is practically illustrated in Schiller's poem, "The Artists," which his translator, Bulwer, ranks amongst his noblest productions, and of which the German master-poet himself says "that he had hitherto written nothing that so much pleased him, nothing to which he had given so much time." It is one of the many pieces in which he describes the progress of man. He represents him as soaring up to the highest perfection by the cultivation of his talents; he looks upon man at the end of the last century, "on the still century's verge," as —

> "The ripest-born of Time!
> August through meekness; free through Reason; strong
> Through Law — and rich with treasures hoarded long
> In thy still bosom."

Banished from the presence of his Creator to that —

> "Dark abyss, Mortality,
> To seek the late return to glory past,
> Amidst the dim paths of the sensual clay,"

unable to view Truth, known as Urania, in her own peculiar splendor, Urania —

> "Laid aside her fiery crown,
> She comes to earth as *Beauty* down."

Thus the goddess of the Beautiful was, according to our poet, the only one that deigned to console man; she painted on the walls of his dungeon the shapes of Elysium (cf. Bulwer). Now, of this beauty Schiller predicates all that the Christian religion teaches us of the operation of the Holy Spirit when imparted to us; and to the exertions of the votaries of that beauty he attributes all the civilization and morality which was brought to the world by Christ and Christianity. (Compare Kleutgen, D. Ideale u. ihre Verwirklichung, Frankf. Brosch. 1868, 4 Jahrj. No. 5.)

I do not deny that art may exert a great influence upon the refinement of morals, and even upon the ennobling of the mind and the formation of the character. But this it can do only by holding up to men their true ideal and last end — God, the Ever Good, the Ever True, the Ever Beautiful; and not by placing before them a false ideal, an imaginary, transitory, unreal beauty. What a vain arrogance is there not in Schiller's verses, which gave the lie not only to our belief, but even to every page of the world's history, promising that art, scattering bloom," will lead humanity on a ladder of flowers from one "Alp of Beauty" to another still higher one; until at the end of Time it will, by a last poetical vibration, glide into the arms of Truth, that has in the meantime resumed —

> "Her fiery crown divine,
> And all effulgent, vailless, shine
> Before her formed and Ripened Son — [Man]
> The Urania of the skies?" —

(Compare Kleutgen, ibid.)

No one can, without shuddering, read the conclusion of this great poem. What else does the poet, than the pagans did, who, in order to destroy the memory of Jesus crucified, erected a statue of Venus on Calvary's Mount? (Compare Kleutgen ut supra.) The Eternal Truth was mistaken, that our end must be attained by humility, mortification, and the way of the Cross! No! Schiller knows better: pride, self-indulgence, and the flowery paths of art will divinize us, will make us like unto God!

Even with all the *licentia poetica* which the most generous critic would accord to the works of Schiller's youthful period, usually considered as closed by "Don Carlos," we must pronounce them unhistorical, fantastic, and demoralizing. And when next he turned professedly to history and philosophy, he made the former a magazine for his surmises and reflections (see his letter to his sister-in-law on this subject), and the latter he degraded to the humble office of handmaid to his speculations. Only after passing through this twofold period he produced works which engaged undisputed admiration, as *e. g.*, his beautiful ballads and his "Mary Stuart."

And what can I say in favor of Goethe, when I hear him proclaimed as the prophet of the New Gospel of *That und Gesinnung*, which is to supplant the Gospel of Christ? Can I allow my pupils to read indiscriminately his works, though David Strauss recommends them as a substitute for the "effete Gospels," though Duntzer glorifies him as the High Priest of Love, though a considerable number of German materialists sail under his flag? I, for one, cannot praise as the most glorious characters of the history of German literature the unfortunate girls and women with whom that poet trifled. I cannot regard his unclean romances as a source of poesy and enlightenment. In short, I cannot become a votary to the Goethe-worship, no matter whether it has been fostered by Emerson or G. Calvert. I maintain that any people who idolize him are in danger of losing their greatest treasures, their Christian faith and Christian culture. "From their fruits you shall know them," says the Eternal Truth. What fruits Goethe's writings produced in an ethical point of view, untold numbers of suicides and debauchees among his followers could declare; and Schiller's idolatry of art has probably produced a harvest of skepticism from which the would-be student of Divinity would have recoiled with horror, had he foreseen it.

I hope that no one will understand my remarks to be any thing but objective. I do not assail any one's private reputation; I would be the last person to try to deprive my native country of the literary glories gained by her grand masters. I only caution educators against the indiscriminate and unfettered use of some of its productions by the young; and I invite the attention of the ripe scholar even to the fact that often Goethe and Schiller ignored or disfigured a religion which, according to the former's avowal, made at the end of his life (see Eckermann), could not be surpassed or set aside by either the progress of spiritual culture, or the expansion of natural sciences, or the elevation of the human mind. And though, even when making his avowal, he did not recognize the supernatural character of Christianity, because in the same breath he declared himself a worshiper of the sun, yet he gave Christianity the preference before all other religions in point of correct ethics. (Compare Baumgartner, Goethe's Lehr u. Wander-jahre.)

It is the right, and even the duty, of the Christian educator, whilst freely acknowledging the many beauties and truths to be found in a masterly and classical form in these writers, to survey critically and, according to circumstances, to combat productions which ignore and assail Christianity and its heaven-inspired principles of Truth and Morality.

Scholars intrusted with the responsible task of educating the minds and hearts committed to their care, and unwilling to sin against their conscience, their God, and their pupils, will be able to sift the commendable, the grand, the noble, the lofty, the ideal, from the immature, the mediocre, the material, and the realistic of those writings. Whatever they will find in them to be repugnant to truth and goodness they will disapprove, censure, and reject. They will caution their pupils, lest they may be infected with deadly poison to their souls, whilst they fancy that they are gathering valuable treasures for the storehouse of their minds. They will be especially careful in regard to this class of Modern German Classics, because they sometimes profess to be Christian; use Christian terminology, and even treat of Christian subjects. Lulled into semi-unconsciousness by the occasional strong fragrance of such lofty Christian professions, the unwary and only partially instructed pupil will soon be corrupted by the poison hidden under an exterior calculated to inspire confidence. (See Wedewer, l. c., p. 31.)

Only expurgated editions of Goethe and Schiller, such as Lindemann's and Hulskamp's, should be placed in the hands of the young. By such editions those dangers are removed which the young would otherwise meet with in the complete works of Goethe and Schiller. In revised works the lover of the beautiful will find so many attractions and lucid explanations that he need not look for other poems, objectionable in point of Christian ethics, and sometimes inferior even in literary merit.

The works of earlier and later Christian poets should also receive more serious attention. Frederick von Spee, Jacob Balde, and Johann Scheffler in the seventeenth century, Klopstock in the eighteenth, and our latest master-poet, Frederick William Weber, the universally revered author of Dreizehn-linden (not to mention many others), may not have attained the high literary standard of Goethe and Schiller, but they represent very fairly the beauties of German style and diction, and at the same time they indelibly impress upon the young reader's susceptible mind the true ideal in art — the ever true, good and beautiful.

X.

THE STUDY OF ENGLISH.

By EUGENE BOUTON, Ph. D.

How much attention the study of the English language and literature should receive in our schools, and how these subjects can best be taught, are unsettled questions. But they must be settled before there is peace in educational circles. That we should proceed from the known to the unknown in the training of the mind has been accepted as a maxim in education. But it is not manifest how this principle is followed in a course of study which attempts to teach the laws and the practice of our familiar and spoken English by first laboring with Latin and Greek, which not more than one in a thousand pretends to become familiar with or to use. It is pretty generally admitted that the most desirable knowledge for a person to have, is that which will give him the most satisfaction, and will be of the most service to him. But the course of study in which ancient languages crowd out our own, does not seem to have gained this reputation. In fact, it is stated with considerable boldness that most classical college graduates can neither read their Latin diploma nor write a creditable English essay, and that they themselves recognize and deplore the fact. Most students of literature maintain that the literary treasures of our own tongue are unsurpassed in richness and extent; but many college graduates are compelled to take the opinions of others on both the richness and the extent of English reading. This statement is, however, becoming less just every year; and the tendency of the time seems to be in the direction of more attention to our vernacular and its literature. It has been maintained that the study of ancient literary forms and of the ancient spirit, is essential to the finest literary taste and the highest skill in literary execution. But some have wondered whether any one can become a great writer by imitation; whether Schiller was not correct in thinking that he could write German better by not filling his mind with Shakspeare's English; and whether the ancient Greeks would have produced much better literary work if they had been able to lean more on others. There are many who doubt the expediency of allowing mathematics to so largely usurp the dominion of intellectual effort, to the exclusion of those finer themes which literature provides and the humanizing influences of poetry and romance.

Against these encroachments, the old curriculum, composed exclusively of Greek, Latin and mathematics, is waging a somewhat unequal contest. Its enemies do not treat it with the respect due to the infirmities of age; but insist that it must be assailed as a tyrant, and be banished from the territory over which it has so long held sway. I do not aspire to the reputation of an iconoclast, but I have little inclination to defend the old curriculum in its assumption of absolute authority. I must maintain that, until a child is fairly familiar with his immediate surroundings and knows his relation to them, and through them to the world at large, he needs to study Greek roots less than the roots of the ordinary vegetables in his vicinity. He will be more likely to learn something beneficial by studying the best means of procuring and preparing the common food which he eats, than by committing to memory the opinions of the commentators respecting the nature of the ambrosia which conferred immortality on the inhabitants of Olympus. Until he can identify five or six of the birds which sing for him day by day, and can learn to love their songs, he will not be very likely to catch a phenix rising from its ashes, or be hung for the murder of a sacred ibis. The average graduate from the Greek, Latin and mathematical course is lamentably ignorant of his surroundings. Unusually fortunate is he, if he is not also practically ignorant of the literary and historical treasures of the languages which he has studied, and of the practical uses to which his mathematics may be put. Many a man can conjugate the Greek verb with correctness and rapidity, and distinguish with nicety the uses of the Latin subjunctive, but is unable to tell in detail the names of the objects and parts of objects in an ordinary room. Much less can he state, with any reasonable accuracy and style, the causes and effects of many of the simplest phenomena which are occurring in his presence.

I believe that in most of our study of ancient tongues we begin at the wrong end, and make the same mistake that a teacher of arithmetic would make if he undertook to teach progression and evolution without first securing the mastery of the fundamental rules. From my experience and observation, I believe that the surest and shortest road to a useful knowledge of Latin and Greek leads through a careful preliminary study of English, and demands continual remembrance of the fact that, since the essential features of the three languages are the same, their differences require the student's chief attention. If this course is followed, and this preliminary study of English is properly pursued, the student can at any time close his account and enjoy the satisfaction of having invested his time and effort in that which he needed most.

If the extent and necessity of actual use be taken as a measure of the importance of any study, we must agree that the study of the English language and literature easily ranks first in all educational work. Expression, both oral and written, forms a large part of the daily experience of every human being. If it be urged that it will take care of itself from imitation of others, it may be answered that such imitation is one of the very things that most hinder the use of good language in the community, and that the same reasoning would apply to most of the work done in our schools. I claim that from the primary school to the close of the college course, the study of the English language and its literature demands at least as much time and attention as that of any other subject or any other language whatever.

This importance appears the same, whether the study is viewed as an evidence of refinement, as a means of communicating and recording thought, as a means of obtaining thought, as a means of influencing men, as a source of entertainment, or as a means of advancement in general society. A person is seldom called upon to exhibit either a knowledge or ignorance of Latin or Greek; but he is very frequently indeed compelled to show either knowledge or ignorance of English. Our literary works are indeed full of allusions to the heroes and myths which occupy so large a place in Latin and Greek; and it is doubtless necessary for us to know about those heroes and those myths in order to fully appreciate our own literature. But we can trace out those stories without learning the languages. As a matter of fact, we do usually get our knowledge of them from works printed in our own tongue. Let us study the language, the literature, and the history of the ancients for the purpose of illuminating our own language, our literature, and our daily private lives. But let us remember that they cannot illuminate the paths we pursue, so long as our own language and literature are unknown to us, and the proper conduct of our private and public lives is not in our thoughts. And, besides, the diligent enthusiasm of Commencement speakers has already indelibly impressed upon the world the facts that Demosthenes and Cicero were eminent orators, and that Greece and Rome were great nations.

Latin and Greek being dead languages, the study of them has partaken largely of the character of a *post-mortem* examination. Their skeletons have been taken apart and put together. All their bones, even the minutest, have been counted, named, classified, and described in tedious detail as wholes and as parts. All their joints, with their various shapes, connections and motions, have been made sacred to the memory of many a midnight hour by students who knew nothing of their own frames. All their muscles, with their attachments, their various forms and uses, their positions, and their scientific names, have occupied hour after hour of study and recitation. The supposed function of every part has been made the theme of elaborate disquisitions. The peculiarities of this, that, and the other individual subject, have been dwelt upon until the fragments of his corpse could be picked out of a confused pile of remains with entire confidence and certainty.

In the midst of this critical examination the course of study has come to an end. The students have been amazed at the knowledge and the skill of the experts who have taken charge of the investigation. The verdict, "He is dead," usual in such cases, is unanimously returned. On Commencement day the funeral is held. Some of the chief mourners afterward dig up the honored dust to reexamine it for the benefit of a new generation. Others bow their heads as they pass the tomb where they suppose the great departed to lie, and, perchance, are led to temporarily recall some of the scenes of the repulsive examination.

Notwithstanding the time that has been spent in this long work, there has been so much to do that few have had time to ask who the subject was, what deeds he performed in his life-time, or how he came to his death. Once in a while it has occurred to some enthusiast that it would be well to see how the subject walked and acted when he was alive. So the corpse has been placed upon its feet and made to move to and fro across the dissecting-room; its limbs have been put through the motions of a living being; its jaws have been worked as if in speech, and the students present have participated in the proceedings with a certain interest which not even the ghastliness of the spectacle could entirely destroy. But the glorious and undying sentiments which the dead man uttered in his prime, the great deeds which he did, the beauty and the strength of his form, the poetry and romance of his life, and the influence which he exerted upon his contemporaries and upon posterity — all these have been forgotten, or at least neglected; while the repulsive details of the *post-mortem* examination have occupied the time and the attention of all concerned.

Until a recent period, essentially the same method has prevailed in the study of English, except that less attention has been given to the dissection of the language itself, and more reliance has been placed upon what the text-books had to say about it. In elementary instruction, grammar has been looked upon as the means by which pupils were to learn how to speak and write the language correctly. How they were to learn to speak and write it at all, or how they were to speak and write it fluently, was scarcely considered. Instruction in grammar consisted almost solely in committing to memory rules and definitions, with their numerous exceptions; in learning declensions, paradigms, and lists of parts of speech; in purely mechanical parsing and analysis, and in correcting false syntax. The rules and definitions were sometimes illustrated by examples; but very generally the examples were learned rather because they were with the rules and definitions, than because they explained them or resulted from them. The declensions, paradigms and lists were learned, not as types of usage, but as individual facts. The parsing and analysis were often the mere repetition of forms, destitute of significance and purpose. The syntax was spoken of as false, not so much because it was untrue to the usage of good speakers and writers as because it was said to be contrary to the rules in the book. That the whole study of grammar had any practical connection with actual every-day talking and writing probably never entered the thought of the majority of pupils. Indeed, teachers allowed the grossest mistakes in language to be made in other recitations, because those matters belonged to the grammar class. It seems strange that such a state of affairs ever existed, but its absurdities are scarcely exaggerated, and, indeed, may be found prevailing in many places at the present time.

It may be unfair to charge the origin and general use of this kind of teaching upon the prevalent methods of classical instruction; but it looks very much as if such an accusation could be sustained. The old plan of teaching children to speak and write the English language was just as sensible and successful as to attempt to teach swimming, base-ball, lawn-tennis, and other athletic sports, or some branch of manual skill, by a minute study of the parts of the body. Such study may be requisite to perfection in those sports; but its usefulness must come after much actual practice has made the learner familiar with his strong points, his weaknesses, and the nature of the sport or other accomplishment in which success is desired. Here and there one more gifted or more zealous than his comrades began to love his composition-work, in spite of its traditional repulsiveness, and, by diligent practice, learned how to write. Debating societies and similar influences fanned in others the spark of eloquence into flame. But, as for teaching children in general to speak or write correctly or in any other way, the old plan of instruction was well-nigh useless.

In the higher branches of English study, including rhetoric and literature, there was perhaps a less lamentable state of affairs. But, as in the earlier study, still in rhetoric the gulf between theory and practice was very wide and very deep. The study of literature was simply a study of biography, in which literary works were known chiefly by name. That such study was useful, is doubtless true; but that it was an effective study of literature, is not true. Pupils formed judgments of literary productions by hear-say, and condemned or applauded simply because such condemnation or applause was found in the books which they studied.

To say that all this is changed, would be to betray an ignorance of educational work. But to say that in primary, intermediate, and advanced work, new and better methods are known and extensively practiced, is entirely within the limits of truth. The sun of a new day in the study of English has not reached the zenith, but it has risen above the horizon and shines brightly enough to make the shadows upon the landscape very distinct. I shall try to indicate some of the desirable methods which are already in use, and others which, in my judgment, ought to prevail in the study of the English language and its literature.

Down at the bottom of all methods of teaching language, lies the oft-forgotten fact that language presupposes thought, feeling, or purpose. It is probably safe to say that, without at least one of these, language never could have existed and never ought to exist. To attempt to teach a person, young or old, to talk or write without any thing to say, is about equally difficult and useless. To allow him to tell only what others see and say, instead of observing and thinking for himself, is to train a parrot, whose remarks may be very wonderful, but will seldom be either very agreeable or very valuable.

To acquire the power and the habit of observing, the child must be brought into conscious contact with many objects on which he may exercise his senses. He must handle, see, hear, taste and smell things for himself. His observation must be so guided and aided that he will grasp the essential characteristics of things, and learn to recognize both the likenesses and the differences which objects present to the senses. Moreover, the objects upon which he is asked to exercise his observation and thought must be such as lie within his range of understanding. That his conclusions may be of worth, he must, in every case, penetrate through the conventional form to the underlying characteristic. He must be fed — not stuffed — with knowledge. Since the power of keeping a large number of consciously stored ideas ready for use and of promptly bringing them forward when they are wanted, is an important part of good thinking, his memory must be carefully trained to grasp and hold every item of valuable information with which he becomes acquainted. Upon the materials thus collected and changed from lumber into furniture, the imagination must be trained to act. He must see in the forms and the phenomena about him, the germs of the things and the events of which he reads, until words always suggest vivid pictures, and the pictures become to him realities. When the mind has acquired this power and this habit of assimilating and vivifying information, it ceases to be merely a cistern of knowledge and becomes a fountain of thought. Expression, both oral and written, will then be original, abundant and valuable.

No person destitute of this power can become a great writer. A lack of such training in school may be remedied by natural inclination, which of its own impulse increases into habit. But sometime and somehow the mind must learn to translate things into thoughts, and give "to airy nothing a local habitation and a name," before its product is worthy the name of literature. When the mind has this power it may even draw upon the thoughts of others with impunity; for whatever it takes from another it will mold into new forms and impregnate with a new spirit. It was this that made Shakspere at once the greatest plagiarist and the greatest original in the language.

The mastery of language involves two things. The first of these is the ability to understand the expressed thoughts, feelings and purposes of others, *i. e.*, to translate words and signs into conceptions. In other words, it demands the power and the habit of listening well and of reading well. The second requisite is the ability to express thoughts, feelings and purposes, *i. e.*, to translate conceptions into words and signs. In other words, it demands the power and the habit of talking well and writing well.

A person who has no power to distinguish one word from another, or one musical tone from another, is practically deaf. If he is unable to distinguish one sentence from another, but is conscious of only a succession of words from which he gains no thought, he is not much more fortunate. Those who habitually disregard what is being said in their presence, are practically in the condition of those who cannot hear at all. In conversation they seldom know what has been said, and either ask for its repetition or ignore it altogether. They attend a lecture, and when it is ended cannot give the merest outline of its substance. The consequence is that they are in many cases ciphers, when they might otherwise be significant figures. No one can afford to lose the opportunities for improvement which occur in his daily intercourse with those about him. It is, therefore, important that the training of a pupil should be distinctly aimed at the acquisition of not only the power, but also the habit of comprehending and remembering what is said in his presence.

The other way in which we derive information and inspiration through the medium of language, is reading. It demands three things. The first is perfect familiarity with the various characters used in written and printed language, with their proper uses and meanings. The second is the ability to gather from these the meaning and spirit which the writer put into them. The third, in the case of oral reading, is to interpret for others the meaning and spirit thus gathered. Mechanical reading, in which the words are spoken correctly, but in which the thoughts are neglected, is as unsatisfactory as that reading of music which gives exclusive attention to the names of the notes, the rests, and the other elements of musical notation, but which neglects the expression of the sounds which the notes and other marks represent. From the reading lesson may be taught also the names, the forms, and the uses of words and signs; or, in other words, the grammatical features of the language. The power and the unvarying habit of noticing correctly the details of a written or printed page are essential to their correct interpretation. Thus the careful observation that is cultivated by the teaching of these details in the reading exercise, is the directest possible means of learning to read, and at the same time is laying the foundation upon which the whole structure of a mastery of English must rest.

To reading belongs the study of English literature. I presume that the traditional gulf between them may impart to this statement a strange sound. So much routine and formality, and, perhaps, dramatic elocution, have sheltered themselves under the wing of the reading class that it may astonish some teachers to hear one claim that pupils in school, as well as their friends outside, should read for the sake of information and culture. It is evident that a child must acquire a certain power of understanding words and signs before he is able to read independently. But it is pretty generally admitted that this understanding will be gained more rapidly, by connecting the child's study with objects and thoughts which enter into his experience and appeal to his sympathies, than by the opposite method. If this is so at the beginning, how much truer is it in the progress of a child's training. Happy are those children to whom the treasures of Mother Goose and the other traditional lore of the nursery are made familiar. They are to them in their tender years, as real treasures as Gray's Elegy and King Lear can be at any subsequent period. Just as soon as a child is able to comprehend the real works of literature, he should read them, and be released from books which contemplate nothing more than the formal acquisition of the ability to read. How many hours, days and even years, are spent in the dull and deadening routine of the reading class. Meantime the golden years are fleeting, and the masterpieces of literature are sealed books, of whose very existence the child is ignorant. If the long series of text-books is deemed indispensable, the teacher ought to connect the fugitive gems and the fragments of standard works with their authors, or the works to which they belong He ought to so aid the pupil in appreciating their beauties and feeling their charm, that he will seek out their companion-pieces and the wholes of which they are parts. Another means of leading pupils to read standard books is to give them additional credit on their school record for each book read. In this way they will often be induced to read one or two standard books each term, and the detail with which they will reproduce what they have read, as evidence of their work, is as amazing to the listener as it is valuable to them.

When the time comes for more formal study of English literature the ideal course is not so evident. It ought to result in a hunger and thirst for literary culture, and such delicacy of taste as can discriminate between the valuable and the worthless. It ought to result, also, in such a comprehensive knowledge of the entire field, as will enable the pupil to make for himself the best choice of literary food. For the accomplishment of these ends, I know of no better course than that which has for some time been pursued in the

Albany Academy. It begins with half a year's work in English poetry, in which the chief aim is to cultivate, by constant reading and class conference, a power to appreciate the form and the spirit of true poetry. The biographies of authors, the chronology of works, in short, the history of the literature is utterly ignored, except so far as it seems to assist in cultivating a love for the literature itself.

Following this has come a year's work on the history, the criticism, the biography, and the reading of general English literature. As an indispensable aid to literary history, the general history of England has been studied; and, as essential to a clear understanding of both, the geography involved has been made a standing requirement. More and more the preparation of lessons has taken the form of intelligent and thoughtful reading. More and more the recitation has become simply a conference of teacher and pupils, in which an approximation to equal rights of speech and opinion has prevailed. More and more have the pupils seemed to reach below the surface, to seize upon the true spirit of literary study, and to show its results in broadened views and in useful information. In short, teacher and pupils have agreed that they were no longer playing at the study of literature, but were gathering a harvest full of value and of satisfaction.

When a pupil has acquired the ability to understand and interpret the words of others in oral speech and in written records, his further use for language must lie in the direction of oral and written expression. The problem of his instruction becomes simply that of teaching him to talk well and to write well. Whatever the method pursued, these ends must be kept steadily in view, and it must be distinctly remembered that the means by which these ends are accomplished are of no consequence, provided the ends themselves are attained. The spelling-book, the copy-book, the language lessons, the grammar, and the rhetoric are simply tools in the hands of the teacher. If the pupil can talk well and write well, when the teacher is through with him, and has not spent an undue amount of time in the process of learning, it is nobody's business whether he has followed the traditional course or not. If, when the teacher is done with him, he cannot talk well and write well, his instruction has not been successful, no matter how many books he has learned.

The two natural divisions of oral expression are conversation and oratory. Of these, the one which has received by far the greater attention in schools is oratory. The one which is by far the more generally useful to nine persons in ten is conversation. In fact, it seems as if the ability to converse well had been taken for granted. Were the assumption sustained by the fact, the course pursued would be commendable. But the fact is that ordinary pupils cannot tell well what they know and think, and that the teacher should in all the oral work of the school make a distinct effort to cultivate in his pupils the habit of clear, correct, and graceful expression. I have used the word *habit* advisedly. It cannot be emphasized too much. The rules and definitions of the books, the rich treasures of the dictionary, and the theoretical views he receives, are of no account to the pupil until they pass from knowledge into practice.

Accordingly, from the child's first entrance into school to the close of his college career, he should be taught and required to make all his answers and statements in correct, definite, and graceful language. His vocabulary should be enlarged by minute descriptions of the things which form a part of his daily life and conversation. It should be made familiar and flexible by constant use on all suitable subjects and occasions. He should be taught to tell in his own language the results of his observation and his reading. He should learn to discuss with candor and clearness ordinary subjects in his school work, and those less familiar in specially arranged contests. Above all, he should be required, in his ordinary recitations, to give without questions a clear, comprehensive, and graceful account of what he has learned and thinks on the topic assigned. He should be able, in a public examination, to tell without confusion what he knows of the work he claims to have performed.

Perhaps I am sketching an educational millenium with too free a hand. But it certainly seems a reasonable thing to ask, as the result of years of instruction. One thing, in all this demand, must not be forgotten. It is that a person's confidence in himself is essential to good oral expression on his part. Whatever exercises, therefore, tend to give him more ease, self-possession, and confidence in his own strength and grace, will directly aid him in oral expression. Declamation, recitation, gymnastics, and music — all have this effect, and are consequently very desirable for this reason, were they of no value in other directions. As a means of furnishing the mind with useful and inspiring thoughts and apt expressions, the memorizing of such passages of literature as seem best adapted to this end is greatly to be desired.

If a copious and ready vocabulary, and habits of accuracy in execution are vital in oral expression, what must we say of them in written expression, where every mark has a meaning, every imperfection is recorded, and where facility is scarcely less desirable than a perfect manuscript? The perverse tendency of instruction to be impractical has been peculiarly manifest in this branch of language-study. I have heard somewhere of a person who exhausted the wits of his friends by asking them to guess how another person had spelled the word " cat." After they had unsuccessfully stretched their imaginations to the utmost, and had in vain suggested all the permutations and combinations of the entire alphabet, he astonished and edified them by the information that the spelling to which he referred was c-a-t. Something like this has for many years been going on in the teaching of written language. The spelling-book has been crammed down the intellectual throats of pupils; they have been drilled in right curves, left curves, lines, and spaces; they have learned the rules and definitions of the grammar; they have parsed and analyzed ; they have corrected false syntax; they have learned with care the distinctions and the cautions of the rhetoric. They have not been required to write to a sufficient extent to make these formidable preparations of much value. At last it has occurred to some that it might be a good plan to set pupils to writing, and make the thing they were trying to teach the subject of instruction. And behold! the discovery has been heralded abroad as a "new education;" and, like most other new things, it is viewed with a degree of suspicion. But it is the true method. Time will both accomplish and vindicate its general adoption.

The old method of language-study concerned itself primarily with teaching the facts and the principles of expression, and largely neglected their habitual use. The new method concerns itself with their use, and acquires the facts and the principles because a knowledge of them is essential to good expression. Composition is made the basis of instruction; how much to continually improve it, is the problem. Hence the child must be required, from his first entrance into school, to write correctly, neatly, and promptly all work that admits of being written. After the teacher has made the written form of a word or a sentence, the beginner must learn to make it himself. The careful and exact copying of dictation exercises, reading lessons, and important portions of text-books, with all the recognized adjuncts of written expression, should be used to cultivate accuracy in details. After pupils have named and described the things which form a part of their daily life and conversation, they should be taught to write out these descriptions with such additions and improvements as more careful study may suggest.

To the progressive teacher there is no need of detailing subjects and devices. The written reproduction of interesting stories, conversations, and readings; the composition of original stories, suggested by pictures or passages of literature; accounts of journeys, meetings, and important public events — all these, and many others, are familiar. Readiness may be cultivated by impromptu compositions on easy subjects, for the writing of which ten or fifteen minutes are allowed. Accuracy and completeness of treatment will result from frequent written examinations, in which correctness and neatness of execution affect the standing. The world of art and the whole realm of nature are open to both teacher and pupil, and ever invite attention. The objects and parts of objects in the school-room will furnish materials for many interesting and valuable exercises. The useful and beautiful objects in the house, the garden, and the field will give an infinite range of subjects at once attractive and profitable. If these subjects were generally used in schools, the amazing ignorance of common things that prevails among the masses would cease. How many persons in an ordinary school district can tell even the names of the trees within its limits? How many know the habits of the birds that sing around their dwellings and fill the forests with music? Yet every school-boy spends time enough rambling over the fields to know every bird by name, to know its plumage, and its habits, and its song. Every plant and every flower, with their structure and their odor, might be familiar to him, if he were taught to observe them in his rambles and required to write about them daily in his school. It certainly seems that, by a proper arrangement of school-work, most pupils might, in addition to ordinary attainments, obtain a vast amount of knowledge concerning the objects around them. Well might we imitate some features of savage education.

"Then the little Hiawatha,
Learned of every bird its language,
Learned their names and all their secrets,
How they built their nests in summer,
Where they hid themselves in winter,
Talked with them whene'er he met them,
Called them 'Hiawatha's Chickens.'

"Of all beasts he learned the language,
Learned their names and all their secrets,—
How the beavers built their lodges,
Where the squirrels hid their acorns,

> How the reindeer ran so swiftly,
> Why the rabbit was so timid,—
> Talked with them whene'er he met them,
> Called them 'Hiawatha's Brothers.'"

If, in order to make room for such instruction, it were necessary to neglect the subjects at present taught, the case would be different; although it is by no means certain that no improvements could be made in the usual course of study. But, important as all this certainly is, it must not be forgotten that no teaching of language can be effective without persistent attention to the thousand and one details of form and use which cover the whole field of penmanship, spelling, grammar, and rhetoric. If the spelling class is to give way to a composition class, the composition class must see that spelling is not neglected. If the penmanship class is omitted, penmanship itself must still be taught. If the forms and uses of words are not taught in special language lessons or in the grammar class, they must be learned nevertheless, and the principles of expression must be habitually regarded, whether they are learned formally or informally. Unless this necessity of attention to details is continually kept in mind, the results cannot fail to be unsatisfactory. Every written exercise must be as perfect in execution as the pupil can make it. If he is not sure he knows how a word is spelled, he must find out before he writes it. If he is not sure what mark of punctuation is needed, he must find out; and he must be persistently held to the use of every mark in its proper place. His penmanship must invariably be plain, regular, and beautiful; and, to this end, should conform to the standard system. When special defects of any kind become prominent, they must receive such time and attention as they require. If they are too numerous or too important to be disposed of in the regular exercises, special exercises must be devoted to them. But such separate classes are not needed in the early stages of instruction, unless there are definite errors to be corrected; and, if there are, the instruction should be aimed directly at those errors.

When enough of such elementary work has been done to make the ordinary forms and uses of words and the ordinary means of expression familiar, and when the process of writing has become a mere matter of manual labor, the problem of composition ceases to be elementary and becomes a question of literary excellence. Then comes a demand for a complete and scientific knowledge of the language in all its details. Not simply its general structure, but its idioms, its niceties of word and phrase, and its critical interpretation, must be mastered by a thorough course of instruction in grammar and rhetoric.

The whole matter of advanced composition should be treated as literary work instead of school drudgery. Pupils should be encouraged to write from their own stand-points, and to assume toward their subjects the attitude of independent investigators. They should choose subjects in which they will feel an interest, and study them in all their branches and bearings. Above all, their work should be original; for whatever value their writings ever have, will be the result of either their own thinking or their own expression. If to literary freedom and refinement they can add instructive and attracttive drawings, their productions will have still further merit and value. To those who have never introduced this feature into composition work, the skill, the enthusiasm, and the benefit which result from it will be a surprise. That the methods here suggested are practical, experience has shown. That they, or others in the same spirit, may become general, ought to be the prayer of every friend of genuine education and of literary excellence

XI.
MEDICAL EDUCATION.—ITS OBJECTS AND REQUIREMENTS.

By Professor F. R. STURGIS, M. D.

I take it for granted that no dissent will be expressed to the proposition that education and training are needed to fit people for any work to which they propose to devote their lives, no matter how humble that work may be, and that the requisite amount of education varies only according to the nature and character of the work which is to be undertaken.

Although the truth of this self-evident proposition is theoretically admitted, practically it is not carried out in many walks of life, and in none is this more true than in the profession of medicine, where so many persons commence its study with insufficient preparation or previous education. As was once said of the English church, that when a man was unfit for any thing else he was always good enough to be a parson, so it may be said of medicine, if a man fails in every thing else, let him become a doctor. No previous education is required to prepare him to become a student of medicine; the curriculum of study is not very long in any of the schools, and there are many schools in which the final examination for M. D. is so superficial as to amount to very little more than a farce. If, perchance, he should find the examination too hard at the school where he has been studying, a very short time will suffice to allow him to present himself at some other school, where the examination is easier, and where he can obtain the coveted diploma which informs the world that he is a man learned in the art and science of medicine, and such is the latitude in the requirements of the different medical schools that he must be a hopeless blockhead if he cannot find some school which will vouch for him.

Should, however, he be denied by all the reputable schools, the case is not hopeless. Although he cannot legitimately obtain his diploma, he can buy one, and that after all is the easiest way of obtaining a license to practice medicine, saving time, trouble and money. Such a statement may sound startling, but it is nevertheless true, as those who will take the trouble to read the facts published in the Philadelphia *Record* upon the breaking up of the schools under the management of Drs. Buchanan, Paine and Miller will see. Nor is this impropriety in the granting of diplomas for the doctorate of medicine confined to the city of Philadelphia.

One prominent reason for this laxness in medical education is due to the facility with which charters are granted by legislators to any concern which calls itself an institution of learning, and this even is not always requisite. The laws of Massachusetts granted the Bellevue Medical College of Massachusetts the right to confer the degree of M. D., although the only law under which it was incorporated was the "public statutes relating to manufacturing and other corporations." This swindle was exposed in November, 1882, by the Illinois State Board of Health, and is so interesting in connection with this subject that I shall quote *in extenso* what is said about it from a work on "Medical Education," prepared by the Illinois Board of Health and published in Chicago.

"The exposure in November, 1882, by the Illinois State Board of Health of the fraudulent Bellevue Medical College of Massachusetts, led to the correction of a flagrant abuse in connection with the issuing of medical diplomas of Massachusetts. The 'Bellevue' was organized under the 'public statutes relating to manufacturing and other corporations,' and its officers, on the trial which resulted from the exposure above referred to, pleaded that they were legally incorporated, and were empowered by the laws of Massachusetts to issue diplomas and confer degrees without any restriction as to course of study or professional attainments. The United States Commissioner before whom the trial was had, held the plea to be valid, and dismissed the case with the following remarks:

"The State has authorized this college to issue degrees and it has been done according to legal right. The law makes the faculty of the college the sole judges of eligibility of applicants for diplomas. There are no legal restrictions, no legal requirements. *If the faculty choose to issue degrees to incompetent persons, the laws of Massachusetts authorize it.*

"As the natural result of this decision, the 'American University of Boston' and the 'First Medical College of the American Health Society,' were promptly incorporated under the same enactment as the 'Bellevue;' the 'Excelsior Medical College' and doubtless others were projected, and this new branch of manufacturing industry, which furnished the degree of Doctor of Medicine for $150, C. O. D., without study or lecture attendance, developed into rather startling proportions. It suddenly collapsed, however, under the passage (June 30, 1883) of an act forbidding any corporation, organized under the public statutes above referred to, from conferring medical degrees, or issuing diplomas or certificates conferring or purporting to confer degrees, unless specially authorized by the Legislature so to do."

Another reason for the growth of illegal schools of medicine is the want of care in allowing schools to be incorporated under laws which never contemplated the formation of medical schools, which is exemplified in the case of the Bellevue Medical College of Massachusetts just quoted, and in that of the United States Medical College of New York city, which latter school was incorporated under a law passed in 1848, entitled "An act for the incorporation of benevolent, charitable, scientific and missionary societies." This school was incorporated in 1878, and for six years was allowed to grant diplomas of Doctor of Medicine illegally, until the late Attorney-General of this State, Leslie Russell, Esq., upon representations furnished by the Medical Society of the county of New York, instituted proceedings against this school in the name of the People of the State of New York to show cause why the charter should not be declared illegal. The case was tried in two courts in New York city; both courts held that the college had never had a legal existence, and the case has lately been argued before the Court of Appeals of this State, which affirmed the decision of the other courts. The College of Physicians and Surgeons of Buffalo had a similar corporate existence and has also been declared illegal.

The above statements are made, not for the purpose of discussing the standing of the schools, but as introductory to what I have to say about medical education, by showing that the schools must first be shown to possess the necessary qualifications to teach medicine, and that if the teachers themselves are unworthy, it cannot be a matter of surprise if the education afforded by them is poor and defective. What then constitutes medical education ; what are its objects, and what is requisite to fulfil the condition embraced under the term? To bring the matter out clearly I shall arrange the subject under three heads:

First. The objects of a medical education ;

Second. The previous education requisite for commencing medical studies; and

Third. The best method of medical training.

If the student were asked to give an answer to the first question he would probably reply that it was to obtain a livelihood and this would be a perfectly natural and, under some restriction, a proper answer. None of us work from a pure love of work, merely because we are devoted to it; there must be some tangible result to be obtained, something in the shape of a reward to induce one to push on in spite of difficulties and discouragements toward the goal, else no one would work. But if this were the only incentive, then the minimum amount that is requisite to attain the object in view would suffice, and so long as the result was attained, it would matter little if the manner in which it were accomplished were good or bad. Now in medicine, it is important to bear in mind that something more than the mere obtaining a livelihood is to be effected, because another important factor comes into play here, to-wit : the preservation of human life and the care of human bodies. So well recognized is this that it has been formulated into the saying, that in nothing does man approach nearer to the gods than by conferring health upon mankind. Certainly in the doctor's hands, much responsibility lies, for to him we look to preserve the health of the community at large as well as of the individual, and it is of the first moment that he should be well equipped for his work, not in theory merely, but in practical knowledge. Nor can the preservation of human health be attained unless the means be equal to the end, and those means lie principally in the knowledge and skill which the physician can bring to bear on the problem, not only of curing disease, but of preventing sickness. The objects then which a medical education seeks to effect are the cure and prevention of disease ; teaching human beings to live in accordance with the dictates of prudence and in obedience to natural laws ; and in cases where sickness overtakes people, to show them the best means of overcoming the disease. In other words, its aims are practical ; and all scientific investigations, although at first they may seem to have no practical value, are really directed ultimately to this end, otherwise they would be an useless expenditure of time, trouble and money, without any excuse for existence. Take an old illustration, but one which is of value, as it has lived long enough to have demonstrated its usefulness — the discovery of the vaccine virus by Jenner, a country physician in Gloucestershire. By a proper use of his eyes he discovered an agency which was to become of the first importance as a means of checking the ravages of one of the most mortal diseases with which the human race is afflicted. This gentleman, a pupil of John Hunter, whose name is honored where-ever medical science is cultivated, and whose method of teaching lay in directing his pupils to use their eyes and their brains, observed, what others had noticed before, that the milk-maids of his section of England were frequently liable to be affected with pustules of the hands, contracted from milking cows affected with the cow-pox, and that they were not liable to contract small-pox. They seemed to be safe against infection. He, in his letters to his old master, John Hunter, mentioned this fact, and the latter urged him to investigate the subject. This he did, with the result of presenting the world with the inestimable boon of vaccination. Take the recent investigations of Koch with the bacilli of consumption and cholera, and of Pasteur with the various animal poisons, more especially of hydrophobia and the germ theories of disease. Although the facts are still under further investigation, and perhaps subject to modification from the accepted results, they will undoubtedly all tend in but one direction, the alleviation of sickness and modifying the virulence of diseases, if not their eradication. These, then, are the objects to be sought for by a medical education, and all the training and all the teaching should be in the direction of using eyes, brain, and indeed every faculty with which man is endowed. The mere perfunctory listening to a certain number of lectures and the cramming to obtain a license to practice medicine is not a medical education; it may turn out a learned blockhead, but it will never make a physician.

Second. Is a preliminary training requisite to enable the intending physician to get the most out of education in medicine? Were I to depend upon the announcements of the schools of medicine in this country, I should say *no!* No previous education is necessary, beyond an ability to read and write, the former because the student will have to use some books, and the latter because the physician will have to write prescriptions. Beyond these two acquirements, the less the medical student knows the better, perhaps; at any rate, his ignorance on other matters will not be a bar to his gaining a diploma. Perhaps this statement will be greeted with the stare of incredulity, but I think you will admit that this is a fair exposition of the case after reading a paper read by Dr. Albert Gihon of the United States Navy, upon this subject before the American Medical Association in 1883, and which shows how ignorant medical men, men who are graduated from reputable medical schools in this country, are of such a simple matter as orthography. Mistakes in spelling are made which would put a school-boy to blush, and which are inexcusable in men of a liberal education, in fact disgraceful. I am sorry to say that I can corroborate the facts contained in Dr. Gihon's paper as the result of the examination for positions as assistant surgeons in the navy; for in my capacity as secretary to a school for medical instruction, I sometimes receive queerly spelled letters from graduates of reputable schools of medicine. So much attention has lately been directed to this subject that some schools of medicine require a preliminary education, at least they claim to, in their prospectuses, but when this claim is examined closely it is found but too often to be a sham instead of a reality. Let me lay before you some of these requirements, and I will take them at random from the book on medical education from which I have already quoted.

There are now one hundred and twenty-three medical institutions of all kinds in the United States; of these, eighty, or a little over sixty per cent, claim to require a preliminary examination of their students, but it is of such a superficial character, or the requirements are so carelessly carried out, as to amount to nothing. For example, at the medical department of Yale College the requirements for examination are (a) a degree in letters or sciences; (b) passage of examination for admission to some college; or (c) examination in mathematics, including algebra, geometry, the metric system of weights and measures, and elementary physics.

It does not specify who is to conduct these examinations, and the requirements are not very useful to the intending medical student, physics really being the only necessary thing in the examination.

The Rush Medical College of Chicago requires for admission, a matriculation examination, which will include the writing of a brief paper on a subject to be given; and an examination in the elementary principles of physics and mathematics as taught in the public schools of the country. The written paper will be sufficient indication of the student's knowledge of orthography, as well as the subject given. Graduates of a " literary or scientific college, academy or high school, or who have passed the entrance examination to a literary college in good standing; or persons having a State or county teacher's certificate; or graduates in medicine; or previous matriculates of this college; or students who desire to pursue a special course of study — other than for the purpose of securing the degree — will be exempt from examination. Students who have completed a full course of study equivalent to that required for admission to this college, may, by special arrangement, be admitted on the certificates of their instructors."

This is too vague, and the last clause is objectionable; it looks like opening a wide door for shirking the examination.

The Chicago Medical College (Medical Department of the Northwestern University) requires for admission, "a certificate of graduation from a literary college, academy or scientific school, or satisfactory evidence, through matriculation examination, of a good English education."

This is too vague. What is meant by a good English education?

The Indiana Eclectic Medical College thinks that for admission "Every student must possess a good English education, including mathematics, English composition and elementary physics. A diploma from a high school or college is preferred."

It is significantly stated under the head of "Remarks": "At the April, 1883, meeting of the Illinois State Board of Health, charges against this college being under consideration, it was resolved that its diploma would be recognized in the future by said Board whenever and so long as it shall appear that its methods and practices entitle it to such recognition," showing that its practices and its theories did not strictly conform with one another.

I have picked out these cases at hap-hazard to show that any of these so-called requirements amount to nothing. Very many schools, and not the poor ones either, require nothing in the way of examination of the candidates, prior to commencing the study of medicine. From these cases it is evident that the requirements are not made to be stringent; indeed, one school naively admits as much. It is the Hahneman Medical College and Hospital of Chicago, Illinois, whose requirements for admission are as follows: "Upon application for admission each student must possess a good moral character, and must present to the registrar satisfactory evidence of a good English education. Such as are graduates of a literary or scientific college, academy or high school, or who have passed the entrance examination to a literary college in good standing; * * * who have a county or State teacher's certificate; graduates in medicine; previous matriculates in this college; and students who desire to pursue a special course of study — other than for the purpose of securing the degree — will be exempt from this requirement, providing they furnish this documentary evidence to the registrar. Students who have completed a full course of study equivalent to that required for admission to this college may, by special arrangement, be admitted on the certificate of their instructors. It is not intended to make this a critical examination; but what is required and insisted upon is, that every student shall possess a fair English education."

Pray, what is the use of an examination if it is not to be critical? What is the use of having any? The whole announcement reads like a clever piece of chicanery; the object being to make the examination a mere perfunctory work, while it would seem to be in the interest of higher medical education. In plain English it is a fraud. And this is the position of many others, although they are not frank or stupid enough to openly acknowledge it.

But there are some schools of medicine which really try to make their practice and profession tally; which really try to find out what the future student of medicine knows before admitting him or her to the study of medicine, and of these the most noticeable are the Halifax Medical College, the Johns-Hopkins University, and the Medical Department of Harvard University. Let us, for a few moments, examine the requirements of these three schools.

The Halifax school requires "for admission, (a) diploma of a recognized university in arts; or, (b) matriculation examination on the following compulsory subjects: English language, including grammar, composition and writing from dictation. Arithmetic, including vulgar and decimal fractions, and the extraction of the square root. Algebra, to the end of simple equations. Geometry, first three books of Euclid. Latin, one book, translation and grammar. Elementary mechanics of solids and fluids, and one of the following optional subjects, viz.: History of England with questions in modern geography; French translation; German translation; one Greek book · History of Nova Scotia; History of the Dominion of Canada."

The requirements of the Johns-Hopkins University are quite elaborate — perhaps needlessly so. They are as follows:

"Three classes of students are admitted to this preparatory course" (to the study of medicine). "First, graduate students without special examination; second, matriculated students; third, special students. The first and third classes are permitted to follow the biological instruction, in part or in their entire range. Special students are those who are not prepared at admission for full matriculation, but who desire to enter upon a three years' course of scientific instruction. They are admitted to the privileges of the University, out of deference to the custom which has heretofore prevailed in this country, of requiring no preliminary examination of those entering upon the study of medicine; but they cannot compete for the degree of A. B. This arrangement, therefore, is a sort of compromise of a temporary nature, and which will pass away with the changes and improvements that time will make in our methods. Nevertheless, the indulgence to this class is only partial, and there is laid down for it an entrance examination in elementary mathematics in Latin, English (including a written composition), French, German and drawing. Matriculates — that is, those who are candidates for the degree of A. B. — are required to pass an entrance examination of a much more rigid character on the same subjects, and in addition upon Greek (a thorough knowledge of French and German will be accepted as a substitute for this), history and the elements of physics, chemistry, physical geography, botany and physiology; this examination is common to all candidates for the degree of A. B. in each of the seven collegiate courses."

"The full course preparatory to medicine — the full length will vary somewhat, according to the student's ability and industry, but 'rarely, if ever, will be completed in less than three years after matriculation' — embraces English, German, French, logic, ethics, psychology, physical geography, ancient history, vocal culture, physical culture, the theory of accounts, physical chemistry and biology; the last, the study of living things, animals and vegetable, in their forms and functions' — is the dominant subject of the course, but the design is to give such liberal culture as will avoid a one-sided or narrow development."

"Opportunities are here afforded to a young man, who expects at a later day to take up the study of medicine, to become proficient in laboratory work while acquiring a knowledge of French and German and continuing his general education. A course is arranged in which physics for the first year, chemistry for the second, and the biological study of plants and animals for the third year, are the dominant topics. At the close of this course the student should have become proficient in the knowledge of the physical and chemical laws which underlie the conditions of life; he should have become familiar with the structure and functions of living things, in their normal and healthy conditions; he should have become skilled in the use of the microscope and other physiological apparatus; and so, when he enters the school of medicine, he should know that he has been well prepared for the study of diseases and of its treatment, by a training in the fundamental sciences, which has not only exercised his eye and hand, but has accustomed his mind to accurate habits of observation and inquiry."

The entrance examination required by the Medical Department of Harvard University is not so stringent, but still it is fair and I hope will be still further improved as time goes on. The following are the requirements: " For admission, all candidates, excepting those who have passed an examination for admission to Harvard University, must present a degree in letters or science from a recognized college or scientific school, or pass an examination in the following subjects: (a) Every candidate shall be required to write, legibly and correctly, an English composition of not less than two hundred words, and also to write English prose from dictation; (b) The translation of easy Latin prose; (c) A competent knowledge of physics; (d) Each candidate shall pass an approved examination in such one of the following branches as he may select: French, German, the elements of algebra, plane geometry, or botany."

I have taken these examples of medical schools which require and those which do not require any preliminary education prior to the study of medicine with a purpose. When we come to examine the question of preliminary education in medicine in this State, we shall find some things which are good and some things which are bad, and in order to suggest improvements or modifications we must know what other schools are doing in order to pick out and to assimilate what will be for our benefit and reject what we cannot use with advantage. Besides which, we wish to know if certain changes in the manner of teaching medicine are feasible or not, and it is fair to suppose that what other States do, we can also do. Let us now turn to New York State and see what the condition is here. In the first place, one thing strikes us at once—there is a lack of system in medical education; the instruction given varies widely. One school gives good instruction; its neighbor gives very poor teaching, and both stand equal in the eye of the law. Not only that; a school sells its diploma without any instruction being given, or if the farce of giving any is carried out, it is of the most perfunctory kind. And yet the diploma of that school is legally good and stands on a par, in the eye of the law, with the diploma of the good school. Now this is all wrong; such a strict supervision should be kept over all the schools that no one of them should be allowed to turn out men who have received a defective medical education. So long as the medical schools are private corporations, owned and controlled by the faculties of the schools, it is useless to expect that the corporation is going to cut its throat to gratify what many of its members think are the whims of doctrinaires, who know nothing about examining men for a degree, nor are possessed of the capacity for teaching. Indeed, judging from the utterances of some of the professors in the medical schools, nine-tenths of the wisdom, learning and ability in the medical world is concentrated in their schools and when it is suggested that there is something rotten in Denmark, they, with one accord, deny it, and say that such a thing is impossible. Now as regards the requirements demanded of the student in medicine. The three principal schools in the city of New York — those which rank as the best — the College of Physicians and Surgeons of the city of New York; the Bellevue Hospital Medical College, and the Medical Department of the University of the city of New York,— demand nothing of their students in the way of requirements. Those which claim to demand some preparatory knowledge on the part of their students are, the Albany Medical College, the Medical Department of the University of Buffalo, the Long Island College Hospital, the New York Medical College and Hospital for Women, the Woman's Medical College of the New York Infirmary, and the College of Medicine of Syracuse University. Some of these requirements are fair, others are worthless. The only colleges which can be considered as really demanding any thing from the candidates for medical instruction are the Albany Medical College, the Woman's Medical College of New York Infirmary, and the College of Medicine of Syracuse University. In the former, (a) graduates from recognized colleges, scientific schools or medical institutions, and (b) students presenting certificates of competency from the censors of the medical society of the county from which they come, will not be required to pass the preliminary examination on joining the school ; (c) all others will be required to pass examinations by a page written at the time, of which the orthography, grammatical construction and penmanship will be considered, and in arithmetic, grammar, geography and elementary physics."

The Woman's Medical College examination is by all odds the most thorough test of the student's qualifications for the study of medicine of any college in this State, as will readily be seen from the following extract from its requirements: "For admission, students entering the graded college course, unless they bring a diploma from some recognized literary school, will be required to pass a preliminary examination in the following branches : 1. Orthography, English composition and penmanship, by means of a page written at the time and place of examination. 2. Definitions and synonyms as found in 'The Scholar's Companion.' 3. Latin, through declensions and conjugations. 4. Arithmetic, in denominate numbers, fractions, proportions, percentage and the roots. 5. Algebra, Davies' Elementary, through simple equations. 6. Geometry, Davies' Legendre, first and second books. 7. Botany, physics and chemistry, as found in 'Science Primers,' edited by Professors Huxley, Roscoe and Balfour Stewart." This is the best and most practical preliminary examination which is given by any school of medicine in this State, and it is to be regretted that it should have been left to women to be the pioneers in this matter.

The requirements of the other colleges may be regarded rather in the light of evasion of a test of qualification than as serious attempts to find out what the future student of medicine knows. Thus the New York Medical College and Hospital for Women demands that the student on admission shall be eighteen years of age, shall have a good moral character, and shall be examined in the English branches before the faculty. But how many or how few "English branches," or what constitutes "English branches," is not stated.

The University of Buffalo (Medical Department) requires for admission "a certificate from the student's preceptor of his moral character, and that he is duly entered and properly qualified to study medicine. The responsibility of sufficient preliminary education rests, of necessity, with the private instructor." This seems to me like a plain shirking of responsibility. It is the duty of the school to find out if the intending student knows enough to commence the study of medicine, and this responsibility cannot and does not rest with the instructor. The school, after having examined him, is the one to decide this point. But the crowning glory in this farce of how not to have any requirements, while pretending to have them, is reached by the Long Island College Hospital. This school has the following requirements: "The faculty earnestly desire to co-operate with the profession in securing a higher grade of preliminary education before students enter professional studies; but until some uniform grade is agreed upon by the leading colleges of the country, the responsibility of such qualifications must rest with the private instructor. For the purpose of testing the general literary qualifications of the students before graduation, frequent written examinations will be required hereafter throughout the whole course of instruction, and these examinations will enter into the graduation of the student on his final examination."

We have now gone over the review of the schools which require or claim to require a preliminary examination of their students, and we have seen in what those requirements consist. Some are good and some are poor. Let us discuss for a few minutes what of these various requirements are necessary and what can be dispensed with. In the first place, I suppose we will all admit that reading, writing and spelling the English language are necessary, and the need of a proper acquaintance with these branches is so evident as not to require any extended discussion. But when we come to a knowledge of the dead languages, there is a wide diversity of opinion. Some teachers contend that what little knowledge is requisite can be picked up by the student while he is studying medicine, and many argue that no knowledge is necessary, because the Latin names and terms can be learned like any new word, without any acquaintance with the language from which it is derived. To such opinion I dissent most heartily. In the first place, education is not teaching a man to repeat words and phrases like a parrot, and for the proper use and application of the Latin terms which enter into medicine, some knowledge of the frame-work of the language is necessary. If this were more insisted upon, we should not hear medical men talking of the *labium major*, nor of the *fenestrum ovalis*, nor see, as I have seen, written upon a diploma *Novi Yorkensi* as the Latin name for our city of New York. Let me hasten to say that this latter was from an eclectic school; but, I regret to say, the regulars are not a whit behind their eclectic brethren in ignorance. It may be said that the physician who writes *labium major* may still be able to practice medicine acceptably, and be a worthy member of the profession. He may do routine work perfectly well, and do it as well as nine-tenths of his professional brethren, but is he likely to advance the knowledge of his art, or to pay that debt which Lord Bacon held that every man owed to his profession? Another point: the man should not be wasting his time, which should be devoted to other things, in picking up information or knowledge with which he ought to be acquainted beforehand. It is not requisite that a man to study medicine should be a profound Latin scholar, but there is a great difference between this and absolute ignorance of the fundamentals of a language which he is obliged to use every day of his life. With that, I think, he should have some acquaintance; hence the Latin language should be required of the future student of medicine sufficiently, at least, to enable him to read easy prose, such as the first two books of Cæsar's Gallic war, and to decline nouns and adjectives and to conjugate verbs. Beyond that it would not be necessary to go. As regards Greek, there is not the same need for the student to be conversant with this language, as it will not enter so largely into his studies, and may therefore be reserved as an optional branch. The modern languages are now coming so much to the front in general use, and so much is done in medical circles by the French, German and Italian physicians, that a man can hardly be considered as a well-equipped physician who is ignorant of all these languages; a knowledge of one of them should be required of the future physician, and in view of the large number of our German fellow-citizens who may need the attention of the coming medical man, as well as the ease with which the language can be acquired in this country, it would be well to insist upon at least a reading acquaintance with this tongue. An ability to read and to correctly translate German should be one of the requisites for entrance upon the study of medicine. A knowledge of physics is another subject with which the student should be familiar, in order to properly understand the diseases of the eye and ear, as well as the correct treatment of fractures and dislocations.

Chemistry (organic and inorganic) is another requirement. In this branch the student should be well grounded, both theoretically, and practically by work in the laboratory, as by this he can devote his time more thoroughly to the study of medical chemistry, which will be needed to enable him to study physiology to better advantage. The same may be said of botany, with a view to its bearing upon the study of materia medica and of therapeutics. Thus far, then, the list of requirements comprises a knowledge of Latin and German, reading, writing and spelling English, physics, chemistry (theoretical and practical), and botany. But there are other subjects in which the future student of medicine should be well taught, viz.: Arithmetic, which he will need every time he writes a prescription, and some knowledge of geometry, to enable him to properly study regional and surgical anatomy. These, then, should be necessities, and I do not think that any of these branches here enumerated can be charged with being superfluities. There is no objection to the medical student knowing other things such as history, as required by the Toronto school, or the branches enumerated in the curriculum of the Johns-Hopkins University, but these are refinements and luxuries, and in presenting this paper to the notice of my professional brethren, my aim has been to present subjects which are not only necessary but which are feasible, and not above what every man of average intelligence and education should be prepared in. Now as to optional studies, should any be required? I think so, for although the list above given embraces nearly all that should be exacted of the future medical student it does not include every thing which is necessary. An acquaintance with some other branches of learning, then, should be added from which the student may select. The optional courses should be comparative anatomy and physiology, Greek, French and Italian. The first branch is in the direct line of their future studies, and by a knowledge of it the students can give more time to the study of the other portions of their medical curriculum. The knowledge of French and Italian, at least a reading knowledge of these tongues, will be of infinite use to the future medical man, the more so as medicine is getting day by day to be a catholic profession, ignoring such distinction as differences of tongue or country, and it behooves the medical man to know what is being done by his brethren in other countries, unless he himself wants to be overshadowed in the struggle which is daily going on in the profession of medicine. Two, then, of these optional branches should be made obligatory. The list then would stand:

Obligatory — Latin, reading of easy Latin prose, Cæsar's Commentaries on the Gallic war, first two books. Written composition to show proper construction of sentences and a knowledge of orthography and syntax.

English — Read English Prose, Macaulay's Essays. Written composition, showing knowledge of orthography and syntax.

German — Schiller, such as Wallenstein, or the Thirty Years' War.

Physics — Atkinson's translation of Ganot's Physics, or some equally good text-book.

Chemistry — Brande and Taylor's Chemistry, or Bloxam's Chemistry, inorganic and organic.

Botany — Gray's Botany, or Wood's Class-Book of Botany.

Arithmetic — Colburn's, or an equally good arithmetic.

Geometry — Pierce's Geometry, first thirteen chapters, or Davies' Legendre, first two books.

Optional — Two of the following branches:

Greek — Goodwin and Allen's, or Felton's Greek Reader.

French — La Fontaine's Fables, or Molière's Le Bourgeois Gentilhomme.

Italian — Dante's Inferno; first two books.

Comparative Anatomy, etc. — Owen's Comparative Anatomy of the vertebrates; Owen's Comparative Anatomy of the invertebrates.

Thus far the future student of medicine has merely advanced to the threshold of his desired profession, he has only been prepared for the course of study which is to result in his diploma of Doctor of Medicine, and although the requirements here urged may seem great as compared with what is demanded of the present race of students, it is no more than every student of medicine ought to be prepared with. Being thus fitted before their entrance into the medical school, it would save so much of that elementary instruction which is the bane of good teaching and the discouragement of the teacher, who going upon the supposition that his men know something about the rudiments of their future profession, attempts to teach them something more advanced, only to meet with the reproof of the Dean of his Faculty that he is shooting above the heads of his students; or else he has the mortification to see the benches empty and his hearers depart to listen to a teacher who gives them something easy to understand. To carry out such a course of preliminary examination as is here sketched out would undoubtedly restrain some who now become students of medicine, and would undoubtedly thin out the large classes of some schools, but with those points we have nothing to do. No man should be allowed to study medicine without receiving a thoroughly good preliminary training, nor would the loss of such untrained men be any detriment to the profession, and certainly as regards the schools it would be little loss to any, except the faculties of the schools themselves, if half of the present schools were swept out of existence.

The third point for consideration is: What is the best method of medical training?

In this country the larger part of the education which a medical man receives is purely didactic — that is, one derived from lectures; and in those few cases where the instruction is called clinical, the opportunities for each student to see and to examine the cases for himself are so small that clinical teaching becomes more or less of a farce. A certain amount of didactic teaching is, of course, necessary, but so much more can be taught and better taught from the exhibition and examination of cases, that clinical teaching must always form the basis of a good medical education. The recognition of this fact has, within the past few years, done much to revolutionize the method of instruction given, but even with all the advances made in medical teaching, clinical instruction is yet in its infancy in this country. But let us take up the didactic side of a medical education first. Most of the schools of medicine make the lecture courses a prominent feature of their curriculum, and these courses are given with but slight variation to all grades of students alike, to the man in his first year as well as the one just ready to come up for his examination for the degree of M. D. There is no gradation; no method of adjusting the course of instruction to the requirements or the fitness of the student. The novice is often instructed in obstetrics or surgery, before he is acquainted with the anatomy of the parts concerned in the branches in which he is being instructed. Now this is all wrong. It is as though a boy were set to reading Virgil before he has been taught the grammatical construction of the sentences he is called upon to parse, or the groundwork of the language he is required to read and understand. In other branches of learning the student is carried up step by step, but in medicine he is turned in to the study of his profession without having acquired the elementary branches which he must first learn before proceeding to the higher ones. It would be well, then, if every school would institute graded courses of instruction, and insist that no student shall be promoted from one grade to the next higher until he has passed an examination to prove his fitness for the advance. In that way the student would be duly prepared to receive instruction with the most advantage to himself, and students who have already gone over the ground would not be obliged to listen to matter with which they were already acquainted. A graded course then should be insisted upon and the number of grades would depend upon the number of years which the school decided upon requiring before allowing the student to come up for his final examination. The minimum time should be three years spent at some recognized medical school, and instruction with a preceptor should not be allowed as part of the time, for in a large proportion of cases such instruction is a sham. Neither should the student coming from some other school be allowed time on any of the branches taught at the school which he may then be about to attend until he has passed an examination in all the branches taught in the lower grades corresponding to the time allowance which he asks for. Thus, if a student wished to be granted a year's allowance, this can be done only upon the condition of his passing a satisfactory examination in all the subjects of the first year; if he wants two years' allowance, upon those studies of the two years for which he seeks the allowance. But no student should be granted more than two years' allowance of time, and then only after passing a satisfactory examination as specified above.

Now as regards the number of courses and the instruction to be given during those courses. As has already been stated, three years should be the minimum time exacted for a medical course, and it would be much better to make it four. Let us take four years then as the length of time required. The first year should be devoted to the study of anatomy (with dissections), normal histology, physiology and medical chemistry, with laboratory work included, and at the end of the year, the student should be examined as to his fitness to be advanced to the second year's course. Nor should he be allowed to move up until he has passed the examination satisfactorily; the second year should be given to the study of pathology and pathological anatomy and histology, materia medica and medical botany, surgery, clinical as well as operative; the third year, to theory and practice of medicine with therapeutics, obstetrics and gynæcology, and diseases of children; and the fourth year, to nervous and mental diseases, ophthalmology and otology venereal and skin diseases, hygiene and forensic medicine. As has been already stated, annual examinations should be held for each of the four grades, but in addition to these, another examination, general in its scope, should be held for the degree of M. D. which should embrace the whole ground gone over in the four years. In this respect the plan here proposed would differ from the courses given at Harvard, where the examinations are "distributed over the entire course instead of being held at the end of the period of study." The examination at the end of each year's study should all be written, but the one for the degree of M. D. should be both written and oral, and in addition, the student should be obliged to make a clinical examination of a patient in both medicine and surgery, furnishing a written diagnosis of a given case, together with a plan of treatment. The term should also be lengthened as it is at Harvard, and made of forty weeks' duration, divided into two terms of twenty weeks each, with six weeks intermission. Besides this curriculum which is purely ante-graduate, every well-equipped school should afford ample opportunites for post-graduate instruction; by that I mean for advanced instruction to graduates in medicine. Almost every branch of medical knowledge will admit of advanced instruction being given, more especially in the domains of surgery, histology, both pathological and normal, hygiene, mental diseases, and gynæcology.

In surgery alone, the fields of ophthalmology and otology, skin, venereal and genito-urinary diseases would amply repay minute and extended study, and the same is equally true of other branches.

Heretofore, medical men, desiring to follow a certain line of study have been compelled to go abroad to do so; there is no good reason for this, except that heretofore the facilities for giving advanced instruction have not been sufficiently utilized, but of late years the faculty has waked up to the possibilities of giving courses similar to those given abroad, and it is to be hoped that the beginning which has been made in this and other cities will be not only extended but improved upon. There is plenty of material and there are capable teachers enough for the work.

Is there any thing in the plan laid down in this article which is utopian and impossible of fulfilment? I do not think so. I believe it to be perfectly feasible. At first the effect might be to prevent many men, who could not come up to the standard marked out, to abandon the idea of studying medicine, but I do not think this would be an injury, because those who would be deterred from the study are those whom the profession of medicine could well spare. I do not believe that the Medical Departments of either Harvard University or the University of Pennsylvania have suffered in the long run, for want of students because they have raised the standard of requirements by having preliminary examinations and graded and longer courses, and I do not believe that any good school would suffer elsewhere. If, then, it is only the weak or disreputable schools which are to be the sufferers, then the sooner some effective plan of weeding is adopted, the better for the community, the profession of medicine, and the reputable schools themselves. For after all it is not a multitude of schools that is wanted, although there is no objection to them provided they are all good and of equal standing as schools of instruction, but well-equipped ones — schools which can give thorough and systematic teaching.

One more point remains for consideration; that is, how can the method of study be made uniform? If left to the schools themselves nothing would be done, on the principle that what is everybody's business is nobody's business. Nor is this meant as a slur on the schools. No reforms or changes are ever instituted until there is a general demand for them, and certainly the medical schools could hardly be expected to carry out changes which might not be to their immediate advantage, merely to gratify what many of them conceive to be a sentiment. But if there were some central body having the necessary authority to enforce a certain standard of medical tuition, the difficulty would be at once met. And this standard should be a minimum one, below which no school can go, but above which they can, if they choose to ; the central body should see to it that the schools come up to the required standard, and if they did not, that they should be debarred from teaching. The public would then know that every medical man had been educated up to a certain standard at any rate, and that no absolutely ignorant person was in practice. Such a body, to whom these powers could be delegated, now exists in this State, in the Regents of the University of the State of New York. Then if, in addition to this, the license to practice medicine and surgery were separated from the possession of a diploma, and this right granted solely by a board having no interest in passing men except upon their merits — by a board, in other words, of State examiners, such safeguards would be established as to preclude ignorant and dangerous persons from practising medicine, and they would redound to the advantage of the lay public as well as of the practitioners of medicine.

XII.
REPORT OF THE COMMITTEE ON NECROLOGY

By Principal JOHN E. BRADLEY, Chairman, Albany High School.

It has been the sad duty of your committee to record, during the year an unusually large number of deaths among the present or former members of the Convocation — many of them of men prominently associated with the interests of education in this State. From the active discharge of the duties of his position and from frequent and most welcome participation in the exercises of the Convocation, we mourn the loss of Professor Benjamin N. Martin; from among those formerly connected with the institutions here represented, we note the removal of ex-President Simeon North of Hamilton College, and Dr. J. C. Gallup, ex-principal of the Clinton Classical School; while from the eminent men of science identified by position or otherwise with the Convocation, we record the names of Arnold Henry Guyot, Elisha Harris and Jacob S. Mosher. Other men of conspicuous usefulness, beloved and honored in their various fields and departments of labor, have also passed away; among them Professor Arthur Spielman of the New York University; Dr. Samuel G. Taylor, late principal of the Adelphi Academy, Brooklyn; Professor M. P. Costin of St. John's College; Henry Bannister, formerly principal of Cazenovia Seminary; Professor E. D. Blakeslee of the Potsdam Normal School and Rev. Dr. Seigmund of Grace Church, New York, formerly professor of Latin at Hobart College. Other deaths among the educational workers of the State, less immediately connected with the Convocation, are those of Orlando Meads, trustee of the Albany Academy; John A. Gillett, classical teacher in the Union School at Waterloo; General S. D. Hungerford, founder of the Hungerford Collegiate Institute; V. C. Douglass, superintendent of schools at Oswego; Samuel A. Bowen, president of board of education at Cooperstown; Alonzo M. Winchester, president of board of education at Sodus, and Thomas Kinsella, for many years president of the board of education of Brooklyn.

REV. DR. SIMEON NORTH.

By Professor EDWARD NORTH of Hamilton College.

Born in Berlin, Connecticut, September 7, 1802; united with the First Congregational Church in Middletown, Connecticut, in May, 1818; graduated from Yale College in 1825; graduated from Yale College Divinity School in 1828; tutor in Yale College, 1827-9; professor of Greek and Latin languages in Hamilton College, 1829-39; married, April 21, 1835, Frances Harriet Hubbard, who died January 21, 1881; elected fifth president of Hamilton College in 1839; trustee of Auburn Theological Seminary, 1840-49; ordained at Winfield, New York, by the Oneida Association in May, 1842; received LL. D. from Western Reserve College in August, 1842; orator of Connecticut Alpha of Phi Beta Kappa in 1847; received S. T. D. from Wesleyan University in August, 1849; resigned the presidency of Hamilton College in 1857; half-century analyst of Hamilton Alumni in 1879; died on College Hill, February 9, 1884; buried in Hamilton College Cemetery, February 12, 1884.

At the last annual meeting of the trustees of Hamilton College, the following memorial minute was reported by Hon. Theodore W. Dwight, and adopted as an expression of respect:

Rev. Dr. Simeon North held special and peculiar relations to Hamilton College as professor, president and trustee.

As professor of Greek and Latin he exhibited profound and earnest scholarship, and exacted of. his students thorough acquirement. He set himself resolutely against superficial attainment. Thoroughly appreciating the niceties of Greek and Latin construction, he was also alive to the poetic or literary sentiment, the grace and charm in the style of his favorite authors.

In his character as president, he has left behind him most reverent and tender memories. We recognize the difficulties of his position in a faculty so organized that he had no more power than the humblest of his associates, while he bore in the eye of the public nearly all the responsibility of the college government. The administration of President North was characterized by steadiness of action, warmth of kindly feeling, a generous appreciation of the student's position, a true soundness of judgment, and practical wisdom in disposing of difficult questions as they arose. His surviving students, without exception, profoundly esteem his great excellencies of character and revere his memory.

As a friend and a man, his qualities were excellent and rare. He possessed true gentleness and simplicity of character, a sincerity and steadiness of friendship which deeply attached to him all who had the privilege to know him.

For many years the late president had withdrawn from active life, and yet from his post of observation he looked out upon the affairs of men with a most intelligent and interested spirit. He never failed to remember a former student, nor to take a special and kindly interest in his success in life.

Dr. North held a high rank as a preacher, and exemplified in his daily life the finest qualities of an exalted Christian character. His death severed the last link that connected Hamilton College with Yale College, whose early methods of instruction and discipline he carefully copied. To his influence much is due for the firm hold which classical studies have taken in the institution to which he gave twenty-eight years of faithful service.

> Twice twenty years of prayerful toil,
>   And where is all their garnered gold?
> Full eighty years in mortal coil,
>   And where is all their struggle told?
>
> No bank could store the priceless gain
>   Wrested from agonies and ills;
> No rhyme could tell the joyful pain
>   Of triumphs bathed in tears and smiles.
>
> Long summer's alchemy transmutes
>   To gold the plowman's anxious sweat;
> Autumn's gay leaves and blushing fruits
>   Enrich the laborer's coronet.
>
> The elm that sees its aged form
>   Glassed in the bright Oriskany,
> Hoards strength from sunshine and fierce storm
>   For loftier commune with the sky.

Rev. BENJAMIN N. MARTIN, D. D., L. H. D.

By Professor JOHN J. STEVENSON of the University of the City of New York.

Benjamin Nicholas Martin, born at Mount Holly, New Jersey, on October 20, 1816, was graduated from Yale College with the class of 1837. He made profession of Christian faith while at college, and immediately after his graduation entered the theological seminary at New Haven.

After completing his course at the seminary, in 1840, he supplied for nearly two years the pulpit of the Carmine Street Presbyterian Church, New York, now known as the West or Forty-second Street Church. He then became pastor of the First (or Russell) Congregational Church of Hadley, Massachusetts, where he remained until 1847. His labors were attended with marked success in both charges, and his memory is still cherished affectionately by the older families of each congregation. During his stay in New York he married Miss Louisa C. Strobel. As the climate of Hadley proved unsuited to Mrs. Martin's health, he resigned the charge in 1847, and in 1848 became pastor of the Fourth Presbyterian Church of Albany. This was his last ministerial settlement.

After little more than a year Mr. Martin gave up the pastorate, but he remained in Albany for nearly three years longer. These were the years which really made the man. While serving as pastor and preacher he had devoted himself earnestly to theology and metaphysics; but between 1848 and 1852, he was thrown much with scientific men at Albany, and he made full use of the opportunities thus afforded for gratifying his native bent toward natural science. These were busy years; he studied, he wrote, he preached; proofs of his labors were found in the journals, the reviews, and in the pulpit.

In 1852, he was called by the University of the City of New York to fill the chair of logic and philosophy, which then covered nearly every branch of mental and moral science, and of political science, as well as of literature and history. He succeeded the erratic, but encyclopedic, Dr. C. S. Henry.

From that date to the day of his death Professor Martin's name was prominent in every good work, and his influence was felt in all directions. His energies were not confined to the discharge of his duties as professor. In many cases his was the unseen hand that did the work, while men of national fame were placed in the front. He cared nothing for the reputation; he sought only the results.

But in later years he could no longer work in the less prominent positions, and, much against his will, oftentimes he was compelled to accept the prominent place to which his services had rendered him entitled. When stricken down he was an effective worker in the Evangelical Alliance, the American and Foreign Christian Union, the Society for the Prevention of Crime, and the New York Academy of Sciences. In each of these organizations he held a responsible office.

In 1862, Columbia College conferred on him the degree of S. T. D., and in 1869, the Regents of the University of the State of New York bestowed on him the degree of L. H. D.

Professor Martin's married life continued for forty-one years, and it was a life so near the ideal, that were it described truthfully the description might be called a romance. Mrs. Martin's death, in the spring of 1883, was a fearful blow, but Professor Martin was not of those who sorrow without hope. His patience while thus stricken preached as effectively as did his active life. But the separation was not long, for on December 26, 1883, he sank under acute bronchitis, dying as he had lived, full of cheerful trust in the God whom he had served with single-heartedness for half a century. The only issue of the marriage was the son, who survives him, and is so well known as a faithful worker in the Convocation.

No eulogy of Professor Martin is needed at a meeting of the University Convocation; but it is well to put on record a little respecting one whose services everywhere were as effective as they were unostentatious. The younger members cannot forget his kindly words, his generous encouragement. Let them not forget his noble example.

Professor Martin's acquirements were remarkable. He was firmly grounded in his metaphysical studies, for ten of his best years had been spent in thorough research; but beside this he was well versed in various branches of natural science. He began his studies in scientific subjects when most of the branches now so important were in their infancy, and it was possible for one to become well-informed in general principles without danger of becoming overwhelmed, as now, by a mass of apparently incongruous facts. With rare power he seized the salient points in each branch; and by careful, systematic study he kept himself fairly well abreast with the general advance during the following thirty years. He was not a professional expert in zoölogy or geology or mineralogy or molecular physics, but he was so well grounded in the general principles of each of these divisions of science, that no geologist or zoölogist or mineralogist ever conversed with him for an hour without gaining some new conception, without feeling broadened, without becoming convinced that he had talked with one who had reached the higher plane of philosophy. It was this that gave him his power as an instructor in metaphysics — as an instructor in any branch. He was not built up on any one side at the expense of the others. Each student under his care soon discovered this. Other instructors taught their specialties, but in Professor Martin's room the whole was gathered together, carefully assorted and stored away, every fact in its own place with those related to it; so that the thoughtful student, when through with Professor Martin's immediate instruction, went away a well-furnished man, often surprising his seniors in age by his stock of general information, so well-assorted and so easily available. Professor Martin was singularly successful in his efforts to cultivate a judicial turn of mind in his pupils, whom he delighted to lead into discussions upon the topics under consideration. He knew well that the instructor's highest duty is not the mere imparting of knowledge, but the development of the man.

That Professor Martin was a great thinker his many essays prove; that he was a great teacher more than a thousand pupils proudly assert; but more than thinker, more than teacher, he was great in those higher attributes which gain for a man not only the respect but also the love of those with whom he is brought into contact. Throughout his life he was an example of that religion which demands of its followers, " Do unto others as ye would that they should do unto you." He, like his Master, went about doing good, and that, too, with utter forgetfulness of self. When he conferred a favor the recipient incurred no obligation; the good deed had brought sufficient payment to the benefactor. He demanded no return of gratitude, and therefore seldom failed to receive it in good measure.

Wherever good could be done Professor Martin was ready to serve. He visited the sick in hospitals; he helped the needy far beyond his ability; he preached freely to feeble churches; he organized and for years kept alive at the University the Friday prayer meeting of students, which was a precious means of raising and maintaining the moral and spiritual tone of the institution.

It is said that the good which men do perishes with them; but the folly of the adage is proved in such a case as this. Professor Martin is not dead; his manly frankness, his whole-souled honesty of purpose, and his greatness of heart which felt all men brothers, gained at once the confidence of those with whom he had to do, and enabled him, insensibly to themselves, to mold them much as he would. He has left no great volumes of published works, though many important and original essays and articles on science, literature and philosophy; and to-day he is preaching from nearly two hundred pulpits in this land. Who can estimate the greatness of the work thus done?

NOTICE OF PROFESSOR MARTIN BY PRESIDENT PORTER.

[From the New York Independent.]

The writer was a friend of this excellent and accomplished gentleman for a little more than fifty years, and counts it both a privilege and a duty to render a brief tribute to his ability and his work. He is the more desirous to do this, because, though Professor Martin was greatly beloved and honored in special circles, he may have failed to take that rank in general esteem and notoriety to which his eminent ability and his excellent work would seem to have entitled him. He was first known to the writer as his pupil in Yale College, of the class of 1837, a class which was unusually brilliant, and has become well known to the public from the names of Chief-Justice Waite, Secretary Evarts, Ambassador Pierrepont, Governor Tilden, Rev. Andrew L. Stone, George Duffield, Rev. E. P. Rogers, and others. Of the south division in this class the writer had special charge, and to this division young Martin belonged, a slender, black-eyed youth, who, though small in stature, seemed never to have been a boy, having always the manner of a self-assured and self-asserting man. He had, moreover, a great deal of manner; but it was so completely the expression of the man as very soon to obliterate the suggestion of affectation and studied effect which it might at first excite. This manner was thoroughly natural, and was retained by him till his death, being obvious to the most casual acquaintances, and prominently associated with his personality. Whatever he may have lost by it, he gained not a little, and that was the impression, which no one could mistake or deny, that he was a chivalrous and high-toned gentleman to the core and heart of his being. Whether boy or man, whether clergyman or layman, whether college professor or man of affairs, Professor Martin was at once and universally recognized as having a knightly soul, which moved and acted in the sphere of honor and truth and courtesy, claiming for himself, indeed, all the rights which were his due, and as quick to accord to others their dues with an equally ready deference. His scholarship in college was finished and elegant, being alike distinguished for logical acuteness and literary finish — all his productions, whether scholastic or literary, being characterized by an exact and elaborate perfection which was native to the man. He was trained by his excellent mother in religious ways, and during his college life came avowedly under the influence of Christian truth, which exerted a more than usually stimulating influence upon his intellect, and a very thoroughly transforming power over his character. Immediately after graduating he entered the Theological Seminary at New Haven, and gave himself, with enthusiastic ardor, to its studies under the guidance and inspiration of the late Dr. Nathaniel W. Taylor. It was at a time of active controversy and ecclesiastical strife, in which the heart and intellect of young Martin was thorougly enlisted, and he became one of Dr. Taylor's most devoted champions and enthusiastic friends. With this attitude of mind and heart he entered upon the work of the ministry. It was unfortunate for his reputation at first, perhaps, that he seemed so much of a partisan, and that his attitude toward those who were antagonistic to the New Haven Theology was so confident and defiant, and most of all that his settlement as pastor, in 1843, was connected with a local and personal ecclesiastical strife. For controversy and discussion Professor Martin was always ready. No sooner did the challenging glove from any quarter touch the ground than he was ready to take it up, and was never known to cry "hold, enough" to any antagonist. The resources of his logic and rhetoric were apparently never exhausted, and his spirit for a discussion was never abated. He was, moreover, in the early part of his ministerial life, profoundly convinced of the grievous wrongs which were done to the good name and the theological and Christian reputation of his principal instructor and the theology which he taught, and was animated with a generous desire to defend his good name whenever it was called in question. To the end of Dr. Taylor's life he maintained the most loyal and grateful concern for his reputation, and after his death contributed a very able statement and analysis of his services to philosophy and theology. But while he retained this loyal and fervent regard for Dr. Taylor's teachings, he was by no means a theological partisan of any man. Very few men can be named of his generation who were more catholic in their tastes, or more great and liberal in their appreciation of different writers and schools, or more generous and truly liberal in their sympathies, whether their sympathies were concerned with men, or their opinions, or with public movements.

Professor Martin found his appropriate place when, in 1852, he was elected professor of philosophy in the University of New York, and became instructor of the students in rhetoric. To his preparation for and his work in the class-room, he gave the best of his energies, and here gained the best reward of his labors — the respect and confidence of his pupils. Much of the administrative work of the institution was also assigned to him. Many of its heaviest responsibilities fell upon him. He met these demands in a laborious and self-sacrificing spirit. No one knows so well as his colleagues, with what conscientious fidelity, with what untiring patience, and with how sweet a spirit he assumed the various burdens which were imposed upon him. Besides the studies which were appropriate to his double professorship, he became specially interested in the various branches of natural history, and the new questions in theology and philosophy, which have been raised within the last twenty years. To this class of topics he gave the most earnest attention, and was never tired of conversing or writing upon them. The few essays which he published upon these themes, are all admirable in matter and form, and his friends have only to regret that his life was so divided and straitened by manifold domestic and public cares and responsibilities, that the fruits of his rare genius and rarer culture have been comparatively so scanty. On the other hand, those who knew him best and loved and respected him most tenderly and sincerely, may point to those which he did produce as the rare and well-ripened products of a gifted and noble thinker.

As a Christian believer, he was at once strong in faith, ardent in zeal and truly catholic in his love. His just and truth-loving mind delighted itself in the living and loving God as manifest in Christ, and his loyal soul held fast to his Divine Master with knightly and affectionate devotion. In whatever society he was introduced his confession of fidelity to Christ and his cause was loving and fervent, and expressed in no doubtful terms. It was to him meat and drink to pray and labor for the Kingdom of God. As a friend and helper, he was generous and untiring. Those who confided in his friendship were certain that he would never betray them, and all who came in contact with him felt that in him truth and uprightness were conspicuously exemplified. Those who knew him best regretted that he was not known more widely, and that circumstances should have seemed to limit his reputation and usefulness. They will all unite in the opinion that, for clearness of thought, felicity of diction, catholicity of culture and justness of judgment, Professor Martin deserves to take a very high place among the Christian scholars of his generation.

NOTICE OF PROFESSOR MARTIN BY EX-CHANCELLOR HOWARD CROSBY.

[From an address made at the funeral.]

It is literally true that a great man and a father in Israel has fallen. In intellectual power, deep piety, and social manner he was an eminent man. I was attracted to Dr. Martin when I first met him. There was a power about him, that for want of a better name, we call magnetic power. He had a large and loving heart. In the University, I marked not only his conscientious faithfulness to the duties connected with his own chair, but also his unceasing labors in the interest of all the students. His influence in the weekly prayer-meeting was such, that I have seen bold scoffers brought to their knees through his instrumentality. The University is indebted largely to him for its wholesome influence during the last thirty years.

He really filled two chairs, doing the work of two men, and doing it with all his heart, never once neglecting a duty. With all his sincerity and ability, he was a modest man, never putting himself forward, although there was not his superior in the United States in the mastery of mental science, and he had few superiors in his knowledge of natural science. With a metaphysical mind that could unravel any problem, and put it before the students in the clearest light, he could at the same time master its relations to natural science. He never dodged a question, but always answered the hardest ones with precision.

Such a man has our University lost. Who can supply his place? How can we find a man in whom so many qualities, found separately in others, are here united ?

His whole daily life was an illustration of what Matthew Arnold calls " sweetness and light " ; the sweetness of natural disposition, and the light of a clear and powerful intellect, and both alike touched, and developed, and ennobled by the indwelling grace of God.

His leading feature, intellectually, was his many-sidedness of thought and of attainment, together with the power of commanding and combining his varied mental resources. Those who had the privilege of knowing him in the University, as an instructor, will not fail to recognize these aspects of his mind and character. Never was there a professor whose class-room afforded a freer field for the discussion of all questions that could legitimately arise in any of the bearings of a subject. Yet he never allowed mere random talk to consume the time either of himself or his classes. Outside of the regular work, moreover, he was ever sought by the students as a counselor, an expounder, a friend, a father. Questions in every department of their other studies were presented frequently to him, in the certainty of a kindly welcome, a ready response, and a lucid explanation. Was there a seeming contradiction between some statements heard from professors in other branches of study? — it was brought to him for solution. Did a student begin to feel interest in some form of science, gathering, in his vacation or on a holiday, some (to him) novel or curious mineral or fossil? — he would show it to Professor Martin at the next opportunity, knowing that a prompt and pleased recognition of it was sure to be given. Was a young man in trouble at home through death or illness in the family circle? or was he uncertain as to his own plans and prospects after graduating? — he well knew where to find sympathy, help, and counsel. Was he unsettled and perplexed by questions of scientific or philosophical doubt, rising up in connection with his reading or his studies, and disturbing the religious faith in which he had been early trained? — how often have such anxious young minds sought and found the clear, calm, patient guidance that they so much needed, from that broad, strong, gentle soul, and that loving fatherly heart!

In all circumstances and all places he was ever the same; not varying or changing with his surroundings, but carrying into every relation the same rare union of dignity and brightness, of affability and scholarship, of earthly cheerfulness and high spiritual purpose and aim. Wherever he went he was a marked man, attracting the notice of others all unconsciously, and winning singular esteem upon very brief acquaintance. Nowhere was this so conspicuous as in summer travel. It was curious to note the manner in which, unsought and undesired, he would become the centre of attraction in a summer hotel, where he had come, an unknown stranger, a day or two before. He never went to such places alone, but always with his wife and son, who formed his entire family, and were bound together by a peculiar bond of affection and companionship, and were largely sufficient for each other's society. Going out with his son for a walk, for instance, it mattered not where, the ramble was sure to yield material of scientific interest and study in some form; and the two would return to the hotel from their reconnoissance, with minerals, shells, fossils, or flowers, gathered with that delight which lovers and students of nature are privileged to find everywhere in their wanderings. Ere long, these objects would attract attention and curiosity among the guests of the hotel; and soon Professor Martin would become the centre of a group of ladies and gentlemen, admiring, wondering, and full of inquiries, to which he was ever ready with answer and explanation. In a few days, these casual acquaintances had grown into a body of warmly appreciative friends.

As the Sabbath approached, he had become already well known as a professor and a minister, and some of the pastors of the place would invite him to preach in their pulpits. Then, as he so loved to do, he would present some earnest aspect of gospel truth in the house of God; and the friends who had admired his social and intellectual attainments, now learned his power and depth as a preacher of the Divine Word. Many very delightful friendships were formed in ways like these, simply from the attraction he exerted upon those with whom he was thrown.

PROFESSOR ARNOLD GUYOT, LL. D.

By Principal J. E. Bradley, Ph. D.

The great eminence of the late Professor Guyot and the distinguished services which he rendered to science and education would entitle him to a place among these notices, although not a resident of the State; but we have more direct reason for honoring his memory here, in the fact that the meteorological observations which he conducted for so many years and the explorations and surveys which have made his name a household word throughout the Catskills and other portions of the State, were to a large extent prosecuted under the supervision of the Regents of the University.

The following sketch has been prepared from materials kindly furnished by Professor Scott of Princeton, and by Mrs. Guyot, who shared his work and enthusiasm to a remarkable degree.

Arnold Henry Guyot was born near Neufchâtel, Switzerland,

September 8, 1807. His early education was obtained in his native town, and it is interesting to note that during his school-life there, he was president of the gymnastic club, and one of the best school athletes. His slight, wiry frame thus received a training in strength and endurance which afterward stood him in good stead, when he undertook the immense labors of glacier-study in Switzerland, and of mountain climbing in America. On leaving Neufchâtel he went to complete his studies in Germany, attending successively the gymnasia of Stuttgart and Carlsruhe. At Carlsruhe he was an inmate of the family of the Brauns, and there met his countryman Agassiz who, with Imhoff and Carl Schimper, was making a vacation visit to his friend Alexander Braun. This period was one of the critical points in Guyot's career. There was formed that close and tender friendship with Agassiz, which lasted until the death of the latter, and found its final expression in the beautiful memoir of Agassiz which Guyot prepared for the National Academy of Sciences in 1877. But of still greater importance was the impulse toward the study of science, which he received from the enthusiastic group of young naturalists with whom he was thus brought into daily and hourly contact. He says of this period: "My remembrances of these few months of alternate work and play, attended by so much real progress, are among the most delightful of my early days.

In 1829, young Guyot went to Berlin to complete the theological studies which he had begun at Neufchâtel; but the love of science was strong within him, and the new field which the lectures of Steffens, Hegel, and Ritter opened up to his view decided him to enter upon the study of nature and his life-work. Having thus decided, he determined to lay his foundations broad and deep, and with this end in view he attended lectures on nearly all departments of natural science: chemistry, physics, meteorology, zoölogy, geology, and physical geography, alike received attention, and his subsequent career showed the great wisdom of this thorough preparation. In 1835, he received the degree of Doctor of Philosophy, and at once proceeded to Paris. Here he resided more than four years, quietly pursuing his preparatory studies, and extending them in vacation by tours of observation through various European countries. He also took up the subject of history under Michelet, and, like every thing else which he touched, made it valuable in the great pursuit of his life — the study of earth and man.

In the spring of 1838, Agassiz came to Paris, enthusiastic upon the subject of glaciers, and this induced Guyot to turn his attention in the same direction. In the summer of the same year, he went to Switzerland, and began his work on the glaciers of that country. The results of the summer's work were presented in a paper before the Geological Society of France during the session of 1838, at Porrentuy. This paper is mentioned in the "Proceedings" of the society ("Bulletin," vol. IX, p. 407), but, owing to a long illness of the author during the following winter, it could not be printed. The great laws of glacial phenomena first enunciated by Guyot in this paper, were afterward announced as new discoveries by other observers, and were the occasion of bitter quarrels. Afterward, when a discussion arose between Forbes and Agassiz, the manuscript was, on motion of Agassiz, and by a formal vote, deposited as a voucher with the Society of Natural Sciences at Neufchâtel, and was printed by that society in 1883. This paper contained the following contributions to the subject: 1. The sloping of the terminal beds of glaciers toward their interior, and their origin as closed-up crevasses. 2. The laminated structure or blue bands of glacier-ice. 3. The cause of the fan-shaped disposition of crevasses. 4. The more rapid motion of the glacier's centre than of the sides. 5. The more rapid motion of the top than the bottom of the glacier. 6. The movement of glaciers which takes place by means of a molecular displacement, whence results the plasticity of the glacier. Later, he added the law of the formation of transverse crevasses in a plane, perpendicular to the steepest slope of the glacier. With rare modesty, Guyot never took part in the fierce discussions caused by the claim laid by others to his own discoveries, contenting himself with a simple statement of the facts published long afterward in his memoir on Agassiz.

In 1839, Guyot accepted a call to the Academy of Neufchâtel, where his friend Agassiz was then settled, and there he remained till his removal to America in 1848. His chair was that of history and physical geography, and he regarded the years of his work there as the period of his greatest intellectual activity. During this time he gave much attention to his glacial work, taking up the geological side of the question, the erratic blocks and ancient extension of the glaciers, and devoting to this work, "absolutely single-handed, seven laborious summers, from 1840 to 1847." This gigantic undertaking was brought to a successful conclusion, though the results were but partially published, inasmuch as the " Système Glaciaire," by Agassiz, Guyot and Desor never went further than the first volume (Paris, 1847). Guyot's collection of five thousand erratic rocks, illustrating eleven erratic basins -- a monument of incredibly pains taking labor — now fills a room in the Princeton Museum.

The political disturbances of 1848 induced Guyot to follow his friend Agassiz to America, where he lived for some time at Cambridge, Massachusetts. He first attracted public attention by the remarkable series of lectures, afterward published in the well-known book "Earth and Man." These lectures were the starting-point of a great reform in the historical and geographical teaching of this country.

About this time, at the request of the Regents of the University of the State of New York, the State granted an appropriation for renewing the system of meteorological observations and providing the stations with better instruments. This was to be accomplished under the joint supervision of the Board of Regents of the University and of the Smithsonian Institute. Professor Henry proposed to intrust the execution of the plan to Professor Guyot. A set of instruments for making meteorological observations was prepared by Professor Guyot for the use of observers, together with tables for the reduction of the observations, and published by the Smithsonian. The book, "Meteorological and Physical Tables," was first published in 1851; was considerably enlarged in subsequent editions in 1858 and 1859, and was swollen to a volume of over six hundred pages in the third edition. This valuable collection has been extensively used both in this country and in Europe, and a steady demand renders necessary a fourth edition, which is now in press (1884). In connection with Professor Henry, he must be regarded as the founder of the system of weather observations and reports, which has resulted in the Government Signal Service.

In 1854, Guyot was elected to the chair of geology and physical geography at Princeton — a post which he filled for the thirty remaining years of his life. Until compelled to cease by the increasing infirmities of age, he devoted all his vacations and spare time to his favorite investigations, making elaborate and careful examinations of the mountains from New England to South Carolina. This work involved an immense amount of hardship and fatigue, and he was fond of describing, with quaint picturesqueness and humor, his experiences in roughing it in the mountains of Pennsylvania and the Carolinas. In 1861, he published in the "American Journal of Science and Arts," the results of his work up to that time, "a memoir which remains to this day the best existing description." Again, in 1880, he brought out another memoir on the same subject devoted chiefly to the Catskills, some of the rougher work for which, was done after he was seventy years old. Many shorter papers on meteorological, physical and geographical subjects were written at intervals, but no complete list of them has ever been prepared. His work during this period is a noble example of what may be done without appropriations or endowments.

For many years, Guyot labored under great disadvantages from the lack of proper appliances, but he never allowed these drawbacks to lower the character of his work. When Princeton's day of prosperity came, he showed that he knew how to apply money wisely, as before he had been able to do grand work without it. The system of scientific expeditions to the West, which has so greatly stimulated the study of natural science at Princeton, and added so greatly to the treasures of her museums, was organized under his direction; and the wonderful growth of all the departments of natural science in the college must be in very large measure attributed to the wisdom and foresight of Guyot.

But even this brief and imperfect sketch cannot close without some testimony to his noble and exalted character, modest, unselfish, and devoted. "He never seemed to be thinking of himself, but always of his subject and his hearers. He cared very little for fame, very much for the study of Nature and the education of man." An earnest and consistent Christian throughout his life, he was ever charitable and tender, never indulging in acrimonious criticism or denunciation of those who differed even most widely from him. Always liberal, he sympathized with and appreciated honest opinion on whatever side it was uttered. He was remarkable for "the beauty in his daily life as well as for his nobly finished work." There is little cause for grief in the quiet close of such a splendid, useful, and complete career as this; nevertheless, we must mourn our irreparable loss, sorrowing most of all that we shall see his face no more. He was a devout believer in the Bible, and his last strength was spent in its defense.

His death occurred on the 8th of February, 1884, after a long illness which was borne with the same Christian faith and entire submission to the will of God, which had so eminently characterized him through all his life, and he died, as he had lived, an humble, believing and trusting follower of Christ.

ORLANDO MEADS, LL. D.

[From a notice by the Rt. Rev. W. C. DOANE.]

Born in 1806, Mr. Meads* had outlived almost all his early friends. A graduate of the Albany Academy and of Union College, he was a man whose education carried out and on and up the course of study, which institutions of learning only begin; just as he passed beyond the mere sufficiency of professional training as a lawyer, into the wider ranges of the great principles of jurisprudence and canon law. "He was a scholar and a ripe and good one;" fresh in his classics, accurate in historical knowledge, familiar with the great English writers in prose and poetry, and critical in his love and knowledge of art. Born at a time when men read books that were worth remembering, and remembered what they read, his range of information was very wide and accurate. His frequent journeyings abroad, with mind and eye open to realize the life of history and art, in the places and pictures which keep them alive, gave to his conversation a wealth and variety and freshness not often equaled or surpassed.

His active interest in all that concerned the dignity of Albany made him prominent in many positions. As the president of the Albany Institute, and of the Board of Trustees of the Albany Academy, he found place for the exercise of his love of science and the higher education of men. As trustee for various public institutions, and of many private interests, he displayed the conscientiousness of his high standards of honor and faithfulness. And though withdrawn for many years from the active exercise of his profession, he was looked up to as an adviser, whose judgment was based upon a thorough acquaintance with the principles and practice of the law.

And to this honorable career as citizen and friend, in his profession and in his public duties, he added the beauty of a blameless private life, of an earnest faith, of an active service of God. His loyalty to friends — to principles, to duty, to God — was the crown-jewel of his nature.

To his Bishop, who writes this faint and feeble tribute of reverent affection, he was as a strong right hand. Seventeen years of almost daily intercourse and intimacy, personal and official, made him

---

*Orlando Meads was born in Albany, June 18, 1806, and died February 11, 1884. He was graduated from Union College in 1826. He received the degree of Doctor of Laws from Hobart College in 1857. At the time of his death he was president of the Albany Institute, and president of the Board of Trustees of the Albany Academy.

dearer and more important every day. The pain of his loss is too intense to put in words, and too sacred to be laid bare to casual eyes.

We thank God for the blessed memory of his good example, for the honor and blessing of his love, for the confidence of his " reasonable religious and holy hope." Like the wondrous pillar that came between Israel and the Egyptians, his death is " a cloud and darkness " to us, but it " gave light in the night " to him as he passed out of the shadow into the light perpetual, which may God make to shine upon his soul. " He is numbered among the children of God and his lot is among the saints."

GENERAL S. D. HUNGERFORD.

By ALBERT B. WATKINS, Ph. D.

Solon Dexter Hungerford, the son of Dexter Hungerford and Marietta Burr, his wife, was born at Watertown, N. Y., March 12, 1818, and died at Adams, N. Y., May, 1884. At the age of fifteen he became a clerk in a dry goods store, where he remained four years. He then accepted the position of book-keeper in the Jefferson County Bank, and at the end of one year was promoted to the position of teller. This office he successfully filled for several years, when he was elected cashier of the Lewis County Bank at Martinsburgh. After filling this position for two years he went into banking on his own account, and in 1845, at the solicitation of the leading citizens of Adams, he opened the Hungerford's Bank of Adams. Through all the changes of laws in regard to finance, through all the fluctuations of business and of credit for nearly forty years, and to the day of his death he here continued in the business of banking. It was a fact in which he took a justifiable and honest pride that in the fifty years in which he had been engaged in banking, nearly forty of which he was the president of a bank, no person ever lost a dollar by the failure of any bank with which he was connected.

He was actively engaged in agricultural pursuits, owned a large farm called the Valley Park Farm, which for many years he managed personally, and at one time was quite extensively engaged in raising thoroughbred Ayreshire cattle. He was for sixteen years a member of the executive board of the New York State Agricultural Society, and for one term filled the office of president. His activity in another direction is shown by the fact that for several years he was president of the Jefferson County Bible Society.

He was connected with the State militia for many years, acting successively as inspector of the twelfth division of infantry, captain of the thirty-sixth regiment of infantry, and brigadier-general of the eighteenth brigade of the fourth division.

He was deeply interested in all public enterprises, and for more than a quarter of a century was a director of the Rome, Watertown and Ogdensburg railroad.

But his interest in educational affairs, and the time and money given by him to advance the cause of education in his native county are the chief facts which make it especially appropriate that these particulars concerning his life should be here presented. Various attempts had been made in Adams to establish an academic school of high rank. In 1864 a large building erected for a hotel came into the possession of General Hungerford. This he offered to give as a proper building for an academic school, if the citizens would raise an endowment fund of $10,000. The offer was accepted, the fund raised, and a charter secured from the Regents for the Hungerford Collegiate Institute. The school was organized and successfully carried on for nearly three years, when the building was burned. In 1870 a fine new edifice, upon a new site, was erected with the avails of the insurance from the old building, secured chiefly through the personal care and foresight of Mr. Hungerford, and from his generous donations and those of the people of the town and surrounding country. To the erection of this building he gave much of his time for many months, frequently expressing the determination that nothing should be left undone to make it the very best of its kind. When the school was opened in the new building in August, 1870, he was present, intensely interested in its prosperity, and greatly gratified with its success; and during the whole of the first year of the school he was seldom absent from the morning chapel exercises. As president of the board of trustees he exerted himself to bring its merits to the attention of all within the circle of his acquaintance, to increase its patronage and extend the sphere of its usefulness. The school was justly a cause of great pride and satisfaction to him, and he rightly considered the part which he was enabled to take in founding an academic institution of superior grade in the village in which he was a prominent citizen the greater part of his life, as one of the most creditable and most useful acts of an unusually long business career. His interest in education was still further shown by the fact that he gave to Hamilton College a fund for the establishment of a metaphysical scholarship which bears his name.

He was married in 1845 to Miss Ann E. Huntington, of Watertown, who died in 1878, deeply beloved by all who knew her. One son, Robert B., was the result of this union. He married for his second wife Mrs. Sara Phelps Ireland, of Binghamton, a lady greatly respected, who survives him.

General Hungerford was a man of exemplary habits, of great energy, of liberality at all times fully proportioned to his means, and deeply interested in all public enterprises, chief and foremost of which was the Hungerford Collegiate Institute, in founding which he had so large a share

PROFESSOR JACOB S. MOSHER, M. D.

By SAMUEL B. WARD, M. D.

At the time of Dr. Jacob S. Mosher's sudden death he was filling many important trusts in his profession, most of which were promotions from others of minor significance. The list of medical places which he had occupied could hardly be made complete without more detail than it was possible for me to verify in the brief intervals of time, stolen from other duties, which I have been able to give to this paper. But a partial statement will show in what esteem he was held as a physician and surgeon and teacher of medicine.

Graduating from this college in 1863, he served in the year following as volunteer surgeon in the army before Petersburg. He was afterward made assistant medical director for the State of New York. He was also military superintendent and surgeon in charge of the State Hospital for disabled soldiers in this city, until it was closed. In 1869, he was appointed Surgeon-General of the State by Governor Hoffman, and served as such until 1873. From 1870 to 1876, he held the position of deputy health officer of the port of New York. His connection with the Albany Hospital ran through several years and was varied and valuable in character; the same was true of St. Peter's Hospital; this membership of the medical staff of these two institutions making large drafts on his time. From 1863 to 1870, he was professor of chemistry in the Albany Academy. His relations to this college are well known to you all,

He was at first professor of chemistry and medical jurisprudence, afterward of the theory and practice of medicine, and was for a long period of time the registrar and librarian. A mere statement of the titles of these positions would not convey to an outsider any adequate idea of the time and energy he expended, or the tact and ability which you all know he displayed, in performing the duties belonging to them.

He was a member of the Albany County Medical Society, and had been its president; having served as delegate to, he had become a permanent member of, the Medical Society of the State; he was a fellow of the New York Academy of Medicine; he had been a delegate to the American Medical Association; he was a member of the body that drafted the law under which the national board of health came into existence; he was chairman of the board of health of this city; he was professor in the Albany College of Pharmacy and president of the faculty; and, lastly, he was president, at the time of his death, of this Alumni Association, this last fact causing this session to be made one of honor to his memory.

This list has been made to follow chronological order as far as possible. He also held other positions of less marked prominence which came to him from the fact of his holding the more important ones which have been named. Indeed his untitled relations to the cause of medicine in the nation, the State, the city and college were numerous, constant and active. He was frequently consulted by officials, both medical and political, as to the filling of medical positions, the laying down and application of lines of policy, in the making or amendment of laws, and as to the effect on the unprofessional mind of certain lines of action. There was no point at which any institution with which he was connected came into contact with public life or affairs, where he was not felt as an authority. No such institution was ever called upon to confront an emergency when his views and energy, and wonderful knowledge of the world and of human nature, and keen foresight of possible contingencies, were not found available and useful — sometimes well nigh indispensable.

His influence in the struggle within the profession itself for larger liberty of thought and action, for a higher and truer friendship among its educated exponents, was second to that of very few men. His service, as a chemist and as a medical expert were in constant request. They were frequently rendered, it is true; but it would be a grave mistake to suppose that they were given in every instance in which they were asked. They were also frequently refused, even when accompanied with large fees; for Dr. Mosher would never espouse on the stand a cause which he believed on careful preliminary examination to be an unrighteous one.

Besides all these ways in which Dr. Mosher appeared before the public he was also a great student, and was endowed with a wonderful memory. He had, as you all know, an unusually large and complete library, and what is far more rare, he knew his books thoroughly and how to use them and their contents to the best advantage. Nor were his books or his lore confined to professional matters alone. During the seven years that I knew him well, many a knotty point was presented to me, in one way or other, for solution, in mathematics, in history, in art, in literature, or in general science. It became my custom to carry them to him, and I can honestly say that I do not remember to have ever come out of his cozy library without having learned just what I wanted to know, and usually much useful information had been gleaned besides. His private studies he pursued to make himself a better physician and surgeon as well as a man of general learning and culture, and all these belong to the not easily reportable portion of his life. They took up much of his time and thinking and work, and connected him with the common lot and labor of his medical brethren. A few of us may be instructors and officials, fewer still are experts or specialists; all of us are doctors; and it was not as a sanitarian, or chemist, or lecturer, or civil servant, or medical witness that our friend desired to shine so much as in the capacity of a general practitioner. In this latter character he was coming out strong in the last few years of his life. He recognized that he had ploughed many fields and the best harvests he had gathered from them were those which he could use in the calls made upon him in the practice of his profession. Public positions were always seeking him; this was because he was unusually qualified by the variety, extent and depth of his information, coupled with absolute honesty and great tact, to discharge faithfully and well any duties that might be imposed upon him, and not because he put himself forward as a perennial candidate for place. In his later years it mortified him to be classed with those who are seeking positions within the gift of governments. I do not mean to say that he was not gratified when offers which carried honor as well as responsibility were made to him; but he was gratified because they were a tribute to the record which he had, unaided, made for himself, and because no one could truly say that he had sought for them. He had definitely begun to appreciate the advantages and pleasures of mixed public and private employments, the combined professional and official opportunities within the grasp of a physician at this center of government, of population, of hospital facilities, of household and office practice and of medical education. He loved Albany; he loved Albanians; and they loved him. He expected here to close in a calm and studious old age the term of his probation upon earth. The summons came to him in mid-life, instantly; but not before he had shown that he meant to root himself here and that his wanderings, unless of a most temporary nature, were over.

As a medical instructor Dr. Mosher was notable for his ability to get interested and to interest others in almost any subject. He never labored perfunctorily, but loved to talk all over, and around, and into, and through, a subject. He always preferred to prepare himself for his lectures, at almost no matter what sacrifice of personal comfort or much needed rest. But when not able to do so he had an art, and a fund of general information to draw upon which made the lecture-hour a sort of symposium of useful knowledge and of conveying to students very valuable, broad views and generalizations of a subject. Lord Bacon says; "Speaking makes a ready man, reading makes a full man, and writing a correct man." When Dr. Mosher was not full of a subject he was always ready with a theory about it; but when he was full of it he relied little upon devices. The glee with which he would tell his friends — for he had a most keen sense of humor — of the shifts to which he had resorted to avoid the discovery, on the part of the class, that overwork had left him unprepared, was most charming and contagious; but he never let students into the secret until they had ceased to be students; for while in social hours he was a companion to all, no lecturer was ever more careful to maintain the dignities of the class room. As an enlightening and enthusiastic lecturer our friend will be remembered by all whose pathway up the steps of science he made clear.

As a physician among physicians Dr. Mosher was always both a learner and a suggester — as good a listener as he was a speaker. He acquired knowledge by hearing it from others who were older or had made special studies and observations. He could add to almost any man's views by experiences, researches or generalizations of his own. His own ideas or views he would, on occasion presenting, put forth for what they were worth and often subsequently decide for himself whether they were sound or not by the discussion they would provoke. How tenacious he was of his own views on a subject which he had considered we all know, but we also know that he had equal consideration for the views of others. He had a natural courtesy which made him always gentlemanly, and, even when earnest in controversy, he extended to others the respect which he did not need to demand for himself, since he always commanded it. Older physicians found Dr. Mosher deferential and fond of learning from them. Those of his own time realized that he liked to compare views with them — and he never got more than he gave in that delightful work. Young practitioners found his heart, his library and his best thought always at their disposal.

As a sanitarian and an executive he held high rank, and he deserved to hold it. Very few, if any, exceeded him in knowledge of epidemic diseases. He had met and combatted almost every variety of them at quarantine, with all the resources of a great government to assist him. But a dull man with the mental grasp of a sponge — no matter how large a one — could never have profited by his opportunities as he did. Whatever he learned there he not only held but he expanded and verified and generalized on. Then he applied the results to the needs of the house, the city, the State or the nation, as called for. Some of the views which he held as to the habits of epidemic disease were original, based on careful observation, truthful, and useful of application in the way of prevention.

In administration he was firm, efficient and full of tact. The devices by which he produced results without loss by friction, and without the process becoming patent to the average observer, were most ingenious and effectual. He was always so cool and quiet in his methods that the forces he put in motion seemed to start themselves. While with unfounded self-assertion and with impertinence he had no patience — and few knew how to meet either as well as he — with mediocrity he could lose time without losing his temper. With men of brains he could be as quick, as plausible, as ingenious, or as sober, as deep and as logical as they. He gave to high officials counsel which was wise because it was disinterested, because it regarded the limitations set to their actions, and because it was tempered by a knowledge of the requirements of public life which seemed almost intuitive, but was, in reality, the result of close observation, for he knew men, he knew classes, he knew communities. The worldly wisdom often thought to be wanting in scientific men was not wanting in him.

His cleverness as an expert was known to jurists. The reasons he gave were founded on facts, and the record of these facts was at hand. He was enabled to anticipate objections, for he had studied both sides, and this gave him great advantages over shallow partisans of some special theory; and nature and art both assisted him in commending his views to a jury by not appearing too anxious about them. Long experience with a temper not easily controlled, had taught him how not to get angry; he well knew, when circumstances justified it, how to anger others, and the expert or lawyer who tried unfair means to antagonize him, found that they were fighting the court and the jury, who, by a process which they did not understand, were under the quiet spell of the man they tried to break down. The study requisite to learn from books all that Dr. Mosher knew from them is within the reach of almost all; the skill with which he used his knowledge was a gift that rests with him in the grave.

His merits as a physician and a surgeon do not need to be dwelt on at length in this presence. Most of us have practiced with him more or less, and know him to have been equipped by study and experience to do well his work as a general practitioner. If he had ever neglected this for public duties he was certainly making up for lost time when he definitely settled down to the business of his later years. He was painstaking in diagnosis; he was cautious in prognosis; he felt that he could rely on certain old remedies, as he could on old friends; he was courteous, but judicial, toward new ones, as he was to recently made acquaintances. No one was more considerate and conscientious toward patients of all classes than he. When friendship went with his calls he was indefatigable; for then sleep, comfort and pleasure were of no account at all in comparison with an exhaustive study of the case in all its possible aspects, and neither sympathy, where it would prove of benefit, nor firmness, where it was required, were wanting. The magnetic personal influence which he possessed in general intercourse with men was not wanting in the sick-room. To the record of his professional excellence in consultation this should be added; he always loyally maintained to the family the position assumed by the attending physician, even if he quietly advised him to modify it; he would make no standing for himself at the expense of others.

That all this is but a suggestion of our friend who has gone before-us I well know. He was a man who entered into our life so fully that to analyze him is almost as difficult as to tell why we loved him. We know that we did love him, and that others did. We do not at all succeed even to our own mind in inventorying him. The brilliant qualities of his heart and intellect were the constituents of a whole man; and it is the man as a whole whom we recall, and of whom, remembering him as he was to his kin, to his friends, to his calling and to this college, we realize "that we shall not look upon his like again."

ELISHA HARRIS, M. D.

By LOUIS W. PRATT, Albany.

A year ago the subject of school sanitation was presented to the Convocation, and in the discussion which followed the reading of the paper many will recall the remarks of an illustrious advocate of sanitary reform, whose life had been almost entirely devoted to the interests of public health. During the past year the record of that well-spent life has closed, and this opportunity cannot be lost of recalling the self-sacrificing, earnest life of Dr. Elisha Harris and of paying a brief tribute to his energy, devotion and success in his profession and in the public service.

Elisha Harris, M. D., was born at Westminster, Vermont, March 4, 1824. While a boy his parents removed to Homer, in this State, where he received his academic instruction from Dr. Woolworth, the late Secretary of the Board of Regents. Associated with him as a boy were also President Bascom of Wisconsin University and Dr. Elisha Mulford. He taught school and studied medicine, graduating at the College of Physicians and Surgeons in New York city. He received the degree of A. M. from Lafayette College. In 1849 Dr. Harris married a daughter of Rev. J. B. Andrews, of New York city, and settled there for the practice of his profession. He was not permitted to remain in private life, however, and in 1855 became, by the appointment of the Governor, Superintendent of Physicians at Quarantine, Staten Island. While at Quarantine Dr. Harris devised the "floating hospital," and made an accurate study of the sanitary questions arising from the defects and inadequacy of the then existing system, which resulted in a thorough reform and the organization of the present efficient service.

At the outbreak of the war Dr. Harris was the first to propose the Sanitary Commission, and, as one of the commissioners, devoted himself to that cause throughout the war. He invented and put in operation the "ambulance car," and was indefatigable in contriving means for the sanitary welfare of armies and the care and treatment of the wounded. At the close of the war he edited the important "Sanitary History of the War."

In 1867 Dr. Harris succeeded in organizing the Metropolitan Board of Health and the system of registration of vital statistics for the city of New York, being sanitary superintendent and registrar until 1876. He also devoted himself to the interests of the American Public Health Association, of which he was the first secretary and afterward president.

In 1880 he prepared the law organizing the State Board of Health of New York, and, on its passage, was appointed by the Governor one of the three State Commissioners of Health, and by election by the board became its secretary and superintendent of the Bureau of Vital Statistics, which position he held until his death. To the vast work of organizing a system of health-boards and registration in the towns, villages and cities of the State, he exerted the force of all his energy and experience, and within four years accomplished almost incredible results. His ceaseless devotion to the duties of his position doubtless led to his death, which occurred, after a brief illness, on the morning of the 31st of January last.

During his life Dr. Harris contributed a very great number of valuable papers to the literature of medicine, and as an authority on sanitary science was unequaled by any man in this country. His remarkable record of public service in medicine and in the organization of health-boards is also unrivaled.

Dr. Harris possessed many kind and affectionate qualities, which endeared him to all who knew him. He labored among the convicts and poor of the State institutions, ever striving to reform what was wrong and generously to relieve all distress.

Another striking quality which Dr. Harris possessed deserves mention on this occasion. It was his constant effort to impart useful information to the people at large concerning the preservation of life and health, and the value and nature of sanitary regulations. Education is a broad term. School teachers and college professors impart much of the training that is termed education, and stand before the world as the exponents of educational interests. But side by side with avowed instructors have stood men like Dr. Harris, seeking the same result, though working through a different channel, whose death is thereby a loss, not only to the medical and scientific world and to the State in his official capacity, but to the University Convocation and the interests of humanity and education, which are deprived of a faithful ally, an earnest supporter, and a warm friend.

REV. MICHAEL P. COSTIN, S. J.

By Professor P. A. Halpin.

At Boston College, on Sunday evening, June 8, the Rev. Father Costin suddenly died of heart disease. The deceased was born in Halifax, August 24, 1838, and was nearly forty-six years of age. He went to Ireland to complete his education, and, after studying some years at Clongowe's College, returned to America, where he entered the Society of Jesus on the 23d of April, 1854. Wherever he was employed as professor, he always left the impression which a mind of quick, large grasp and clear, acute perception must necessarily make on young minds. In spite of continued ill-health, he taught, with unfailing regularity, the higher branches of mathematics and the sciences for nearly twenty years at St. John's College. Though devoted principally to the teaching of mathematics, there was no branch of learning with which he was not familiar. He was equally eminent in philosophy, theology, literature and the sciences. He spoke and wrote English like a master, and the students of this college were never weary of listening to his beautifully simple and lucid explanations of the Gospels at the Sunday Mass. He was a most genial companion. His students admired and loved him and his death will be regretted by all. In a word, he was a great, good man, and the world is a loser by his demise, of one whose intellect entitled him to rank with the thinkers of the age; whose virtue purified and hallowed the sphere in which he moved; whose genial character and loving nature made friends fast and true wherever he went. With Father Costin's life a shining light has been quenched, and many a young and many an old heart has been deprived of a model and a friend. Such an expansive heart was his, so open to every thing that betokened suffering or wretchedness, that he applied himself to learning the deaf and dumb language, so that the speechless children might have the consolations of our holy religion. It was always a moving spectacle to see him surrounded by the deaf-mutes of St. Joseph's Institute, Fordham. How they loved him! How their affection was returned with the fullest measure! The big heart is at rest, and the great mind is in possession of the magnet of all minds, Infinite Truth.

PROFESSOR ARTHUR SPIELMANN.

[From The University Quarterly.]

Arthur Spielmann, Adjunct Professor of Civil Engineering in the University of the City of New York, died in New York of typhoid pneumonia, November 29, 1883. Professor Spielmann was born in Hoboken thirty-seven years ago, and graduated from the New York University with the class of 1867. He immediately engaged in the practice of civil engineering, and in 1869 formed a partnership with Professor Charles B. Brush, under the firm name of Spielmann & Brush, which was only dissolved by death. He has been prominently identified with all the principal public improvements that have been made in Hudson county, N. J., during the past fifteen years. It was through his indefatigable researches and as an expert engineer that Attorney-General Gilchrist was furnished with the data that enabled him to win the up town street improvement suits of Hoboken whereby the city was saved from the payment of several thousand dollars of improvement certificates issued on over-estimates of material.

The firm, of which he was the head, was connected with the Hudson river tunnel as engineers in charge, when the work was begun, and at the time of Mr. Spielmann's death, he was engaged in making soundings for the new tunnel to be built under the same river at Communipaw. The recently-completed water works of the Hackensack Water Company, which supply Hoboken and the adjacent towns, were built by the firm. He was engaged on the Bulls Ferry road improvement and many sewer improvements. He devoted a large portion of his time and money to the solution of the problem of proper drainage of the low lands of Hoboken.

In 1882, he went abroad and spent his time in the study of drainage, visiting Holland for that purpose, and consulting distinguished engineers in England, France and Germany. He was frequently called upon as an expert by public corporations and private parties, especially on matters relating to foundations.

He compiled official property maps of New York city, and also of Hudson county, which have been of invaluable aid to the legal fraternity. His topographical and sanitary map of Hudson county, N. J., for the National Board of Health, is a monument to the ability, skill and knowledge of the subject which has claimed so much of his time.

JOHN CHESTER GALLUP, M. D.

By Professor EDWARD NORTH.

Born in Brooklyn, Windham county, Conn., February 27, 1812. Graduated from Berkshire Medical College, at Pittsfield, Mass., in 1833. Practiced medicine in Attica, 1834–6; in Mount Clements, Mich., 1836–9; in Fentonville, Mich., 1839–49; in Palmyra, 1849–55. In 1859, married Marilla Houghton, of Ingham University, LeRoy. Principal of Houghton Seminary, in Clinton, 1861–80. Elder in the Presbyterian Church in Clinton, 1864–84. Died in Clinton, April 15, 1884.

Twenty-three years ago Dr. Gallup entered upon the crowning work of his life as the founder and conductor of Houghton Seminary, in the village of Clinton. He was then in vigorous health, a tried and approved teacher, already rich with the wisdom that comes through various experiences, with intellectual powers well trained for meeting the perplexities and difficult duties of a large educational enterprise. He began his work in 1861, when plans for the higher education of young women called for the most heroic exercise of that Christian faith which is the substance of things hoped for. Never in all its history had our nation seen a darker period. Our specie currency had suddenly disappeared and all business was disorganized. Our young women were thinking less of books than of battle-fields and hospitals and sad farewells to brothers and lovers. Dr. Gallup launched his venture on a troubled sea, when the skies were black with a coming tempest. He had faith that the Union would weather the storm, and that Houghton Seminary would help to satisfy the higher needs of the nation's new career.

Under this prayerful, skillful and enterprising guidance, with the competent and consecrated aid of Mrs. Gallup, Houghton Seminary soon won for itself the attachment and support of many loving and faithful friends. Dr. Gallup prospered by devoutly recognizing the Giver of all true prosperity, and by loyalty to the highest standard of intellectual, social and spiritual culture. Houghton Seminary had no other endowment than the blessing of heaven upon thorough work in all branches of instruction. Its diploma has been from the outset a badge of actual scholarship and high character. Its graduates have gone out from year to year, not veneered with a shallow, deceptive polish, but substantially furnished for each good work and influence, and for all the uplifting, gracious ministries of womanly power. These graduates are widely known and sincerely honored (some of them in foreign fields) as teachers and authors, potent with the voice and pen, as wives and mothers, rejoicing in household and society duties, always and everywhere examples of thoughtful and well poised womanhood. They are the living agencies through which Dr. Gallup's beneficent work as a teacher will be continued and multiplied. His best eulogy is found in the grateful testimony of his pupils to that enthusiasm, and that hearty devotion to his chosen work which released him from bondage to a text-book, and brought all his wealth of personal experience and anecdote to illustrate and enforce the lessons of the class-room. Dr. Gallup was a successful teacher, because he was a true man, with all his manhood and attainments consecrated to the service of his Master.

JOHN A. GILLETT, A. M.

By CHARLES T. ANDREWS.

John Adams Gillett, A. M., was born in Charlotte, Vermont, October 18, 1798, and died at his residence in Hector, Schuyler county, New York, May 5, 1884. Professor Gillett was of Huguenot descent. His father, Daniel Ordway Gillett, was at Dartmouth under the famous president Wheelock, and, during his active life, a Congregational minister.

The younger days of John A. Gillett were passed under the direct instruction of his father. His love of books and facility in acquiring knowledge early manifested themselves. After one year in the Schenectady preparatory school, he entered Union College, being there at the same time though not in the same classes as the Hon. Wm. H. Seward, under the presidency of the celebrated Dr. Nott.

After leaving college he read law in the office of Judge Woods, of Granville, and was admitted to the bar, at a court held in the central part of the State, receiving his "parchments" as solicitor and counselor at law. Without returning home he entered the law office of Judge Gray, then a rising young attorney at Elmira. He also, for a short time, was the "counselor" in a law firm at Havana, New York.

But the practice of law was distasteful to him. He was a born teacher, and after a few years he resumed his chosen profession in the old Elmira Academy.

Under the patronage of Dr. Tompkins, Professor Gillett opened the Peach Orchard Select School in 1841, about the same time that Starkey Seminary was founded by the Christian denomination, directly opposite, on the west shore of the lake. Academies and high schools were then less numerous than they are now, and Professor Gillett's pupils came from all parts of the State, from other States and from Canada. For twenty years the school flourished, and Professor Gillett, earning a competence, taught and studied, living among his books a quiet life which the student may well envy.

The establishment of union schools throughout the State, and the outbreak of the Rebellion, tended to reduce the patronage of Peach Orchard Select School; and, in 1863, Professor Gillett accepted the position of classical teacher in the Waterloo schools, under the principalship of J. S. Boughton.

It was a delight to hear him read Shakespeare or Milton, Virgil or Homer, as with perfect emphasis and inflection he rendered the thoughts of the writer in the language in which they were written. In history and biography he was equally well versed; and as a Bible student he was familiar not only with the sacred text, but with all denominational interpretations thereof. He was eminent as a mathematician, and astronomical investigations were his particular delight. Had he possessed the requisite voice he would have been an orator. As a lecturer, his thorough acquaintance with his subject, his power of lucid statement, his faultless inflections and impressive gestures always interested his audiences. He was a forcible writer, his style being chaste and vigorous, but his publications were confined to a few fugitive pieces.

STEPHEN G. TAYLOR, Ph. D.

By Professor JOHN J. ANDERSON.

Dr. Stephen G. Taylor was born at Sanbornton, N. H., March 23, 1819, and died in Brooklyn, N. Y., March 20, 1884, aged sixty-five years. He graduated at Dartmouth College, Hanover, N. H., in 1847, and afterward received from the same institution the degree of A. M., and from the Regents of the University of the State of New York that of Ph. D.

Dr. Taylor was my most intimate companion, outside of my own family, for at least a score of years. He was a rare, good man. He had a heart to feel for the woes of others and a hand ready to help the needy. I have had to do with many men in my life-time; I have been in the society of many; I have listened to the utterances of many, when the restraining eye and ear were not present, but I never met with a man of greater purity of thought than my lamented friend possessed. Not an offensive word ever escaped his lips, nor would he permit any such word to come from the lips of others in his hearing without manifesting in some way his grave displeasure.

Dr. Taylor was not a great man, as the world is in the habit of measuring greatness. He was too modest and retiring to find a place among the world's great men. He was a good scholar, thoroughly mastered every subject to which he turned his attention, and made a happy use of his acquisitions in the class-room, but he was not gifted in an extraordinary way as a writer or a speaker. What he wrote bore the impress of truth and clearness. It had nothing to recommend it in the way of ornament. What he said was put forth in quiet tones, without apparent effort. Whether he stood before his large school, embracing several hundred pupils, in the character of a lecturer, or among a few friends discussing some topic of interest, or sitting by his own fireside with none but his family about him, he was ever the same in manner and tone. He was a fluent talker and an earnest one, but never a loud one. He loved his home. No man ever appreciated more the comforts and advantages of a well-regulated home. No man enjoyed more the society of his family and of the many friends that esteemed it a favor to visit him.

As a teacher he was eminently successful. Teaching was his life work. From Dartmouth, whence he graduated, he went forth to teach. His first experience was among the schools of New England; then he spent a couple of years in an academy at Tarrytown in our own State, thus preparing himself for founding a classical school in the city of Brooklyn. In this institution, he made for himself such a name, that upon the opening of the now famous Polytechnic Institute of Brooklyn, he was invited to a place among its corps of teachers; and, accepting the invitation, transferred the larger part of his school to this new enterprise. In this position he remained, discharging his duties with perfect faithfulness, until he was called to be the principal of the then new school established by the Board of Education, known as No. 15. Under his care No. 15 grew to be the most flourishing school in the city. It still enjoys its old reputation, though another is at the head of it. While in charge of No.

15, Mr. Taylor, without any effort on his part, without, indeed, as much as a single hint of any kind from him, was solicited by the trustees of the Adelphi Academy, to take the supervision of that institution; and by the unanimous vote of those gentlemen he received the appointment. His work in that excellent school is well known. There he spent the last eight years of his life. He made it, with the co-operation of his excellent assistants, the magnificent school it now is. When he took charge, it sprang into a new life; pupils filled its rooms; its accommodations were increased; an addition, costing $20,000, was built to it; and yet it was not large enough, and applicants for admission had to be turned away.

It was while he was doing his crowning work in the Adelphi Academy, that the Regents of the University, recognizing his merits and appreciating the long and valuable service he had rendered in the cause of education, did him and themselves the honor of conferring upon him the degree of Ph. D.

ALONZO M. WINCHESTER.

By Principal ELISHA CURTISS.

Alonzo M. Winchester, President of the Board of Trustees of Sodus Academy, died April 12, 1884, at Mannsville, Jefferson county, N. Y.

The deceased was born in Orwell, Vt., August 12, 1812. He received a good education in the schools of his native town, and took a complete course at Castleton Academy.

He removed to Sodus, May 22, 1835, and engaged in teaching. He taught successfully select schools for several years. When the first meeting was called February 3, 1852, to consider the propriety of establishing Sodus academy, he was chosen secretary. He has been identified with the best interests of the academy ever since, and for the past twenty-five years or more has been president of the board of trustees.

In 1863 he was elected school commissioner, and during his term of office materially advanced the cause of common school education in his district.

www.ingramcontent.com/pod-product-compliance
Lightning Source LLC
Chambersburg PA
CBHW030748250426
43672CB00028B/1366